THE AUSTRALIAN TRADE PRACTICES ACT 1974

Studies in Industrial Organization

Volume 19

The titles published in this series are listed at the end of this volume.

The Australian Trade Practices Act 1974

Proscriptions and Prescriptions for a More Competitive Economy

Edited by

David K. Round

University of Adelaide, Australia

Springer-Science+Business Media, B.V.

A C.I.P. Catalogue record for this book is available from the Library of Congress.

ISBN 978-90-481-4491-4 ISBN 978-94-015-8324-4 (eBook)
DOI 10.1007/978-94-015-8324-4

Printed on acid-free paper

Originally published by Kluwer Academic Publishers in 1994.
Softcover reprint of the hardcover 1st edition 1994

Review of Industrial Organization

Volume 9, No. 5, October 1994

Special Issue

The Australian Trade Practices Act 1974. Proscription and Prescription for a More Competitive-Economy

Guest editor: David K. Round

Review of Industrial Organization **9:** 459–473, 1994.

EDITORIAL INTRODUCTION

Twenty Years of Modern Antitrust in Australia: She'll Be Right, Mate

DAVID K. ROUND*
Department of Economics, University of Adelaide, Adelaide, South Australia, 5005, Australia

Key words: Australian antitrust, antitrust history, Hilmer report, enforcement, competition.

I. 1974 – The First Modern Milestone in Australian Antitrust

In 1976, I published a paper on Australia's new antitrust legislation (which had come into effect in 1974) in *Industrial Organization Review*, the journal established by the late Gene Boyle which was the forerunner to *Review of Industrial Organization*. Given the absence of previous effective antitrust laws in Australia, I warned, *inter alia*, that a controversial and difficult path lay ahead of the Trade Practices Act 1974 (hereafter "the Act") because:

> "[a] problem with the legislation is that its language is loose in the part that matters most ... Firm guidelines should have been provided on how to interpret "substantially lessening competition" ... The definition of competition undoubtedly will prove to be a major obstacle to the harmonious operation of the Act in the early stages ... A structural approach to competition in Australia can only serve as a crude first approximation; investigation of conduct is the only efficient and equitable way to determine whether competition is present [but] [s]uch an approach has the disadvantage that it is difficult initially to lay down formal guidelines as to what constitutes competition." (Round (1976, pp. 146–147))

It is pleasing to report, twenty years after the introduction of the Act, that while my crystal ball had been well-polished and did foresee the problems which would occur with its implementation and enforcement, the Act is now widely accepted in the business community.[1] Its goals have been embraced by governments with different philosophies about the business sector and, largely, by the business sector itself. Judges, lawyers and economists have produced between them a truly Australian approach to antitrust,[2] which has reflected overseas trends in both law and economics but which has also developed a unique Australian structure and flavor, both in terms of its administrative machinery and in enforcement. Strong precedent has resulted, based on commonsense and a practical approach to antitrust, administratively as well as judicially, rather than one based on doctrinaire political, legal or economic thinking.

It is perhaps not unexpected that Australia has developed its own antitrust style. The nation came late to the modern antitrust scene, and so it had the opportunity to borrow and blend from other countries' laws and to take advantage of their antitrust experiences. In addition, the highly concentrated nature of Australian markets – due in part to their relatively small size, in part to the mergers of the 1950s and 1960s which were unchecked by antitrust activity, and in part to the traditionally highly protectionist nature of consecutive governments – meant that a more tailor-made law was needed to allow for the special Australian business environment. Many in the business sector in the early 1970s expected (perhaps "hoped" might have been a better choice of word) the new law to contain few sharp teeth, so that firms could continue to do as they had done in the heady days of unfettered freedoms. What emerged, however, was a tough set of specific prohibitions on various types of anti-competitive conduct, misuse of market power, vertical practices and mergers that were necessary and practical, and which were sensibly enforced and adjudicated upon.

The papers in this issue provide a historical as well as an analytical review of Australian antitrust in the last twenty years.[3] A common theme emerges in all the papers – of uncertainty and indecision to start with, of mistakes being made, but of a gradual synthesizing of political, legal and economic views over the two decades since 1974. Each paper is self-contained with respect to the historical and institutional background necessary to understand its particular focus. While this may lead to some duplication of coverage (but not necessarily of interpretation and analysis) for those reading the entire issue, it does mean that a reader who is interested in the Australian antitrust treatment of only one type of firm conduct can expect to find the complete picture in the chosen paper.

II. 1994 – New Directions for Australian Competition Policy

The second major milestone of Australian antitrust occurred in August 1993 with the release of the report of the National Competition Policy Review (1993), referred to widely as the Hilmer Report after the Chairman of the Review, Professor F.G. Hilmer. The review was established at the request of the Prime Minister and all State Premiers to produce guidelines for the role competition policy would play as a major element underlying Australia's push for deregulation and micro-economic reform. Recognizing that competition policy is more broadly based than competition law, the Hilmer Report (which is likely to be acted upon around the middle of 1995) has provided a blueprint for a more modern interpretation of competition policy, including antitrust, in Australia for at least the next decade.

Many of the Report's recommendations are controversial. They seek to apply the Act to State government business operations (which are mainly in utilities, and which will lose their "Shield of the Crown") and statutory marketing authorities; to produce structural reform of all public monopolies; to ensure that new competitors in such reformed markets be assured of access to essential facilities; to provide that the Act applies to all incorporated and unincorporated firms in Australia; and to embrace services as well as goods.[4] The Report argues that there should be no regulatory restrictions on competition unless such restrictions can be justified as being in the public interest. It proposes that the Trade Practices Commission (Australia's antitrust agency) be renamed the Australian Competition Commission and be expanded to include and extend the task formerly carried out by the Prices Surveillance Authority, namely the oversight of prices charged by firms operating in markets where effective competition is absent. In addition, it recommended that a new National Competition Council be established, which would be a "high level and independent analytical and advisory body" with a key role to play in assisting governments make policy decisions on all matters relating to competition. All these recommendations are aimed at producing an effective, unified national competition policy that will help improve efficiency in Australian markets and enhance the international competitiveness of Australian firms.

Several papers in this issue refer to the implications of the Hilmer Report for competition policy reform. It is too early to judge the long term effect of its proposals, many of which are recommended for phasing in over the next two to four years. They are still being assessed at Commonwealth and State level for their likely overall impact. However, just as the Act in 1974 engineered a new series of pro-competitive attitudes in Australia, it may confidently be expected that the Hilmer Report will provide the guiding philosophy and framework for the next stage of Australia's antitrust development, and for competition policy more generally. Of course, this pre-supposes full co-operation between the Commonwealth and the States, together with provision of sufficient resources to permit the implementation and enforcement of the proposed reforms.[5]

III. The Last Twenty Years – Competition Comes of Age in Australia

For most of its twenty years the Act was the responsibility of the Commonwealth Attorney-General. In 1993 it was shifted to the portfolio of the Assistant Treasurer, an important regulatory move by the Australian Government. Because of its strong commitment to a policy of deregulation and micro-economic reform, and in the interests of achieving a co-ordinated approach to regulatory reform,[6] the Government decided to centralize Ministerial responsibility for various regulatory authorities and their governing Acts within the Australian Treasury, the most senior and influential Commonwealth Government policy department.[7] Thus, it is apposite that The Honorable George Gear M.P., Assistant Treasurer of the Commonwealth of Australia, and Minister responsible for the Act, has written the foreword to this issue. His paper provides some valuable insights into the policy development, administration and enforcement of the Act, and into its future application. He concurs with the Hilmer Report's findings that there is more to competition policy than antitrust laws, but at the same time he acknowledges the "pivotal part" which the Act has played and will continue to play in the future. He argues that competition laws should apply uniformly and universally across Australian business, which suggests that this aspect of the Hilmer Report's recommendations will be supported by the Commonwealth Government. Finally, the Assistant Treasurer highlights the key competition-enhancing role played by trade policy and foreign competition in recent years in Australia, and he suggests a need for greater co-operation between different nations' antitrust authorities, as well as a greater focus on the extra-territorial application of national competition statutes.

The authors of the next three papers provide their own "broad picture" overviews and analyses of the history, enforcement and interpretation of the Act.

Without a doubt the most influential person in Australian antitrust has been Maureen Brunt, a leading industrial organization academic and commentator since the late 1950s, who has spent most of the last twenty years as a member of the Trade Practices Tribunal, Australia's antitrust administrative review body. Brunt's input into the key decisions of the Tribunal, especially in the important early days after 1974, laid the intellectual foundations for the balanced use of theoretical and applied economics in the unique Australian analytical approach to antitrust enforcement. Indeed, the methodologies established by the Tribunal for the identification of market boundaries and for the assessment of competition have been endorsed and used as precedent by both the Federal Court of Australia, the court of jurisdiction for the Act, and the High Court of Australia, the court of final appeal for Australian antitrust issues. In a comprehensive and challenging paper, Brunt provides a stocktake of Australian antitrust over the twenty years of the Act. After an illuminating survey of the patterns of Australian business (mis)conduct which led to a gradual recognition that legislative controls were necessary in order to revive competitive spirits, she analyzes our "extraordinary" antitrust achievements to date, and identifies several notable features of antitrust law and procedure in Australia. These include our approach to the task of market definition, our dual legal and administrative systems of enforcement, the development of a pure market power standard, and the treatment of vertical price and non-price conduct (which is at odds with currently prevailing American practice). She attributes these distinctive features to three main factors – the small Australian economy, the limitations of the courts in carrying out economic regulation, and "history", beginning with the visions of two men who each served as Attorney-General. She suggests that these combined characteristics might be so unique to Australia that the Australian antitrust phenomenon may never be replicated anywhere else in the world.

As to the future, Brunt warns that the recommendations of the Hilmer Report present "a decisive rejection of the Act and its institutions as controlling mechanisms in the deregulation and privatization process", but accepts that this might be an appropriate stand to take. However, she cautions that considerable care will be needed in handling the interface between the Act and the proposed new regulatory regime. And, consistent with the observations of several other authors, she notes that even though the Act is "economic law", there still exists a tension between economics and the law in Australian antitrust which will take some time to eliminate. Yet she ends on a positive note, declaring that we have achieved "a coherent body of antitrust jurisprudence that has relevance not just to the terms of the statute but to the nature of the economy and the characteristics of the legal system." Nevertheless she believes that a major challenge remains in the need to develop feasible and universally-applicable operational tests to enable the determination of what constitutes a "substantial lessening of competition" and "substantial market power", the two key thresholds which underlie the major prohibitions contained in the Act.

Neville Norman has been involved in Australian antitrust cases – by his count about 100 of them – for at least as long as the Act has been law. As an academic and raconteur, his expert economic evidence has been provocative and influential in many of these cases. As an economist who has sought constantly over the last twenty years to convert lawyers to the economist's way of thinking, he provides an unequalled historical insight into Australian antitrust as economists, lawyers and judges have struggled with the concepts of market, competition and market power. He argues that a major factor inhibiting a speedier acceptance of antitrust in Australia was the uneasy relationship between lawyers and economists, at least in terms of their basic approaches to the subject and its key concepts. In evaluating the way the Australian authorities have overcome these problems he highlights, as did Brunt, the key role played by the Trade Practices Tribunal in moulding Australian antitrust practice and attitudes. He believes that Australian antitrust has reached a stage of "considerable maturity" in its enforcement mechanisms, and that the Australian antitrust approach has been more ideologically balanced than in many other countries, and has concentrated on more relevant dynamic behavioral phenomena like entry barriers rather than paying too much attention to static structural conditions like market shares and market numbers. This approach has occurred, he argues, independently of the parallel underlying developments in economic theory, which provides testimony to the abilities of the Federal Court judges and Tribunal members whose commonsense and economic reasoning abilities were ahead of, or at least contemporaneous with, economists' theoretical developments.

In her conclusion, Brunt agreed with Klaus Hopt that there are certain inevitable stages in the development of antitrust law, no matter what country is being considered, but argued that the ultimate limits of action differ between countries. In a similar vein, Norman concludes that it may be true, as Kahn has argued, that there will never be an end to regulatory policy evolution, but argues that it is essential to ensure that policy neither swings as a pendulum nor goes round in circles. He suggests that Australian antitrust has avoided this and has experienced "a balanced progression". In a fortuitous anticipation of the paper by Mr Justice French, Norman argues that while we have achieved much in the last twenty years, there is still room for cross-fertilization and better understanding between the two professions, and that "[f]urther balanced progress will require the joint venture of law and economics of which antitrust is comprised to become more efficient, and perhaps a little less "competitive"."

Unlike the situation in the United States, few Australian judges have been prepared publicly to discuss the issues on which they are called to sit in judgment. Fortunately, however, two or three judges of the Federal Court have regularly attended conferences of lawyers and economists, giving papers and debating antitrust issues. Mr. Justice Robert French is one of them.[8] As a barrister practising in commercial matters he was for a time an Associate Commissioner of the Trade Practices Commission before his appointment to the Bench. He has now given judgments in several important Australian antitrust cases, and has produced what arguably is the definitive judgment on market definition in Australia.[9] In his contribution, Justice French provides a legal view of Australia's antitrust history. He touches on the famous *Coal Vend* case of 1911, Australia's first antitrust case (and perhaps the best first-instance antitrust judgment written in this country), and on various State antitrust laws, of which relatively little has been written. He also reflects on the interactions and conflicts between the law and the discipline of economics in the realm of antitrust, and, using market definition as an exemplar, evaluates the judicial search for a methodology of market definition.

Justice French notes that "[a]t the interface of law and economics judges are well clear of their syllogistic haven. The boundary between fact and law becomes blurred." This has caused problems for the judiciary especially with market definition, which "requires purposive and normative evaluation which cannot be characterized as mere fact finding",[10] although he acknowledges that the Federal Court's approach has evolved from a "fairly traditional judicial" one to an approach which is rather "more sensitive to the economic questions". He acknowledges the role played by economists on the Trade Practices Tribunal in providing judges "with some of the vocabulary and methodology which is necessary to the proper application of competition law." Yet while he admits that "some judgments might be correct and often are in law, it is not entirely clear on what economic grounds they are right", he notes with some comfort, one suspects, that "in further mitigation of the sins of judges ... even economists do not share universal satisfaction about the state of economic theory in relation to antitrust."

His Honor's main theme that the two disciplines can assist and re-inforce each other productively with constructive dialog echoes Norman's position. He cites as evidence of this a new Federal Court rule which permits economic testimony to be heard as argument or submission rather than in traditional evidentiary form, arguing that "what now passes for expert evidence might be put in its proper place at the bar table."[11] Thus he rejects suggestions made by some commentators that the judicial system is an inappropriate vehicle for making decisions on competition in markets, and foresees that judges will be the final adjudicators for the foreseeable future, "short of some apocalyptic constitutional change", although this will be arm in arm with economists, at least now in spirit.

The next four papers concentrate on individual sections in Part IV of the Act, which contains the main competition provisions.

David Round and John Siegfried discuss sections 45 and 45A of the Act which relate to price-fixing. Round is an academic economist, now in his seventh year as an Associate Commissioner of the Trade Practices Commission, who is also currently an Associate Member of AUSTEL, the Australian telecommunications regulator. Siegfried is an industrial organization researcher, antitrust scholar and expert witness who has been a frequent visitor to Australia in recent years. They relate that antagonism towards price-fixing gradually built up in Australia from 1967 (before which it was as entrenched a business habit as kangaroos were numerous in the country), and that with price-fixing for goods being made illegal per se under the 1977 amendments to the Act, attitudes towards such conduct changed markedly. However in a review of all twenty price-fixing cases heard under the Act, they show that collusive habits still persist, although a recent amendment to the Act raising the maximum corporate penalty for an offense to AUST$10 million, and for an offence by an individual to $500,000, may well cause a speedy change in the attitudes of both corporations and executives. Australian judges have been sympathetic to price-fixers, especially if price-fixing has occurred in response to poor trading conditions or to cut-throat competition that has led to losses. Round and Siegfried perceive that these relatively low fine levels suggest that it might take some time for the judiciary to treat price-fixing with the same condemnation as most economists do.[12] It appears that light penalties and perhaps a greater concentration of enforcement resources in other areas have signalled to the business community that it might still be economically rational to fix prices, and there has yet to develop in Australia any social stigma associated with being known as a corporate or individual price-fixer.

Round and Siegfried show that price-fixing has occurred in a wide variety of markets, albeit more commonly amongst small firms in local retail markets. The economic features of some of these markets do not fit in with traditional theoretical expectations about the characteristics of collusive firms and markets. Unlike the position in the United States where the courts have developed a structured analysis of cartel situations, the Australian courts have not as yet developed a consistent economic methodology for assessing whether price-fixing has occurred in the absence of direct "smoking gun" evidence.[13] This is perhaps to be expected, given that the Trade Practices Commission has brought few cases other than ones for which it had solid evidence of formal meetings having been held to fix prices. If events display such a "concurrence of time, character, direction and result", judges will infer a pre-arrangement to fix prices. The courts look for evidence that communication took place between the parties, expectations were raised and an obligation was accepted (by only one party – obligations do not have to be mutual). However, if the respondents can show their conduct is consistent with "ordinary commercial considerations" allegations of price-fixing will be dismissed. In addition, with so many highly concentrated markets in Australia, informal industry pricing mechanisms can operate which make it hard to detect and prove price-fixing in court.

Section 46 of the Act, which seeks to control the misuse of market power, including predatory pricing and other activities designed to eliminate or damage an otherwise efficient competitor, is analyzed by Philip Williams, an academic economist and frequent expert witness.[14] To support his belief that economically efficient behavior demonstrates the existence of a competitive market, he evaluates the *Queensland Wire Industries (QWI)* case, the major case heard under section 46 so far in Australia, as well as other Australian and New Zealand cases which he believes were inappropriately assessed by the courts (at least with respect to efficiency matters). These cases mainly involved a defendant with substantial market power in the supply of an input downstream to a less vertically integrated rival. Williams finds that no monopolist has as yet raised a successful efficiency defense, despite the indication given by the High Court of Australia in *QWI* that efficiency defenses were arguable. He argues that only inefficient conduct should be prohibited under section 46, as competitive markets demand efficient behavior of their participants.

Courts in New Zealand appear to have been more prepared than Australian courts to consider efficiency defenses. Williams spends some time analyzing the *Clear* case (which involved access to essential telecommunications facilities for a new entrant to the market as a consequence of deregulation), in which there was considerable input from the American economists Baumol, Willig and Kahn. The first instance decision was based on a notion of economic efficiency that would have preserved the incumbent monopolist's profits. This caused difficulty for many economists, especially as the charging regime pricing rule (which would not have applied symmetrically to the two parties) proposed by the Court would not have produced an efficient result in a world of positive transactions costs. In addition, the Court's solution involved regular reviews of prices and costs of the two telecommunications firms – the very regulation which the New Zealand Government had sought to avoid in deregulating the industry. In a postscript written shortly before this issue went to press, Williams notes that the Court of Appeal has now overturned the first instance decision. It rejected the inclusion of a monopoly profit component in an interconnection charge as anti-competitive, and found that the actions of the incumbent in offering only onerous terms for interconnection were designed to put the entrant at a competitive disadvantage and prevent it from successfully entering the market.

Williams concludes his paper by questioning those aspects of the Hilmer Report which recommended structural separation as a means of overcoming problems of vertical integration, and if this is not possible, the use of price regulation to secure access. He claims that the Report has misinterpreted the High Court in *QWI* in arguing that any refusal to supply by an essential facility constitutes a breach of section 46, saying it has overlooked the question as to whether such conduct is inconsistent with behavior in a competitive market. Additionally Williams regrets that the proposed introduction of a new access regime might by-pass the efficiency-based principles which the High Court has laid down. The suggested principles for access pricing ("fair and reasonable prices") are, he argues, inconsistent with the goals of economic efficiency which the Report acknowledges should underlie competition policy.

Vertical non-price arrangements are covered by section 47 of the Act, while resale price maintenance is prohibited per se in section 48. Both sections have been the subject of a considerable amount of legal and administrative action since 1974. Vertical practices are assessed in this issue by Ian McEwin, an academic economist who became so immersed in antitrust issues in the last few years as an economic adviser that he began to study law, and has just graduated as a lawyer. He brings a two-sided perspective to his consideration of the efficiency-enhancing versus anti-competitive aspects of vertical arrangements in Australia. Vertical conduct, he suggests, is "probably the most complex area" of Australian antitrust, a complexity partly caused by the detailed list of vertical practices which the Act prohibits.

At least in legislative terms, the Act disregards the Chicago school's position on vertical practices. Some vertical non-price restraints are illegal per se, while others are subject to a competition test, although all non-price vertical restraints may be authorized (and many have been) by the Trade Practices Commission on the grounds that they lead to public benefits which outweigh any anti-competitive detriments (the test is slightly different for third-line forcing). All except third-line forcing may be notified (a special procedure that gives statutory exemption from prosecution to the parties until such time as the Commission can demonstrate that the conduct is anti-competitive and does not produce a net public benefit). McEwin observes that most of the action on non-price vertical practices has been administrative rather than judicial. Formal consideration of economic efficiency issues has not been common in these determinations, where the focus has been more on the extent of entry barriers and seller market power. When the courts have considered the impact of exclusive dealing (which usually has involved a manufacturer refusing to supply a retailer who stocks a rival manufacturer's product) on competition, McEwin notes that they have focussed on the effects of the constraints on the competitive process (as directed by the Act), rather than on efficiency as such.[15] When the High Court had to consider third-line forcing, however, it based its decision on a literal interpretation of the Act and less on economic analysis, to avoid, it is suggested, the possible commercial consequences of finding a normal business practice illegal.

In contrast, vertical price restraints in the form of resale price maintenance are illegal per se (and have been so since 1971, before the Act was introduced), the legislative and judicial stand being much tougher than in the United States. There has been much litigation involving this type of conduct, and here the Trade Practices Commission has established an impressive win-loss record. The courts see resale price maintenance as preventing price competition. Free-rider justifications have played little, if any, part in cases decided so far, not surprising given that the practice is illegal per se and therefore no opportunity exists for such defenses to be argued in court. Nevertheless, some cases have argued the existence of benefits from the provision of dealer services made possible by resale price maintenance. The Hilmer Report has recommended that while the per se prohibition should remain, authorization on efficiency grounds should be available for resale price maintenance, so long as the demonstrated efficiency benefits outweigh any perceived anti-competitive detriments. McEwin concludes his paper by noting the sorry state of section 49 of the Act covering price discrimination, which is based on the Robinson-Patman Act and which has never been litigated by the Commission, and whose repeal has now been recommended by three committees of inquiry.

Section 50 of the Act covers mergers. Prior to 1974 there was no legislative control on mergers, and few comprehensive economic studies of merger activity exist in Australia.[16] Brian Johns has considered many mergers in his career. He left a professorial post (during which time he was also a member of the Trade Practices Tribunal) to become Director of the Bureau of Industry Economics (an independent research body created by the Australian Government to undertake research into all aspects of Australian industries), where he directed a major research study on mergers (Bureau of Industry Economics (1990)). From there he went to the Trade Practices Commission as Deputy Chairman. He is now a member of the International Air Services Commission, which allocates overseas route capacity to Australian airlines, and still serves as an Associate Member of the Trade Practices Commission.

In his paper, Johns outlines the history of merger policy in Australia since 1974, noting that for most of this period tight control over mergers has been eschewed in favor of legislation designed to facilitate acquisitions which offer the potential to lower costs and enhance the international competitiveness of Australian industries. However, it is indicative of mixed feelings about mergers in Australia that, more than any other area of antitrust in this country, legislation against mergers has swung like the pendulum Norman argues we should avoid. Over the two decades of the Act, several public inquiries have been held on the need to regulate mergers. As a result, Australia has moved from a prohibition of mergers likely to produce a substantial lessening of competition to a far less interventionist policy of proscribing only those likely to lead to a position of market dominance or control. Next the criterion for prohibition was based only on dominance, and currently the legislation has reverted to the more stringent substantial lessening of competition standard. At all times, however, authorization has been available for mergers, where, if efficiency or other benefits can be shown to outweigh the acquisition's anti-competitive detriments, it can be approved by the Trade Practices Commission. In other words, Australia has employed a market power standard (of varying degrees of stringency) that under certain circumstances can be overridden by an efficiency standard.

Johns' paper indicates that, while there have been a few major judicial and administrative merger decisions,[17] court action and authorization applications have been less common than under the other major sections of the Act. He suggests two main reasons for this relative lack of activity – the high threshold test of dominance that existed from 1977 to 1992 (which allowed many mergers to proceed "which were likely to substantially lessen competition in the relevant market"), and a view by governments that in a small open economy prohibitions on mergers could stand in the way of achieving scale economies and thus damage the international competitiveness of Australian firms. He questions whether this latter justification is sound, arguing that "it is competition which forces firms to upgrade their performance." Unfortunately, with so few cases having been considered, Australia suffers from a lack of hard data on the public benefits of mergers and on how these measure up against the anti-competitive detriments of the acquisitions. The limited empirical evidence that exists on mergers does not provide convincing support for a general conclusion that they yield positive net benefits.

Just as the United States looms large on Canada's doorstep, so too does Australia in relation to New Zealand. The two countries are steadily moving closer together, at least in terms of commercial activity and government trade and economic relations treaties, and Australian lay assessors have been appointed to sit alongside judges on the High Court of New Zealand to hear antitrust cases. In view of their geographic proximity and closeness of economic, business and political cultures, New Zealand's somewhat younger antitrust legislation is quite similar to the Australian law, although there are some notable differences with respect to exclusive dealing and resale price maintenance, amongst other things. This issue concludes with a paper by Alan Bollard, formerly an academic and at the time of writing the paper Director of the New Zealand Institute of Economic Research, the country's leading independent research organization. He is now Chairman of the Commerce Commission, New Zealand's antitrust regulator. In his paper, Bollard analyzes the role assigned to antitrust policy in a small open economy with high levels of domestic market concentration which is undergoing massive economic liberalization, and in which imports are generally expected to act as a constraint on domestic market power. He believes that antitrust legislation and enforcement in New Zealand has been "relatively permissive", especially with respect to mergers, such that it can be characterized as "highly enabling" for the major corporate restructuring which the deregulatory process was designed to achieve. Notwithstanding this, he finds little evidence that there has been any significant increase in the already-high levels of market concentration in New Zealand.

Bollard highlights the differences that have developed between Australian and New Zealand antitrust, despite the fact that the Australian Act provided the model for New Zealand's Commerce Act. He notes that the Commerce Act is driven by efficiency-focussed micro-economic theories, even though its stated objective is to "promote competition in markets within New Zealand", and shows how New Zealand has developed its own differentiated antitrust jurisprudence, borrowing from several jurisdictions apart from Australia.[18] In particular, it has drawn on American legal precedent, on American economists as expert witnesses in cases involving conduct by dominant firms with respect to essential facilities, and on

American developments in microeconomics (notably contestability theory, at least in philosophy if not in explicit consideration) that appeared to offer a "light-handed regulatory option".

Despite these differences, significant legislative and administrative interaction still occurs on antitrust issues between Australia and New Zealand, although New Zealand has recently become more liberal than Australia in its prohibitions on anti-competitive conduct and in its anti-merger provisions. With the Closer Economic Relations Trade Agreement made between Australia and New Zealand in 1988 and the creation of a trans-Tasman free trade area, there came the hope of further harmonization of business laws between the two countries, especially as the concept of a trans-Tasman market has been incorporated into the two countries' statutes with respect to the misuse of market power. Further harmonization would now seem to be a matter for the future, especially in view of some of the recommendations of the Hilmer Report, whose overall focus, despite the goal of increasing efficiency in Australian markets, is still the promotion of competition, and which has not made the achievement of competitive markets subservient to an "efficiency at all costs" attitude.

IV. Future Prospects

"She'll be right, mate" is a common Australian saying that translates as "no worries" or "things will be fine". This phrase aptly sums up Australia's two decades of the Trade Practices Act. Born into an hostile environment, with its enforcers and practitioners flying blind in the face of little hard empirical evidence on the conduct and performance of firms in Australian markets, there developed at first a grudging and then a steady public acceptance of the goals of the Act and of its enforcement procedures. The partisan attitudes that have characterized American antitrust, in terms of political and legislative approaches, enforcement philosophies, judicial pronouncements and schools of economic thought, have been largely absent in Australia. A broad consensus that antitrust was needed came about steadily. Australia has witnessed an antitrust evolution rather than a revolution. It has based its statutes on both the British and American antitrust laws and approaches and its judges have not ignored what has been decided in British, American and even European cases. But in the final analysis, the last twenty years of Australian antitrust has been as uniquely Australian as the by-now internationally recognized Aussie greeting of "g'day, mate".

The Trade Practices Act has been undoubtedly effective over the last two decades, almost unobtrusively so in many ways, in changing the collusive, coercive, exclusionary and predatory nature of Australian business. The spirit of the Act and of the Trade Practices Commission lurks constantly in corporate boardrooms in 1994, a vast change from the position in 1974. Few would claim that enforcement of the Act has not resulted in a more efficient, competitive business environment in Australia, although some assert that the Commission's market-oriented approach to assessing proposed mergers is inappropriate, because of the commercial delays which such investigations can produce. Overall, Australia enters the last half-decade of the twentieth century in good shape, both in terms of its antitrust achievements as well as in terms of the potential improvements in efficiency and competition, and hence social welfare, which should be derived from implementation of the Hilmer Report's recommendations. As far as competitive rivalry is concerned, a new frontier awaits Australian markets, firms and executives. Consumers will be well served. And for this, the Trade Practices Act 1974 will have been both the foundation and springboard.

Notes

* I am most grateful to Geoff Shepherd, General Editor of *Review of Industrial Organization*, for his invitation to edit this special issue which evaluates the first two decades of Australian antitrust under the Trade Practices Act 1974, and for his encouragement and unfailing cheerfulness throughout the whole project.

[1] The *Industrial Organization Review* paper was written before but published after the pioneering March 1976 decision of the Trade Practices Tribunal (Australia's quasi-judicial review authority for administrative antitrust decisions) in the case widely known as *QCMA* (*Re Queensland Co-operative Milling Association Ltd., Defiance Holdings Ltd. (Proposed Mergers with Barnes Milling Ltd.)* (1976) ATPR 40–012). This decision, which is referred to in most of the papers in this issue, was a landmark judgment which set the framework for the Australian way of assessing competition in markets. While its reasoning was not easily understood by many legal practitioners or accepted at first by the business community, it has become the very cornerstone of Australian antitrust. Without this decision the lengthy period of misunderstanding predicted in my 1976 paper may well have occurred, to the detriment of Australian industry and public welfare.

[2] This observation is confirmed by many of the authors in this issue, especially Brunt, Norman and French.

[3] For more detailed discussions of the Act and its enforcement, see Corones (1990), Hurley and Wiffen (1994) and the journal *Australian Business Law Review*, published by The Law Book Company Limited, North Ryde, New South Wales, Australia.

[4] As well as these broad recommendations, some important changes to specific sections in the Act have been recommended where the current legislation was thought to be "clearly deficient from the standpoint of a national competition policy." Among these are suggested changes to prohibit price-fixing for services as well as goods; to eliminate the per se ban on third line forcing, making it subject to the substantial lessening of competition test applicable to other vertical non-price practices; to permit resale price maintenance to be authorized on public benefit grounds; and to repeal the specific prohibition on price discrimination (such conduct could still be illegal under section 46 of the Act which deals with the misuse of market power).

[5] At the time of writing this introduction, the practical details of implementing the Hilmer Report's recommendations were still being evaluated by the Commonwealth and State governments. While some of its more controversial recommendations will require significant inter-government co-operation and compromise, especially with respect to reforming public monopolies and providing third-party access to essential facilities, other less contentious recommendations such as fine tuning of the Act and restraining monopoly pricing behavior are likely to be implemented by legislative change without much delay.

[6] In 1976 I had called for centralization of control over some of Australia's major regulatory authorities, arguing that:

> "[t]here is as yet no evidence of any attempt being made to co-ordinate the efforts and philosophy of all the Government's advisory, assistance and regulatory agencies. The danger of conflict between these various agencies looms as a threat to balanced regulation. A much more general,

co-ordinated view of business and its operating environment needs to be taken ..." (Round (1976, p. 150))

[7] Not all of the regulatory bodies have been centralized. For example AUSTEL, the telecommunications regulator, remains subject to the Minister for Communications. It is thought necessary, on the grounds of technical expertise *inter alia*, at least in the medium term, that a specialist regulatory body be retained for this industry which is in the throes of massive pro-competitive deregulation (based on new entry) at a time of sustained technological advances. The Hilmer Report argues that its proposed competition policy framework can be best executed by enforcement being concentrated in one authority, rather than in a series of industry-specific regulators, in order to avoid regulatory capture, to ensure consistency in regulatory approach, to avoid wasteful duplication of scarce skills, and to minimize regulatory costs.

[8] At the time of writing this introduction, Justice French had just been appointed President of the Native Title Tribunal, a new court established to handle claims by indigenous Aboriginal people over Australian land. Hence his expertise will largely be lost to the Federal Court, at least in the short run, as he deals with a likely heavy case load in the Tribunal (although he does retain his commission as a Judge of the Court).

[9] This was in an appeal case before the Full Federal Court, in which His Honor delivered the majority judgment. See *Singapore Airlines Limited v Taprobane Tours WA Pty Ltd* (1991) ATPR 41–159.

[10] This point was made strongly by the High Court of Australia in its landmark 1989 judgment (*Queensland Wire Industries Pty. Ltd. v. The Broken Hill Proprietary Company Limited & Anor.* (1989) ATPR 40–925), when it was made explicit that a clear linkage exists between determining market power and the process of market definition.

[11] This rule has not as yet been taken advantage of. The Australian antitrust community awaits with interest the first application of this new dimension for antitrust economic argument.

[12] At the time of writing this introduction, at least four other price-fixing cases were in the early stages of court proceedings. Also, the Federal Court has just found two Cairns tour booking agents guilty of price-fixing aimed at preventing a competitor from offering significant discounts (*Trade Practices Commission v. Caravella & Anor* (1994) ATPR 41–293); it continued the pattern of leniency by fixing penalties of only $5000 and $500 for the two defendants.

[13] Few price-fixing cases have been heard by the courts in the last five years, a period in which the economic sophistication of the judiciary has improved markedly.

[14] Given the high degree of market power held by the two or three largest firms in most important Australian markets, it came as no surprise in 1974 and for some time thereafter to find that these firms were being very cautious in their conduct, lest what had previously been regarded as commercially acceptable behavior now be targeted for antitrust action. Section 46 has the ability to strike at the conduct of many Australian firms, and private plaintiffs have used it with increasing frequency in recent years, after a hesitant early period in which potential litigants sought to discern just what the section prohibited and what proof might be needed to secure a favorable judgment. The *Queensland Wire Industries* judgment, *supra* n. 10, eliminated most of the uncertainty as to what it would take to breach this section, and the Trade Practices Commission (1990) moved quickly to publish shortly thereafter a guideline for its administration and enforcement of the section.

[15] There is a dearth of empirical literature to help guide the courts on the effects of such practices in Australia. For the last twenty years, empirical studies of industrial organization topics generally have not been a major industry in Australian economic research circles (see Round (1974) for a review of such research in Australia as of the early 1970s). Research grants and better data availability have tended to favor empirical research into macro-economic issues.

[16] A comparative review of the two major academic studies is provided by Ravenscraft (1987).

[17] The Trade Practices Commission has produced two sets of merger guidelines, in 1986 and a draft set in 1992 (as yet not finalized). The 1986 guidelines never appeared to be particularly influential, and, while the most recent set is used internally by the Commission in its consideration of whether to oppose certain mergers, it does not appear to have attracted any significant public comment.

[18] Further evidence of a more liberal approach to business conduct in New Zealand is provided by the fact that the term "public benefit" has been interpreted very widely under the Commerce Act to include private benefits to firms, unlike the more consumer-oriented interpretation given to the term in Australia (which has been controversial, as is noted by Maureen Brunt in her paper in this issue).

References

Bureau of Industry Economics (1990) *Mergers and Acquisitions*, Research Report 36, Canberra, Australian Government Publishing Service.

Corones, S.G. (1990) *Competition Law and Policy in Australia*, North Ryde, The Law Book Company Limited.

Hurley, A. and G. Wiffen (1994) *Outline of Trade Practices and Consumer Protection Law*, Sydney, Butterworths.

National Competition Policy Review (F.G. Hilmer, Chairman) (1993) *National Competition Policy*, Canberra, Australian Government Publishing Service.

Ravenscraft, D.J. (1987) 'Australian Mergers and Takeovers: A Review of Recent Evidence', *Economic Analysis and Policy*, **17**, 221–238.

Round, D.K. (1974) 'The Industrial Organization Vacuum in Australia', *Economic Record*, **50**, 169–198.

Round, David K. (1976) 'The 1974 Australian Trade Practices Legislation', *Industrial Organization Review*, **4**, 142–150.

Trade Practices Commission (1990) *Misuse of Market Power. Section 46 of the Trade Practices Act 1974*, Canberra, Trade Practices Commission.

Review of Industrial Organization **9:** 475–482, 1994.

FOREWORD

A Minister's Perspective on Twenty Years of the Trade Practices Act

GEORGE GEAR
Assistant Treasurer, Commonwealth of Australia, Parliament House, Canberra, ACT 2600, Australia

I. Introduction

The Trade Practices Act 1974 (hereafter 'the Act') has played a pivotal role in the Australian economy over the first twenty years of its operation. During this time there has been an increasing recognition of the role which competition plays in enhancing economic efficiency, and in contributing to sustainable economic growth and improvements in living standards. The competition and consumer protection provisions of the Act have been crucial in this regard by fostering a more competitive business environment and helping to ensure that the benefits of microeconomic reforms are passed on to consumers. It seems most commentators, while perhaps arguing for some changes, consider the Act has generally been successful in maintaining competition within markets and promoting fair trading behavior.

The development of competition policy more generally has also kept pace with the 'internationalisation' of the Australian economy. In particular, opening the economy to increased international competition has highlighted the need to increase competitive pressures in some areas of the domestic economy – in particular by expanding the coverage of the Act to formerly exempt areas.

This paper provides a brief outline of the Act and its objectives, explores the historical development of competition law in Australia, and examines the role of the Act in the broader competition policy framework. Finally, it suggests some likely future directions for the development and enforcement of the Act.

II. Outline of the Act

The Act has two main parts. Part IV deals with anti-competitive business practices, and its content will strike a familiar chord with students of antitrust in other jurisdictions. It prohibits collusive price-fixing, other forms of anti-competitive horizontal or vertical agreements, the misuse of substantial market power, anti-competitive price discrimination, and certain mergers. Part V contains consumer protection provisions aimed at preventing unfair trading practices, such as misleading or deceptive conduct and false and misleading representations and advertising.

The Part IV provisions are of most relevance from an industrial organization perspective and thus form the focus of this paper. While these provisions will be emphasised, the important role of the Part V provisions in preventing consumers from being exploited through unfair trading practices should not be underestimated.

The agency with the primary responsibility for enforcing the Act is the Trade Practices Commission (TPC), although there are also rights of private action. A notable feature of the Australian system is the power given to the TPC to authorize a number of forms of conduct that would otherwise breach Part IV of the Act if it considers that there is a net benefit to the public arising from the conduct.[1] Authorization exempts a party from legal action under the Act for that particular conduct, and is an important characteristic distinguishing the Act from many overseas competition statutes.[2]

III. Objectives of the Act

While the Act does not have an explicit objective, it is generally agreed that the primary goal of its antitrust provisions is to promote market competition, and thus to increase economic efficiency.

It is generally accepted that strong competition is the best means of developing a more efficient economy which can generate higher sustainable living standards for the community. Competition provides the spur for companies to search for ways of providing better value to consumers through better quality or more reasonably priced goods. Competition also ensures that resources are used efficiently to produce those goods and services which are highly valued by the community.

Nevertheless, the competition policy provisions of the Act are not about enhancing competition for its own sake. There may be situations where competition does not achieve economic efficiency, or would conflict with other important social objectives. For example, there may be cases where tying agreements among some firms may deliver enhanced value to consumers despite some lessening of competition, or a merger may result in a firm increasing its operating efficiency (for example due to achieving significant economies of scale or scope). These types of situations are addressed by the authorization process, where breaches of the Act can be given immunity on public benefit grounds.

IV. History of Competition Law in Australia

The development of a set of national laws in Australia to deal with restrictive business practices has not been without its difficulties, and this is reflected in some features of the current Act. The first law controlling anti-competitive business behavior was the Australian Industries Preservation Act 1906. Drawing upon the

United States' Sherman Act of 1890, it prohibited certain conduct that restrained trade or commerce, or destroyed or injured Australian industries by unfair competition. The Act was little used after a restrictive interpretation of Commonwealth (federal) constitutional powers in 1910 substantially constrained its operation.[3] The Commonwealth was unsuccessful in its attempts to overcome the constitutional limitations through a series of referenda in the first half of the century.[4]

The 1950s and 1960s witnessed growing evidence of the cartelisation and concentration of Australian industry, with detrimental effects on competition in the economy. A number of Royal Commissions enquired into restrictive business practices, highlighting the relatively wide extent of such practices.[5] For example, in 1961 there were over 600 trade associations in Australia, of which an estimated 58–66 per cent engaged in anti-competitive practices.[6]

A further attempt was made to enact a national competition law in 1965, when the first Trade Practices Act became law. While a significant advance over the previous situation, the delays inherent in this Act's system of registration of certain agreements and possible disallowance if contrary to the public interest,[7] have been described as "an invitation to make hay while the sun shines."[8] Initially, there was no prohibition on resale price maintenance.[9] The 1965 Act was held invalid by the High Court in 1971 on constitutional grounds.[10] However, the ruling clarified the Commonwealth's constitutional powers in the regulation of business conduct, indicating a constitutional basis for future attempts at regulating trade practices. Replacement legislation was enacted in 1971.[11]

A change of Government in the following year led to a new approach to competition law, and the current Trade Practices Act became law in 1974. Unlike previous legislation which provided for administrative investigation of conduct, the new Act was based on prohibition of particular forms of conduct. The Act relies on the Commonwealth's constitutional powers over corporations, interstate trade and commerce power and some other powers. While this is sufficient to ensure coverage of much of the most significant sectors of Australian business, there are also important sectors in which coverage is minimal or partial.

Following the report of the Swanson Committee,[12] significant amendments to the Act were made in 1977, which among other things introduced tougher prohibitions against price fixing and the now familiar "substantial lessening of competition" test. In the same year, the Act was extended to the Commonwealth and its agencies, but not to the States or Territories, in so far as they carry on a business. In 1986, the Government amended the prohibition on misuse of market power and extended the merger provisions to certain overseas mergers.[13]

In 1992, the Act was amended in response to the reports of the Griffiths Committee[14] and the Cooney Committee.[15] The amendments included changing the merger test to prohibit mergers that substantially lessen competition,[16] and increasing the maximum penalties for breaches of the competition provisions from \$AUST250,000 to \$AUST10 million.

In 1993, the National Competition Policy Review (the Hilmer Review) reported on the best means to give effect to a national, universally applied competition policy.[17] The Committee proposed a framework of laws, principles, processes and institutions intended to address competition policy issues, an essential element being that the Act should be extended to cover all forms of business conduct. The Committee also recommended some relatively minor amendments to the competitive conduct provisions of Part IV of the Act.

A number of recent reviews have also been conducted into different aspects of the Act, including the operation of the secondary boycott provisions of the Act,[18] the international liner cargo shipping provisions of the Act,[19] and the adequacy of remedies.[20]

The large number of reviews of, and amendments to, the Act reflect the evolution of competition law in Australia and overseas – both in terms of theoretical developments and case law and also the interest in, and the importance of, competition law in this country. The Trade Practices Act has now been generally accepted as an essential part of Australia's business environment, bringing about a significant change in entrenched forms of business conduct.

V. The Act in the Context of Broader Micro-Economic Reform Policy

V.1 A Broader Role for Competition Policy

Until recent times competition policy in Australia has been treated synonymously with competition law. While laws such as the Trade Practices Act have an important role in promoting competitive behavior, it is now generally accepted that a wider range of laws and policies also have important influences on the strength of competitive forces within the economy. This was recently highlighted by the Hilmer Review,[21] which noted that competition policy in its broadest sense encompasses all policy dealing with the extent and nature of competition in the economy. The Hilmer Committee considered that competition policy should consist of six elements, which are represented in Table 1 below. These elements reflect the potentially broad scope of competition policy – of which the Trade Practices Act is but one important element.

As noted above, the Hilmer Committee recommended that the Act be extended to cover all forms of business conduct. However, the Committee recognised that applying the provisions of the Act will have little or no effect on competition in a market where, for example, anti-competitive market structures or regulations prevent the establishment of effective competition. In such cases, a wider range of competition policy measures may be required.

V.2 Competition Policy, Deregulation and Micro-Economic Reform

Over the past decade the Australian business community and government policy-makers have become increasingly aware of the need to develop a more competitive,

Table I. Elements of competition policy

1. Limiting anti-competitive conduct by firms (eg. prohibitions on price-fixing, misuse of market power, and certain mergers).
2. Reforming regulation which unjustifiably restricts competition (eg. removal of statutory barriers to entry in areas such as domestic aviation and telecommunications).
3. Reforming the structure of public monopolies to facilitate competition where these are to be opened to competition or privatized (for example structurally separating natural monopoly elements from potentially competitive activities).
4. Providing third-party access to certain facilities that are essential for competition.
5. Restraining monopoly pricing behavior (prices surveillance and monitoring by a government prices agency).
6. Fostering "competitive neutrality" between government and private businesses when they compete (i.e. facilitating competition on an equal basis).

efficient and dynamic economy. One key means of achieving this objective has been to increase the openness of the domestic economy to foreign competition, by reducing barriers to foreign trade such as tariffs and quotas. Reductions in barrier protection have enhanced competition in a number of sectors in the domestic economy, notably manufacturing, and have increased pressures on businesses in these sectors to innovate, reduce costs and improve their quality of service.

Greater external competition also reduces, to some extent, concerns over relatively high levels of domestic industry concentration. In the Australian context, the influence of the external sector on domestic competition was recently acknowledged in the introduction of a new merger test, accompanied by factors to be taken into account in considering whether a particular merger is likely to substantially lessen competition in a market. These factors include matters such as the level of import competition in the market, and barriers to entry (including entry from overseas firms).

The link between trade and competition policy is also reflected in arrangements pursuant to the Closer Economic Relations Trade Agreement between Australia and New Zealand. Under these arrangements, Australia and New Zealand have enacted provisions prohibiting misuse of market power in trans-Tasman markets,[22] rather than apply anti-dumping measures to trade between the two countries. Such issues are also currently being considered by the OECD's Competition Law and Policy Committee, of which Australia has been an active participant.

The increased pressures from international competition have also highlighted the need for a greater degree of competition in Australia's non-traded sector. Some non-traded industries have traditionally faced little competition. For example, until recently telecommunications was dominated by a statutory monopoly, and interstate domestic aviation was a statutory duopoly. State-based statutory monopoly utilities supply a large proportion of the electricity and gas markets, and some agricultural commodities are subject to statutory marketing board arrangements. Importantly, these arrangements are not generally invalidated by the Trade Practices Act, as the anti-competitive result does not involve voluntary conduct by businesses of the kind prohibited by the Act.

The increasing recognition of the substantial costs of a lack of effective competition in these vital sectors has led Governments, not only in Australia but around the world, to begin dismantling these types of anti-competitive regulatory arrangements. The gains from such reforms to date have been substantial and further gains are achievable. However, international experience has demonstrated the need to ensure that the gains from reform are not captured by firms engaging in anti-competitive conduct, rather than being passed on to producers and consumers in the form of lower prices or higher quality products. The Act will therefore play a central role in ensuring that the benefits of micro-economic reform are realised in full.

However, the current Act is less effective than it might be, because of the continued exemption of important sectors of the economy from its coverage. There are two major exceptions to the coverage of the Act. First, the 'Shield of the Crown' doctrine, which provides that a statute will only be found to bind the Crown (Government) by express words or necessary implication, provides exemption for some State and Territory government businesses. (Since 1977 the Act has expressly bound the Crown in right of the Commonwealth and its authorities in so far as they engage in business.) The second exception lies in the Commonwealth's limited powers under the Australian Constitution. These limitations allow a number of unincorporated businesses, including some businesses in some professions, to escape the operation of the Act unless they engage in interstate or overseas trade or commerce.

There is no economic or social rationale for these exemptions from the Act, as has been recognised by most commentators. A major aim of the Commonwealth Government is to extend the reach of the Act in co-operation with the State and Territory Governments, so as to apply the Act uniformly and universally across Australian business.

VI. Future Directions

The Trade Practices Act has played a crucial role over the first twenty years of its operation in helping to create a competitive business environment in Australia. The Act will continue to play a pivotal part in the broader competition policy framework, particularly in areas which have recently been opened up to competition and brought under the coverage of the Act. Implementing the recommendations of the Hilmer Review will be an important milestone in bringing about a national, universally applied competition policy in Australia.

However, global competition is also expanding the focus of competition policy in Australia, as elsewhere. The recent growth in international merger activity has heightened the need for increased co-operation between the competition authorities of different nations, and placed greater emphasis on the convergence of anti-trust processes and greater focus on the extraterritorial application of national competition statutes.

Moreover, with the successful conclusion of the GATT Uruguay Round, and as recognised in the November 1991 OECD Trade Committee Symposium, competition policy is likely to be a major new issue on the international trade policy agenda of the 1990s. This recognition has been motivated by the evidence of increasing interactions, both positive and negative, between trade and competition policies.

Clearly, competition policy can no longer be considered to be purely domestic in nature. It is in the international arena, along with expanded domestic coverage of the Act, that many of the main challenges for the future development and application of competition policy lie.

Notes

[1] Authorization cannot be granted for misuse of market power, resale price maintenance, price discrimination, and some price agreements. Note that authorization decisions are appellable to the independent Trade Practices Tribunal.
[2] The Commerce Act of New Zealand has a similar authorization provision.
[3] *Huddart Parker & Co Pty Ltd* v *Moorehead* (1910) 8 CLR 330.
[4] Referenda were held in 1913, 1919, 1929 and 1944. See Nieuwenhuysen, J.P. (ed.) (1976) *Australian Trade Practices: Readings*, second edition, London, Croom Helm Ltd., p. 300.
[5] Royal Commissions on Restrictive Trade Practices were conducted in Western Australia and Tasmania. See Walker, G. de Q. (1967) *Australian Monopoly Law*, Melbourne, F.W. Cheshire Pty. Ltd., p. 15.
[6] Hunter, A. (1961) 'Restrictive Practices and Monopolies in Australia', *Economic Record*, **37**, 25–52.
[7] Collusive tendering and bidding were prohibited, but a defence was available if the agreement was registered and not made for the purposes of a particular auction or tender – a general practice of collusive tendering was permissible.
[8] Taperell, G.Q., R.B. Vermeesch and D.J. Harland (1983) *Trade Practices and Consumer Protection*, third edition, Sydney, Butterworths, p. 19.
[9] Such a prohibition was enacted in 1971.
[10] See *Strickland* v *Rocla Concrete Pipes & Ors* (1971) 124 CLR 468.
[11] The Restrictive Practices Act was enacted in 1971. A Restrictive Trade Practices Bill and a Monopolies Commission Bill were introduced into Parliament in 1972, but lapsed with the election of a new Government in 1972.
[12] See Trade Practices Act Review Committee (the Swanson Committee) (1976) *Report to the Minister for Business and Consumer Affairs*, Canberra, Australian Government Publishing Service.
[13] Trade Practices Revision Act 1986.
[14] See House of Representatives Standing Committee on Legal and Constitutional Affairs (the Griffiths Committee) (1989) *Mergers, Takeovers and Monopolies: Profiting from Competition?*, Canberra, Australian Government Publishing Service.
[15] See Senate Standing Committee on Legal and Constitutional Affairs (the Cooney Committee) (1991) *Mergers, Monopolies and Acquisitions: Adequacy of Existing Legislative Controls*, Canberra, Australian Government Publishing Service.
[16] Previously mergers and acquisitions had been prohibited where they resulted in, or enhanced, a position of dominance.

[17] National Competition Policy Review (F.G. Hilmer, Chairman) (1993) *National Competition Policy*, Canberra, Australian Government Publishing Service.
[18] Senate Standing Committee on Education, Employment and Training (October 1993) *The Operation of Sections 45D and 45E of the Trade Practices Act 1974*, Canberra, Australian Government Publishing Service.
[19] Brazil, P. et al. (1994) *Liner Shipping Cargoes and Conferences*, Canberra, Australian Government Publishing Service. Part X of the Act regulates outward cargo (liner) shipping services operated by conferences and provides certain exemptions from the provisions of Part IV of the Act, including: fixing freight rates; imposing cargo restrictions; loyalty agreements with shippers; and practices essential to the conference service and of overall benefit to exporters.
[20] At the time of writing, remedies under the Act were being examined by the Australian Law Reform Commission, with particular emphasis on the remedies available under the consumer protection provisions of Part V.
[21] *Supra* n. 17.
[22] The Tasman Sea separates Australia and New Zealand.

Review of Industrial Organization **9:** 483–526, 1994.

The Australian Antitrust Law after 20 Years – a Stocktake

MAUREEN BRUNT*
Graduate School of Management and Law School, University of Melbourne, Carlton, Victoria 3053, Australia

Abstract. The Australian Trade Practices Act 1974 is a court-centered law of the American type. After 20 years it has much to its credit – the abandonment of cartelization and the achievement of a coherent body of antitrust law focused upon market power as the central concept. The law has some distinctive features: the approach to market definition; the possibility of authorization on grounds of public benefit; the treatment of verticals. The challenge now is to expose the exempt sectors to the Act and to design a compatible regime for the corporatized and privatized utilities.

Key words: Australia, antitrust, cartel, authorization, exemptions, privatization

I. Introduction

The "Australian antitrust law" is an apt characterization of the restrictive practices provisions of the Trade Practices Act 1974 ("the Act"). To label the statute an antitrust statute highlights its two essential features: first, that the objective is the promotion of effective or workable competition; and second, that the means employed are court-centered, requiring the interpretation and enforcement of statutory terms by courts of law.

The enactment of this type of law in 1974 constituted a distinct break with the past. After two decades, what have we achieved from this approach? What have we learnt? What are the unsettled questions? How might the Act and its implementation be improved? Does it require reshaping to meet the challenges of the '90s? And, most fundamentally, what are the limits of a court-centered competition policy?

These are questions of immediate and obvious interest to Australian readers. Overseas readers may well approach the topic from a comparative perspective: Are there, as Klaus J. Hopt suggests in a fascinating paper (1987, pp. 297–306), certain inevitable stages in the development of antitrust law which proceeds through the control of cartel conduct and mergers to reach its "limits" in the "abuse control of market-dominating companies"? Are there standard conceptual and practical problems that any national system must encounter?[1] Hopt would say that national differences are largely to be explained by variations in timing of the stages of development, and perhaps by the existence of federal structures such as the EC (pp. 306–310). Or can there be fundamental inter-country differences that stem from distinctive features of the economy such as size and openness to trade and to investment; from the historical legacy of restrictive practices and degree of market concentration; from the nature of the legal system and the relationship between legal and administrative institutions; and from differences in political systems and social values? Australia has a population of only 17 million. Inevitably its markets must be more concentrated than American markets; not all can be opened to international trade. What does antitrust look like in an economy such as this?

II. Anatomy of the Law

Australia is a federal system, the Commonwealth and the six States, with a division of powers laid down by the Australian Constitution. For constitutional reasons, the law is directed in the main to the activities of corporations. There is a significant list of exempt or exemptible activities (ss. 51 and 172(2)).

As a preliminary to our stocktake it is convenient to summarize the main features of the Act as at the end of 1993. While there have been important amendments to the Act over the years, the basic structure has remained much the same.

II.1. The Statutory Prohibitions

The explicit objective of the Act, derived both from its overall structure and some of its terms, is to promote and regulate competition between business firms.[2] The core of the restrictive trade practices law is to be found in Part IV of the Act, containing what are colloquially known as the "prohibitions", a specification of conduct that will breach the Act (if not granted "authorization"): anti-competitive agreements, primary collective boycotts, secondary boycotts and related concerted arrangements, "misuse of market power" (initially termed "monopolization"), anti-competitive exclusive dealing, resale price maintenance, anti-competitive price discrimination, and anti-competitive mergers.

The statute itself lays down which practices are to be treated as per se illegal in the courts: price-fixing (subject to some exceptions), primary boycotts, third line forcing, and resale price maintenance (RPM). All the rest are subject to a statutorily-specified competition test, most often expressed as conduct that "has the purpose, or has or is likely to have the effect, of substantially lessening competition."

Actions for breach are brought in the ordinary court system, albeit with exclusive jurisdiction given to the Federal Court (subject to appeals to the High Court by special leave). Only civil actions are available. There are no jury trials.

II.2. Authorization and the Dual Adjudication System

For some conduct that might otherwise contravene the Act, exemptions may be sought on a case-by-case basis by way of an application for "authorization" on grounds of net public benefit. An application is made in the first instance to an administrative body, the Trade Practices Commission ("the Commission"). The

Commission's decisions are subject to review by another administrative body, the more formal quasi-judicial Trade Practices Tribunal ("the Tribunal"), consisting of a judge of the Federal Court and lay members. There is thus in Australia a dual adjudication system, with the *courts* required to decide whether a practice lessens competition (per se or subject to some statutorily-specified competition test) and the *administrative bodies* required to decide whether, exceptionally, a particular proposed practice would likely result in a benefit to the public that would outweigh any likely anti-competitive detriment.

The resulting structure is set down in Table 1. Note that, when account is taken of the possibility of authorization, the number of practices that are per se illegal is cut back to two: price-fixing with respect to goods (subject to exceptions) and RPM. So, for instance, while price-fixing with respect to services is per se illegal in the courts, it is subject to an overall rule of reason under the dual adjudication system.

II.3. Enforcement

Enforcement in the courts is by way of both public and private actions, and for a wide range of sanctions and remedies – pecuniary penalties, injunctions, damages (compensatory, not triple or punitive) and compensatory orders (compensation for past loss and avoidance of future loss), and divestiture in a merger case. While the Act empowers both the Attorney-General and the Commission to enforce the Act, in practice the Commission has taken almost exclusive public enforcement responsibility. As in the United States, many more actions are instituted by private parties than are instituted by the Commission. Most of these private actions are settled or discontinued; nevertheless, to date, more significant judgments on the merits have stemmed from private than from public actions.[3]

II.4. The Trans-Tasman Connection: The New Zealand Commerce Act

From time to time in what follows, reference will be made to cases decided under the New Zealand Commerce Act and to trans-Tasman law (the Tasman is the sea that lies between Australia and New Zealand). The Commerce Act 1986 is modelled upon the restrictive practices provisions of the Australian Act. The Commerce Act also has a comparable list of prohibitions and a dual enforcement system. The New Zealand Commerce Commission has similar functions to the Australian Commission. Australia and New Zealand have a common legal heritage and cultural tradition. The New Zealand statute was enacted as an element of what is known as CER, the Closer Economic Relations, initiated in 1983 by the Australian New Zealand Closer Economic Relations Trade Agreement. Originally CER was viewed as a free trade agreement; but now its character is in the process of development to something more, a large measure of economic integration and harmonization of business law. In consequence there is now a body of competition law appropriately

Table I. The structure of the Trade Practices Act as at 1993

	Prohibited practice	Section	Per se illegal in court?	Authorization available?
1.	Anti-competitive agreements and covenants	45, 45B	No	Yes
2.	Primary collective boycotts: "exclusionary provisions"	45, 4D	Yes	Yes
3.	Price-fixing agreements between competitors			
	(i) Goods generally	45, 45A	Yes	No
	(ii) Services generally	45, 45A	Yes	Yes
	(iii) Covenants	45C	Yes	Yes
	(iv) Price-fixing exceptions			
	– Joint venture pricing	45A(2), 45	No	Yes
	– Price recommendation agreements (50 or more persons)	45A(3)	No	Yes
	– Buying groups' pricing	45A(4)	No	Yes
4.	Secondary boycotts; collective arrangements between union & supplier	45D, 45E	No	Yes
5.	"Misuse of market power" ("monopolization")	46, 46A	No	No
6.	"Exclusive dealing"			
	(i) Generally	47	No	Yes
	(ii) Third line forcing	47(7), 47(8)(c), 47(9)(d)	Yes	Yes
7.	RPM in relation to goods	48, Pt VIII	Yes	No
8.	Price discrimination in relation to goods	49	No	No
9.	Mergers	50, 50A	No	Yes

labelled trans-Tasman law, albeit differing as between Australia and New Zealand in some particulars. We find we learn from each other, whether moving in step or even a little out of step.

III. The Initial Challenge

Now I take you back to the 1960s and early 1970s. The challenge at that time to Senator Lionel Murphy, Attorney-General, inventor of the 1974 Act, was to rid Australia of unjustified restrictive practices and to do so by a means that was revolutionary for Australia, an antitrust law. Perhaps the best way to set the scene is to quote from contemporary accounts.

It is not easy to convey to persons not in Australia at that time "the web of anti-competitive restriction" that governed business activity (the phrase of the first Chairman of the Trade Practices Commission, R.M. Bannerman (1984, p. 157). It was an interlocking pattern of horizontal and vertical restrictions upon pricing and freedom of entry, often organized by a trade association or linked trade associations. The challenge was not only to meet the pervasiveness of restrictive practices but to respond to their precise form, and in a cost-effective manner.

Karmel and Brunt in *The Structure of the Australian Economy* wrote in 1962 (pp. 94–95):

> "Restrictive practices have a long history in Australia and have come to be regarded by businessmen and consumers alike as normal business behaviour. Indeed, certainly until very recently, the average businessman would have been rather hurt to hear his trade agreements described as restrictive. For example, the Western Australian Royal Commission on Restrictive Trade Practices and Legislation (1958) reported this exchange as indicative of business attitudes to price agreements.
>
> Question: Can you indicate why you are not in favour of Government control and yet are in favour of private control in regard to price fixation?
>
> Witness: Yes, because firstly, we stand primarily for free enterprise and the voluntary conducting of our affairs without being bound by a statute."

"Orderly marketing", "fair shares", "protection all round" were features of the Australian value system in the first 50 or 60 years after the formation of the Australian Commonwealth in 1901. These values were expressed in comprehensive tariff protection, the Australian Arbitration System for the settlement of industrial disputes, and the use of marketing boards for primary production – not just in the cartelization of business.

There were, it is true, individual voices questioning the Australian system of restrictive practices from time to time, such as the economists H.C. Coombs and P.H. Karmel (Masterman and Solomon (1967, pp. 33–35)). Various Tariff Board and other official reports commented upon price-fixing, market-sharing and exclusive dealing arrangements encountered in the course of their inquiries on particular industries (Australian Proposals, "Tables of Trade Practices" (1963, pp. 10–18)). The Labor Party and the trade union movement were prone to criticize monopoly profits and prices, aggregations of ownership, and to question calls for wage restraint in the absence of competitive prices (Masterman and Solomon (1967, pp. 34–35)). The Joint Committee on Constitutional Review (1959, pp. 113–120), a Parliamentary Committee whose legal secretary was the noted lawyer J.E. Richardson, recommended that the Constitution should be amended to enlarge the Commonwealth Government power to legislate to control harmful restrictive trade practices generally. But there was an obvious lack of popular and business support to control, or even question, restrictive practices and monopolies until the mid-1960s.

The Western Australian Royal Commission (1958) was the first comprehensive public investigation into restrictive trade practices that Australia had ever had. To some extent that inquiry was motivated by the prevalence of collusive tendering.[4] But as noted below there were other factors at work in Australia at that time that led to a number of investigations in quick succession: Alex Hunter's influential articles in 1961 and 1963, the Tasmanian Royal Commission Report in 1965, R.D. Freeman's study of trade associations initiated in 1959 as an undergraduate thesis and published in 1965, and perhaps most significant of all, the systematic documentation of restrictive practices over a period of three years undertaken by the Commonwealth Attorney-General's Department on the instructions of a notable Attorney-General, Sir Garfield Barwick (Australian Proposals, "Tables of Trade Practices" (1963)).

It was Alex Hunter, newly arrived in Australia from the UK, who first surveyed Australia-wide trade practices with a critical eye. In 1961 he generalized as follows:

> "Restrictive practices in Australia follow a pattern remarkably similar to that found in the United Kingdom. But two differences of emphasis are worth mentioning. Collusive tendering appears to be much more common than in the United Kingdom. The volume of complaint from municipal and State government departments is consistently high; and it is significant that the Western Australian Royal Commission was prepared to recommend total prohibition of this particular practice. Also, it seems certain that the practice of tied contracts, or "full line forcing", [by which he meant what is more usually termed "requirements contracts"] is more prevalent in Australia. This is to be expected given the high degree of concentration in industry." (Hunter (1961, p. 32)).

He commented that "Australian habits of restriction are remarkably similar to British even to rules, regulations and titles of associations" (p. 27n), but noted "This is not surprising in view of how much of Australian industry had its genesis in British industries (radio and electrical goods, paint, hardware, footwear, tyres, chocolate, pharmaceuticals, etc)" (p. 32n).

The listed industries are all consumer goods industries (at least in part). Later work documented that the restrictive practices extended back into the bowels of Australian industry – into such areas as small engineering tools, cement, sheet steel, plywood, wholesale electrical supplies, flour mills, glass merchants, malleable pipe fittings, paper bags, vitreous china sanitary wear, and valves. Later work also documented forms of vertical dealing of a comprehensive kind including exclusive dealing; RPM and vertical discount structures; and reciprocal trading, with the stop-list being the prime technique of enforcement, whether administered by individual suppliers or through the collective boycott of the trade association. There was a concept of "legitimate channels of trade": only approved dealers could be supplied. For example, only "approved dealers" might be supplied pharmaceuticals, certain toiletries, bicycles, some furniture, venetian blinds, plywood, timber, hardware and certain steel products – and no doubt much more.

In what proved to be a memorable passage, Karmel and Brunt wrote (1963, p. 66):

> "It is said that in a nudist colony nakedness goes unnoticed. Similarly in Australia, structural monopoly and oligopoly, along with Big Business [by which was meant size in relation to the economy as a whole], are so common as to be taken for granted."

They found (pp. 77–88) that what was unusual in Australian market concentration (by comparison with the US, Canada and Great Britain) was not the prevalence of oligopolistic markets (for this was true also of those economies) but the frequency of monopolistic and *tightly* oligopolistic markets. The work made a striking comparison of the degree of market concentration in manufacturing as between Australia and the US: for 1957–58, Australian industries in which the first 8 firms accounted for 50 per cent or more of national sales employed *at least* 60 per cent of the manufacturing work force. In the United States in the 1950s such highly concentrated industries employed less than 30 per cent of the manufacturing workforce.[5] Karmel and Brunt (pp. 84–85) went on to identify 19 important cases of single-firm monopoly in Australian manufacturing within the private sector.

In 1963 Sir Garfield Barwick published a long table of restrictive practices in a "wide variety of industries" to accompany his G.L. Wood Memorial Lecture, "Trade Practices in a Developing Economy." The theme of that address (1963a, p. 2) was that these practices, "plainly defensive in outlook and objective" were "out of accord with the real requirements of Australia's present position in the world" and "alien to the political convictions" associated with a liberal society and free enterprise economy. He gave examples of practices "which suggested injury to individuals with no overall benefit to the public" (p. 2):

> "To mention but one or two, traders found themselves unable to obtain supplies because they were not members of an appropriate trade association; and could not obtain membership of the association, not for any reason connected with personal suitability or financial responsibility but for some reason, e.g. that their turn-over was not large enough, designed to keep the membership of the association exclusive and limited. Lately, a further instance was publicly disclosed in which the rules of an association precluded the entry to its ranks of a migrant until he had been ten years naturalized. Exclusive dealing arrangements in a variety of forms constituted a self-assessed tariff protection. Public authorities' attempts to obtain their requirements by public tender were held up to public mockery by the submission of identical tenders, in one instance from nineteen suppliers each quoting the quite improbable sum of £27,578 14s. 2d. for the job."

In 1965 my paper "Legislation in Search of an Objective" drew together the findings of these various investigations and commented upon the characteristics of these restrictive practices as follows (Brunt (1965, pp. 371–372)):

> "The usual vehicle for the trade agreement is the trade association. Further, of some estimated 1,250 trade associations in Australia, it would seem safe to say that at least two-thirds have as part of their function the organisation of restrictive agreements. While just about every restrictive practice known to man is used in Australia (other than those subject to common law restraints), price agreements, both horizontal and vertical, are undoubtedly the most common. For instance, the recent Tasmanian Royal Commission into the activities of 70 trade associations found 59 to be operating restrictive agreements ... Finally, mention should be made of what is distinctive in Australia (at least by comparison with Britain and the United States). First, there is not only an unusually high incidence of restrictive agreements, but these agreements also have an unusual stability clearly associated with the high degree of market concentration. Second, another consequence of high concentration, unilateral vertical practices such as tying clauses and requirements contracts are fairly common. And finally, "orderly marketing" in Australia is a term which comprehends restrictive practices of the more extreme kind such as level tendering, collusive bidding, collective boycotts and reciprocal trading."

The "normality" of Australia's "orderly marketing" arrangements of that time cannot be better conveyed than by this story (quoted in Brunt (1965, pp. 364–365)) told to the Tariff Board in 1963 by a ball bearing distributor who wanted to compete:

> "Mr Coke, the company's representative, said: 'At one time our list prices for normal bearings did not agree with other bearing distributors' lists.'
>
> 'We found many companies questioned incorrect prices and our accounts department received so many complaints that we changed our list prices to agree with other distributors.'
>
> 'In actual fact, many of our prices were lower than other distributors' lists, and we found that our invoices were being corrected by a number of companies, and we were actually being paid more than we had charged certain customers.'"

But the times were changing, as evidenced by these very inquiries and by the passing of a precursor to our current statute, the Trade Practices Act 1965, the final product of Barwick's labours in this area while serving as Attorney-General from 1958–1964.[6] We are yet to see a definitive history of restrictive practices in Australia that would examine the political and social factors, not just the economic, at work in this century. It is intriguing merely to list what must have been some of the important influences in mid-century that were beginning to undermine the traditional Australian way of life: the expansive and confident post-war years; the vast migration movement that was to destroy our small homogeneous society of seven million British and Irish settlers; the consciousness of changes in the wider world that led to the UK statutes to control monopolies and restrictive practices in 1948 and 1956 and to the Treaty of Rome in 1965; and finally Sir Garfield Barwick's liberal vision of a free enterprise society.[7]

The 1965 Act was tentative and experimental, however. Beyond banning collusive bidding and collusive tendering, it merely required the Trade Practices Commissioner to review restrictive practices on a case-by-case basis to decide whether they should be submitted to the Trade Practices Tribunal for a determination as to whether they were in the public interest (in which case they were banned). The stance of that law is well conveyed by its ambivalent long title: "An Act to preserve competition in Australian trade and commerce to the extent required by the public interest." Lionel Murphy, introducing our present trade practices law into the Commonwealth Parliament, characterized the 1965 Act as "one of the most ineffectual pieces of legislation ever passed by this Parliament" (27 September 1973). Yet, in the environment just described, the 1965 Act was a necessary precursor to the 1974 Act. While much is made these days of the vision and reforming zeal of Lionel Murphy, the breakthrough came with the passing of the 1965 Act. The Act gave rise to the systematic documentation of horizontal agreements through its registration requirement; it enabled the testing and rejection of the public interest claims of some specific price-fixing and RPM agreements in the Trade Practices Tribunal; and the stage was set for a less ambivalent approach.

Even so, the 1974 Act constituted a distinct break with the Australian past by virtue of its unequivocal objective, its comprehensiveness and its character as economic law. In a lecture in the series "The Monash Trade Practices Lectures" (1975, pp. 2–3), I said this of the Trade Practices Act as economic law:

> "We begin with a statute; it is to be interpreted and enforced by courts of law; necessarily we are in the hands of lawyers. Yet fundamentally the Trade Practices Act (together with its implementation, its interpretation and enforcement) is an instrument of economic policy; its subject-matter, anti-competitive conduct of business enterprises within markets, is economic; the very terms used in drafting the statute (e.g. "conduct likely to have the effect of substantially lessening competition in a market for goods or services") employ economic concepts; the statutory criterion for determining whether anti-competitive conduct is in the public interest calls for analysis of economic processes.
>
> There is much competition policy that can proceed with comparatively little participation by the law, e.g. tariff policy, nationalization, policy with respect to mineral leases and government procurement. Yet while the new Act establishes a large role for administrative and quasi-judicial bodies (the Trade Practices Commission and the Trade Practices Tribunal) its central feature *at the level of technique* is that it relies upon the court control of competitive methods and indirectly of market structures.
>
> This is an approach that Australian economists and lawyers, no matter how much they may applaud the legislation in principle, find disconcerting in

practice. Many economists prefer to keep their own professional work "clean" (even at cost of relevance). To many an economist it comes as something of a shock that, if he is to act as economic adviser, his comprehensive and subtle analysis of the implications of some business practice (say, the exclusive dealing of the X co. operating in the Y industry) for his conception of "competition" and the "public interest" must be subjected to the requirements of the legal process. For the economist, the first novelty is undoubtedly that he must learn "to read the statute." The second is that judgment of a practice will stem from evidence and argument bearing on articulated issues that can be tested in an adversary setting; in this sense the formal requirements of "verification" are both stringent and narrow (leading many an economist to cry out in bewilderment, "but they are not talking about the real issues", a remark, to be sure, that may be prompted by less defensible reasons). The third novelty, finally, is that the legal process places particular reliance upon certain techniques for establishing breach of the law – the use of per se rules, rebuttable presumptions, and short chains of reasoning stemming from the evidence. One cannot, therefore, read more into a statute than the courts can handle. Further, it is unwise to read more into a statute than can give rise to legally enforceable (efficient) remedies.

As for the lawyers, the Act challenges them to enter a new world. There is naturally some resistance to interpreting a statute in light of economic policy objectives; to conceding indeed that interpretation will be more than a "legal matter" if relevant economic concepts are drawn upon; to formulating standards of liability in light of available remedies of an economically relevant kind; to agreement that some relaxation of the traditional rules of evidence is appropriate; to allowing a larger role to pre-trial discovery, written proofs and even, as appropriate, written argument; and, finally, to blending elements of economic and legal analysis in argument before the courts. Yet it is plain that what the new law calls for is a drawing together of economics and the law."

Our Trade Practices Act was largely inspired by American antitrust but in some fundamental ways we were travelling alone. There was the dual adjudication system, effecting a sharp division of function between judicial enforcement of breach and administrative granting of exemption on public benefit grounds, to some extent perhaps inspired by the EEC and UK structures but with quite distinctive institutional arrangements and statutory criteria. There was the statutory mix of prohibitions, some per se and some made subject to a statutory rule of reason. And finally all this was to be grafted on to the Anglo-Australian legal system with its common law traditions and practices – the adversary system, the common law evidentiary rules, the focus of civil litigation upon private dispute resolution, the traditional literal approach to statutory interpretation, the judges and counsel largely innocent of formal training in economics.

IV. What Have We Achieved?

Set against this background, the achievements are immense. They can be catalogued under two heads: the impact upon business conduct and the functioning of the economy, and the acceptance of the statute as economic law.

It is, indeed, extraordinary what a revolution has occurred in Australian business attitudes to restrictive practices over the last two decades. These days it is not restrictive practices but competition that is regarded as the norm, with exemptions requiring justification. There is now broad acceptance of the code of business conduct established by the law, with the result that much of the law is self-enforcing. No doubt there have been important additional, reinforcing factors at work such as growth and structural change, trade liberalization, direct foreign investment, deregulation, and the international spread of competition law. The 1980s, in particular, saw the floating of the exchange rate, the deregulation of financial markets, the virtual elimination of tariffs and other forms of protection (apart from those on motor vehicles and on footwear, clothing and textiles), and the elimination of much (not all!) direct regulation of business firms such as licensing and price control. It is clear, nevertheless, that the Trade Practices Act itself has played a major role. These other factors and the new competition law have been mutually reinforcing.

Naked price-fixing, both horizontal and vertical, has largely been eliminated. So likewise has overt cartelization, for example primary boycotts, if not granted authorization. As R.M. Bannerman wrote (1984, p. 160) in his retirement review, "The classic price agreements that still occur today are under cover." As earlier noted, it has been a feature of Australian restriction that horizontal and vertical agreements and arrangements have been interlocking and reinforcing. But now the vertical practices that remain have changed their character, have been "purified" of their explicit horizontal content to become unilateral practices. Trade association activity has been transformed.

Much of this success has been built upon the enactment of the per se prohibitions upon price-fixing, RPM and primary boycotts.[8] Some commentators have complained that the Act's prohibition of primary boycotts is too blunt an instrument, in that it lacks a competition test. But it has served the times; and its bluntness has been saved by the possibility of authorization. There has also been considerable success in eliminating some "naked" restrictions (e.g. some ties and market sharing arrangements not capable of authorization) subject to the relatively straight-forward and understandable competition test.

The level of domestic market concentration remains high, but its significance has changed. When restrictive agreements were rife and markets protected, there was little possibility that concentrated markets could be effectively competitive. Nowadays it makes sense to ask whether firms in concentrated markets possess market power, and the courts routinely attempt to assess the condition of entry when faced with evidence of high market concentration. Much enforcement attention is now given to merger and misuse of market power. The merger provision has been strengthened. Previously mergers were permitted up to the point of single-firm monopoly (the "high-dominance test"). But now, through amendments implemented in 1993, mergers are subject to a competition test: s. 50 prohibits mergers and acquisitions that have the effect of substantially lessening competition in a substantial market.

Turning to the evolution of the law itself, there have been formidable barriers to achieving an effective, economically relevant regulatory law. These are the barriers that arose, and still arise to a degree, from the inherited characteristics of English law noted in the previous section. The very concept of a statute as economic law, embodying a blend of economic and legal concepts and requiring mixed economic-legal reasoning, was novel.

The statute itself is lengthy and intricately structured. For instance the prohibition of "exclusive dealing" (a term used in Australia for a broad range of non-price vertical practices) requires five dense pages. The Act is a kind of lawyer's jigsaw puzzle. One possible outcome could well have been form without substance. And, indeed, there was some tendency to this in the beginning.[9]

However there is no longer any doubt that the Trade Practices Act is economic law, though the characterization was not fully affirmed until February 1989. That was the date the High Court brought down its judgment in *QWI*,[10] a decision that is notable not so much for its detailed finding regarding B.H.P.'s refusal to supply QWI with Y-bar as for its policy content and overall approach. There is here no hint of narrow formalism but rather a willingness to get to the economic substance of the statutory terms. Note that it is not just that the terms of the statute are to be interpreted in light of the policy objective; the very statutory terms have mixed economic-legal content. Thus Mason C.J. and Wilson J. (p. 50,008):

> "But the object of s. 46 is to protect the interests of consumers, the operation of the section being predicated on the assumption that competition is a means to that end ... In fact, the purpose provisions in s. 46(1) are cast in such a way as to prohibit conduct designed to threaten that competition – for example, s. 46(1) prohibits a firm with a substantial degree of market power from using that power to deter or prevent a rival from competing in a market. The question is simply whether a firm with a substantial degree of market power has used that power for a purpose proscribed in the section, thereby undermining competition, and the addition of a hostile intent inquiry would be superfluous and confusing ..."

Thus Deane J. (p. 50,011):

> "... the essential notions with which s. 46 is concerned and the objective which the section is designed to achieve are economic and not moral ones. The notions are those of markets, market power, competitors in a market and competition. The objective is the protection and advancement of a competitive environment and competitive conduct ..."

At the same time, the "essential notions" are transformed. We are concerned not with economics but with economic law. The interpretation of the economic concepts must be subject to the statute – to the language of the relevant section of the Act and the work done by that section in the overall scheme of the Act. Thus to give an example, Deane J. says in the market definition exercise in *QWI* (p. 50, 012):

> "in the case of an alleged contravention of the provisions of s. 46(1), there will ordinarily be little point in attempting to define relevant markets without first identifying precisely what it is that is said to have been done in contravention of the section."

Further, it is plain enough that the specification of economic concepts and the character of the economic analysis must be cut back to accommodate the procedural characteristics and approach to proof of courts of law.

Yet if the achievements of the law are impressive, the Act still lacks universal coverage of business activity. The principal exemptions are:

- State government business enterprises, principally the public utilities: gas, electricity, rail and urban transport, water, port authorities;
- statutory marketing authorities;
- unincorporated entities, especially the professions; and
- overseas shipping.

Adopting a conservative stance for the exercise, we can say that something over 10% of Gross Domestic Product must originate from the State business enterprises, the professions, and agricultural industries using marketing boards.[11] Moreover, a statistical calculation of this kind underestimates the importance of some of the exemptions, the public utilities and some of the professions, for the efficient and progressive functioning of the economy. Significantly, these very exemptions are now being widely questioned. Following the Prime Minister's Statement of 12 March 1991, "Building a Competitive Australia," in which he called for "a positive examination of all we can do ... to widen the ambit of the Trade Practices Act", there was established an Independent Committee of Inquiry (the National Competition Policy Review (1993)) headed by Fred G. Hilmer ("the Hilmer *Report*").[12]

V. What Have We Learnt?

The language of the Australian statute is distinctive and elaborate. Nevertheless we have learnt that lying behind the statute there is available a universal antitrust logic to inform the terms of the statute and the implementation of its policy. The juxtaposition of this logic and the statutory terms has given rise to a distinctive and elaborate jurisprudence, yet one that is compatible with overseas legal regimes.

Few of the prohibitions contained in Part IV of the Act are of a per se character. Rather the courts are required to apply a statutory rule of reason which is, however, couched in very general terms: in terms of the impact upon or relation to "competition in a market" or alternatively, depending upon the context, "market power."[13] The test for authorization by the administrative bodies, the Commission and Tribunal, is likewise expressed in terms of high generality, requiring the weighing of "benefit to the public" against the detriment to the public constituted by any "lessening of competition."

Great input has been required from the courts and administrative bodies to give appropriate economic content to the statutory terms. However a position has now been reached that it is recognized in both the courts and administrative bodies that there is a fundamental unity in the subject-matter of the Act: the Act seeks to control the creation, the extension and the use of market power. It is generally, though not perhaps universally recognized in the courts when dealing with "the prohibitions," that "competition" and "market power" are not different criteria but variants of the same criterion. The Australian approach, albeit still evolving, has become largely to identify competition with constraints upon market power. This recognition has been aided, no doubt, by the fact that a market methodology is mandated by the statute: in every section, other than those dealing with per se prohibitions, the courts are instructed to assess competition or market power in relation to "a market."

Thus Dawson J. in the landmark High Court case *QWI* quoted approvingly the Kaysen and Turner definition of market power (p. 50,015):

> "'A firm possesses market power when it can behave persistently in a manner different from the behaviour that a competitive market would enforce on a firm facing otherwise similar cost and demand conditions.' (Kaysen and Turner, *Antitrust Policy* (1959), p. 75)."

Compare the Trade Practices Tribunal in the *Media Council (No. 2)* application (1987) (p. 48, 436):[14]

> "[W]e adopt as our general concept of anti-competitive conduct any system (contract, arrangement or understanding) which gives its participants power to achieve market conduct and performance different from that which a competitive market would enforce, or which results in the achievement of such different market conduct and performance."

Note also Mason C.J. and Wilson J. in *QWI* (p. 50,008):

> "In identifying the relevant market, it must be borne in mind that the object is to discover the degree of the defendant's market power. Defining the market and evaluating the degree of power in that market are part of the same process, and it is for the sake of simplicity of analysis that the two are separated."

In this unifying vision the courts, Tribunal, Commission and practitioners have been guided, it is plain, by some of the fundamental discussions in US antitrust. For example, in the first case before the Tribunal, *QCMA*,[15] the Tribunal quoted the famous passage from the 1955 *Report* of the US Attorney-General's National Committee to Study the Antitrust Laws (p. 320):

> "The basic characteristic of effective competition in the economic sense is that no one seller, and no group of sellers acting in concert, has the power to

> choose its level of profits by giving less and charging more. Where there is workable competition, rival sellers, whether the existing competitors or new potential entrants into the field, would keep this power in check by offering or threatening to offer effective inducements ..."[16]

Australian antitrust is also indebted to one strand of US antitrust in finding assistance in the structure-conduct-performance paradigm. That analytic scheme was also introduced in *QCMA* when the Tribunal said (p. 17,246):

> "Competition expresses itself as rivalrous market behaviour ... In our view effective competition requires both that prices should be flexible, reflecting the forces of demand and supply, and that there should be independent rivalry in all dimensions of the price-product-service packages offered to consumers and customers.
>
> Competition is a process rather than a situation. Nevertheless, whether firms compete is very much a matter of the structure of the markets in which they operate. The elements of market structure which we would stress as needing to be scanned in any case are these:
>
> (1) the number and size distribution of independent sellers, especially the degree of market concentration;
>
> (2) the height of barriers to entry, that is the ease with which new firms may enter and secure a viable market;
>
> (3) the extent to which the products of the industry are characterized by extreme product differentiation and sales promotion;
>
> (4) the character of "vertical relationships" with customers and with suppliers and the extent of vertical integration; and
>
> (5) the nature of any formal, stable and fundamental arrangements between firms which restrict their ability to function as independent entities.
>
> Of all these elements of market structure, no doubt the most important is (2), the condition of entry. For it is the ease with which firms may enter which establishes the possibilities of market concentration over time; and it is the threat of the entry of a new firm or a new plant into a market which operates as the ultimate regulator of competitive conduct."

The listed factors are now referred to as the *QCMA* factors and, as explained below, the importance of the condition of entry in assessing market power (or competition) occupies a central place in Australian antitrust logic. At the same time, it cannot be said that courts and practitioners are altogether easy with the concept of freedom of entry and its application to the legal process.[17] That is a development for the future. In this, too, it might be said that Australian law has something in common with the American.

The *Avis-Ansett* merger case of 1978 is an early example of how it came to be recognized that the concepts of market power and competition are but the inverse of each other, with substitution the unifying concept.[18] In that case Northrop J.

was called upon to assess whether Avis was "dominant" in the car rental market in accordance with the statutory test at that time. He began his analysis of "dominance" (p. 17,717) as a "word to be construed in its ordinary sense of having a commanding influence on"; but in the end he came to a finding that a firm could not be dominant if it were operating in a market characterised by "keen and effective competition" (p. 17,726). Thus in determining whether Avis was dominant in the car rental market, the Court paid particular regard to the "capacity of Avis to determine prices for its services without being consistently inhibited in its determination by other firms." It did not regard profit figures as being "of real assistance in determining dominance ... What is of more importance ... is the ability of operators to enter the market and sustain their entry" (p. 17,720). While Avis was "by far the largest operator in the car rental market in Australia," its policies were constrained by the competition of both national *and* local operators (p. 17,726):

> "If the service provided by any one operator deteriorates, other operators will gain custom therefrom. If the rates charged by any one operator become too great, the operator will lose custom to other operators. The possibility of new entrants to the market is always there. The possibility of a local operator extending its business so as to become a national operator is very real. The market is expanding and the existing operators are fully aware of their competitors and potential competitors. All these factors tend to suggest that Avis is not in a position to dominate the car rental market in Australia."

Similarly in the *Arnotts* merger case of 1990,[19] the Full Court of the Federal Court equated "dominance" with a "high degree of market power"; referred to the High Court's exposition of "market power" in *QWI*; quoted the "useful list of criteria" in *QCMA* (the *QCMA* factors); referred to *Continental Can*, *United Brands* and *Hoffman la Roche* in the European Court; and then proceeded to a detailed analysis of the evidence relating to barriers to entry and competitive pressures on market shares (pp. 51,788–51,793). The Court prefaced its consideration of market definition and dominance by saying (at p. 51,782): "The role of s. 50 is to maintain competitive markets by restraining monopolisation and prohibiting mergers that will produce a non-competitive market."

The methodology that is evolving in the courts might be termed a *truncated* structure-conduct-performance approach. It is an approach that recognizes the *causal* importance of market structure, especially the condition of entry, as placing constraints upon the firm's ability to "give less and charge more." But it is also recognized that the relevant *evidence* may relate to structure, conduct and performance. It is one thing to say, as in *QWI* (p. 50,009): "It is only when for some reason it is not rational or possible for new entrants to participate in the market that a firm can have market power." It is another to establish that significant barriers to entry exist. Thus in the recent case *Pioneer Concrete*[20] we find Lockhart J. referring both to the importance of the condition of entry and endorsing and applying the performance criteria of competition advanced by the economist Neville Norman, namely (p. 41,000):

"(i) enable products to be delivered consistently to consumers or users efficiently in the range and qualities desired;
(ii) avoid inefficient practices, excessive costs, delays and product-related faults;
(iii) pressure suppliers to adopt best-practice methods of production and distribution; and
(iv) reward efficient operators and penalize less efficient operators (including by failure and exist [*sic*] from the market)."

The methodology is truncated in the sense that evidence and argument are taken only as far as might be necessary to establish whether there is significant discretionary power and if so, whether it is sufficiently significant to qualify for a finding that it is "substantial" as is required by the statute. But to repeat, the touchstone is discretionary power, with and without the conduct at issue, not efficiency or market performance. As explained in the next Section, Australian antitrust for the most part uses a pure, or relatively pure, market power standard (with little normative content) in the courts.

In the architecture of the statute it is envisaged that efficiency considerations are matter for the Commission and Tribunal. Explicitly, the dual adjudication system remits to the Commission and Tribunal the task of assessing net "benefit to the public," i.e. market performance with and without the conduct for which authorization is sought. To what extent the underlying economic subject-matter, in logic, permits this division of labour is discussed in the next Section.

A word of caution is in order. Admittedly the above account represents the way the writer would like to think the law is developing. To a degree the wish may be mother to the thought. And certainly, if one combs through the cases, deviant statements and analyses can be found.[21] It may be that the administrative bodies, which consistently and systematically use a structure-conduct-performance approach to their authorization work, see with greater clarity the essential unity of antitrust analysis. It was, for example, the New Zealand Commerce Commission that enunciated with admirable clarity and forcefulness in two of its determinations in 1987, only one year after the enactment of the Commerce Act (*News* and *Weddel Crown*): "The antithesis of competition is market power."[22]

The caution is directed especially to s. 45 matters. There have been few cases in the courts (as distinct from the administrative bodies) relating to anti-competitive agreements, i.e. provisions in "contracts, arrangements or understandings" that have the "purpose" or likely "effect, of substantially lessening competition." The courts and practitioners are arguably still feeling their way.[23] The focus has been upon developing a legal test of "arrangements and understandings" (communication, mutual expectation, obligation) rather than upon the meaning of "competition."[24] To equate "competition" with "rivalry," whose presence can be ascertained by inspection of "the facts", is an approach that may still have some attraction. However what is required is a finding that there is independent market rivalry that is both non-discretionary – that is, constrained by market forces – and thorough-going – that is, in the words of *QCMA*, extending to "all dimensions of the price-product-service packages offered to consumers and customers" (p. 17,246).

In the development of Australian law there has been a kind of dialogue between the administrative bodies, the courts, lawyers, economists and the Parliament to achieve clarity and sense. That process has been informed, in somewhat eclectic fashion, by overseas developments – as has suited perceived Australian requirements. Very recently, for example, in amendment of the merger law to install a criterion of the acquisition having the likely effect of "substantially lessening competition in a market", the Parliament was fortified by the somewhat similarly worded Canadian law and moved to introduce, in the Canadian manner, a statutory list of factors that must be taken into account when assessing competitive effect. Again, in early days it was decided that the European "abuse" approach to monopolization was preferable to the structural American approach, and there was enacted in s. 46 an Australian variant that prohibited "taking advantage" of market power with the purpose of damaging the competitive process. The 1986 amendments to s. 46 lowered the market power threshold from substantial market "control" to possession of a "substantial degree of power in a market" and sought to clarify the concept of market power by reference to the approach developed in European cases:

> "s. 46(3) In determining for the purposes of this section the degree of power that a body corporate or bodies corporate has or have in a market, the Court shall have regard to the extent to which the conduct of the body corporate or of any of those bodies corporate in that market is constrained by the conduct of:
>
> (a) competitors, or potential competitors, of the body corporate or of any of those bodies corporate in that market; or
>
> (b) persons to whom or from whom the body corporate or any of those bodies corporate supplies or acquires goods or services in that market."

In Australia this approach has been found helpful in emphasizing the discretionary character of market power, thus focusing attention upon the need to identify constraints upon the firm's production and selling policies. But this has by no means shut out the characteristic American emphasis upon the power to raise prices. Indeed the "European" independence of behavior test and the price elevation test are seen as amounting to much the same thing, as for example in this passage from *QWI* (per Mason C.J. and Wilson J. at p. 50,008):

> "Market power can be defined as the ability of a firm to raise prices above the supply cost without rivals taking away customers in due time, supply cost being the minimum cost an efficient firm would incur in producing the product ... Section 46(3), which was added in 1986 by the Trade Practices Revision Act, provides that in determining the degree of market power a court should

consider "the extent to which the conduct of [the defendant] in that market is constrained by the conduct of ... competitors, or potential competitors ..."

We have reached a point, it seems, where we have sufficient confidence in our ability to handle antitrust issues that we can walk with some discrimination around overseas authorities. We are becoming wary of importing overseas "doctrines" such as the "essential facilities doctrine" or the "failing firm doctrine" too literally without regard to policy objectives, statutory terms, factual circumstances, or characteristics of the economy. The recent assessment of the relevance of the US "failing firm doctrine" by the New Zealand High Court (Wylie J. and Mr R.G. Blunt) is of interest:[25]

> "At the risk of expressing a heresy, in our opinion in New Zealand at least there is neither the need nor the justification for a "doctrine". Properly applied the Act is perfectly capable of coping, in terms of competition law, with the consequences of the financial or other failure of a participant without the Commission or the Court endeavouring to engraft thereon some special doctrinal rules of general application and thus elevating them to a discrete branch of the jurisprudence. Put simply, we think that the question of actual, imminent, or probable failure of a participant in a merger proposal is nothing more than a question of fact to be determined by the tribunal and taken into account in assessing questions of dominance and, if necessary, public benefit. It is likely that the impact of such a fact when found will vary infinitely according to the circumstances. Therein we think lies the danger of elevating such a question of fact into some comprehensive doctrine which, if it is permitted to do so, will emerge as a straitjacket confining the true function of the tribunal.
>
> Lest this should be thought to show scant respect for the United States authorities ... it must at once be said that the statutory context there is very different."

Yet if Australian and New Zealand antitrust has taken off, with the case law feeding upon itself, we recognize that there is much to be learnt from overseas authorities and learning. Fact situations can be "typed". Differing approaches to standards of liability, proof and remedy can be instructive. Where we are now most in need of assistance, it seems to me, is in developing standards of liability that would effect some economy in what is required to be proved, as well as developing more effective legal techniques (e.g. "managerial" or interventionist judging, relevant and economical discovery). We can agree with Frank H. Easterbrook (1984) that a "market power filter" gets to the economic essence of antitrust, but too many of our rule of reason cases are taking too long and costing too much.

VI. Some Distinctive Features of Australian Antitrust

The previous Section emphasized the universality of "antitrust" economics to encompass the Australian variant. It was concerned to make large generalizations.

When the perspective shifts to detail, it is seen that there are some distinctive features of Australian antitrust. The topics to be taken up in this Section are: market definition; dual adjudication and authorization; the market power standard; and the treatment of verticals.

Some might think our use of a structure-conduct-performance framework requires explanation, if not justification, in view of the disparaging references that are sometimes encountered in the literature, such as "the discredited structure-conduct-performance approach". However what is discredited, in my view, is (1) any concept of market structure that would exclude the condition of entry and (2) over-reliance upon market concentration as *the* significant element of structure or *the* significant explanator of market conduct and performance. All that needs to be said, I think, is that in Australia these days the paradigm is used with a consciousness of points (1) and (2) – as indeed is the case with the US *Merger Guidelines* produced jointly by the Department of Justice and the F.T.C (1992). It is, indeed, striking how generally useful the structure-conduct-performance approach, properly interpreted, remains for free enterprise economies; and how adaptable it is to shifts of emphasis (e.g. efficiency considerations) and developing concepts (e.g. transaction costs).

VI.1. Market Definition

Three features of the Australian approach are of special interest to economists. The first is that market definition has become the routine first step in most litigation, whether in the courts or administrative bodies. Unlike some overseas jurisdictions, market analysis is not a topic reserved for the consideration of monopolization and merger. So far as the courts are concerned, a market methodology is mandated by the statute: wherever conduct is subject to some form of competition test, the Act instructs the courts to appraise competition or power "in a market"; and market is defined to include "goods or services that are substitutable for, or otherwise competitive with" the goods or services of immediate interest: s. 4E per a 1977 amendment. The amendment was designed to emphasize that it is an economic concept of market that is relevant and not, as had occurred in an early case, some dictionary definition.[26]

The second feature goes to the role of production substitution: cross-elasticity of supply. It has become standard practice in Australia to identify the market by reference to both cross-elasticity of demand and cross-elasticity of supply, stopping short of the creation of entirely new capacity for entry. The approach was initiated in the early *QCMA* case in the Tribunal (p. 17, 247):

> "We take the concept of a market to be basically a very simple idea. A market is the area of close competition between firms or, putting it a little differently, the field of rivalry between them ... Within the bounds of a market there is substitution – substitution between one product and another, and between one source of supply and another, in response to changing prices. So a market

is the field of actual and potential transactions between buyers and sellers amongst whom there can be strong substitution, at least in the long run, if given a sufficient price incentive ..."

It was explicitly affirmed by the High Court in *QWI*, for example by Dawson J. (p. 50,014):

> "The basic test involves the ascertainment of the cross-elasticities of both supply and demand, that is to say, the extent to which the supply of or demand for a product responds to a change in the price of another product. Cross-elasticities of supply and demand reveal the degree to which one product may be substituted for another, an important consideration in any definition of a market."

There is some difference from the approach espoused by the US Department of Justice in its *Merger Guidelines* (1982, 1984 and now the latest edition of 1992, jointly with the FTC). To clarify the difference consider, with Areeda and Hovenkamp (1993, p. 619), the three possible approaches that might be taken to defining the market, given the existence of cross-elasticity of supply as between product A and product B:

> "(1) define the market as A plus B, including the full capacity of both firms; (2) define the market as A and include within it the capacity of particular B firms that could easily make A or perhaps only that portion of their capacity likely to be devoted fairly promptly to A production in the event of a significant rise in its price; or (3) define the market as A alone and include only current A production but appraise the results in the light of the relative ease of entry by B producers and others."

The current Australian approach is generally to define the market as the first of these, the US *Guidelines* the second. Examples from the Australian cases would be the Australian steel and steel products market (*QWI*), the Australian car rental market comprising both national and local operators (*Avis-Ansett*), an Australia-wide market for the towage services of large harbor tugs (*Tugboat Merger* in the Tribunal).[27] From a formal point of view each of the three approaches should give the same answer if pressed through to the stage of entry analysis. Yet there are issues of emphasis, practicality, economy, and analytic coherence.

These assume some importance, in that the Commission (1992) has recently proposed in its draft *Merger Guidelines* that Australia move closer to the American approach, at least in relation to merger:

> 4.32 "... in order to establish the relevant market for a proposed merger, the Commission is concerned to establish the potential sources of competitive, that is close, substitutes for the product(s) of the merging parties. Substitutability is viewed here from the perspective of consumers. The question which the Commission seeks to answer in establishing mar-

> ket boundaries is what are the alternative sources of supply which the customers of the merging firm can turn to?" ...
> 4.37 "Conceptually the process of market definition can be viewed as establishing that area of product, functional and geographic space within which a hypothetical current and future profit maximising monopolist would impose a small but significant and non-transitory price increase from the competitive price levels."

What would be the implications of this proposal? Certainly there would be easier comparability with North American practice. Arguably there could be an advantage in throwing emphasis upon the pricing discretion a merged entity might have for individual products within specified geographic areas: it would be an approach more attuned to a Lerner-type measure of market power. As against this, the existing Australian practice could well claim consistency with the Australian approach to market power, to be congenial to business and judicial modes of thinking, and to suit the Australian economy.

The established approach to market definition throws up for initial consideration firms, establishments and divisions of firms that are in close competition over some geographic area – e.g. banking services in Australia (given that we have a branch banking system) as distinct from commercial banking services or home lending etc. The emphasis is thus upon a related set of activities of business entities. In a manner congenial to Edward S. Mason's perspective (1939), this approach to market definition is consistent with the Australian emphasis upon the necessity to identify the market constraints upon the price and production policies of firms (or divisions of firms), irrespective of whether the formal legal question is couched in terms of "competition" or "market power". Indeed, it reinforces it.

This is a fundamental consideration. In addition, from a practical point of view the approach enables a quick, rough-and-ready view of the number and size distribution of competitors. With such generally high domestic market concentration there is no need for the computation of sophisticated concentration indexes, such as the HHI: the number and size distribution of competitors can be discerned by simple inspection! Moreover, much less can be permitted to turn upon market concentration as a pointer to liability: too many firms would be vulnerable. And if one does wish to compute simple concentration ratios of the 4-firm variety, as the Commission does in order to establish safe havens or benchmarks, the relevant data (capacity or sales figures for plants or establishments that may be expected to have a high cross-elasticity of supply) can be readily available from business sources.

A third feature of the Australian treatment of market definition is our use of the concept of sub-markets. Australia has a concept of sub-markets different from that used in American law. The crucial distinction lies in the fact that the Australian concept is designed and used as a tool of analysis and not as an element of a legal standard to attract liability. In Australian practice a sub-market refers to an area of competition that is narrower than a market, for example in the *Tugboat Merger* case, the individual port as against the Australia-wide market for towage services by large harbor tugs.

The sub-market made its first appearance in *QCMA*. In that case the Commission had submitted that the flour trade should be broken down into four geographic areas, claimed to be markets, in which the proposed acquisition might assume heightened significance. The Tribunal's response was to say that these are not markets, but sub-markets (p. 17,247):

> "Sub-markets are the more narrowly defined, typically registering some discontinuity in substitution possibilities. Where the defining feature of a market is the existence of close substitutes (whether in demand or supply), the defining feature of a sub-market is the existence of still closer and more immediate substitutes. Sub-markets may be especially useful in registering the short-run effects of change; but they may be misleading if used uncritically to assess long-run competitive effects."

In scanning the figures relating to sub-market shares it was true that the two merging firms had a stronger market presence in particular geographic areas (p. 17,251):

> "But this is merely to say that particular firms currently have some competitive advantage in particular areas, with which we would agree. Indeed, this is an important reason why we think it relevant, in this case, to specify sub-markets as well as markets. Yet we do not think we could understand the current and likely strategies of Defiance, QCMA and others in these sub-markets unless viewed as an element in the total Queensland picture."

In *Tooth and Tooheys*' application to the Tribunal,[28] the concept was more carefully developed; it was also put to somewhat different use (p. 18,197):

> "[W]ithin the bounds of the market, substitution possibilities may be more or less intense, and more or less immediate: the field of substitution is not necessarily homogeneous but may contain within it sub-markets wherein competition is especially close or especially immediate. There may be, too, certain key sub-markets such that their competitive relationships have a wider effect upon the functioning of the market as a whole. In these matters we have found that the identification of relevant sub-markets may be rather helpful in clarifying how competition works."

Tooth and Tooheys was an application to the Tribunal for authorization of the two brewers' solus trading arrangements ("ties") for bulk beer sold in hotels in the State of New South Wales. The product market was found to be bulk and packaged beer. Two functional levels were distinguished, the wholesale market extending roughly over the whole of N.S.W. and the retail market comprising distinctive licensing districts and local trading areas.

The two brewers produced over 90 per cent of product sold in N.S.W. They held ties over hotels accounting for 75 per cent of the trade in bulk beer but only 23 per cent overall when account was taken of the sales of packaged beer and of the significance of outlets other than hotels, such as clubs and liquor merchants. The question was whether a "23 per cent tie" could be regarded as significant. The Tribunal distinguished a sub-market of especial importance for the functioning of the market as a whole, namely the sale of bulk beer in hotels in the Sydney and Newcastle Licensing Districts. The licensing laws placed an absolute limitation on the numbers of hotels within these two largest metropolitan districts; together they accounted for over half of the State's beer sales; and there was (p. 18,216):

> "clearly great strategic significance (from a competition viewpoint) in controlling the Metropolitan hotel trade, both for its own importance as an outlet for beer and for its importance in taste formation in the State as a whole."

Thus whereas in *QCMA* sub-market organization had no significant impact on long-run competition – the geographic area was "just a sub-market" – in *Tooth and Tooheys* the tie organization in the sub-markets was found to be of considerable importance for competition in the relevant market, the N.S.W. beer market. There is a discernible shift in the use to which the sub-market concept is put in this case. Yet it still fulfils its role in furthering the analysis of the functioning of the market as a whole. It is interesting to observe that this latter concept has a close affinity to the "sub-group structures within industries" analysed by Caves and Porter (1977) – and interesting, too, to note that the concept was derived independently, in response to the fact situations thrown up by these early Australian cases. Both variants are now well-established in Australian antitrust, whether used dismissively – "just a sub-market" – or constructively, as in the *Tooth and Tooheys* manner, to weave a competition story.

VI.2. Dual Adjudication and Authorization

Perhaps the most distinctive feature of our trans-Tasman law is the partitioning of subject-matter between the courts and the administrative bodies, with the courts required to apply statutorily specified competition tests, and the administrative bodies required to assess on a case by case basis claims for exemption on grounds of net public benefit. The test for authorization is couched in terms of high generality: it requires the establishment of likely "benefit to the public", and a weighing of this against any likely detriment to the public from any lessening of competition.

In the early days, when restrictive practices were so pervasive in Australia, it was unclear to legislators how many of them might be "justifiable" (Barwick's word) – or why. While it was thought that in the small developing Australian economy, there might well be efficiencies that were dependent upon scale or agreements, this was not the only consideration. It was thought to be unwise to be doctrinaire. At the same time, it was thought to be appropriate to give business firms the opportunity to demonstrate that their acquisitions, practices and agreements were in society's interest. And so the Commission and Tribunal were given a broad and open-ended criterion for authorization. The statutory test was not couched in terms of efficiency, or consumer welfare, but "benefit to the public."

Faced with this challenge, the Tribunal has established a framework for the authorization exercise, using the structure-conduct-performance approach to analyze "the functioning of relevant markets with and without the conduct for which authorization is sought."[29] The starting point is the wide ambit given to "public benefit" in *QCMA* (p. 17,242) as "anything of value to the community generally, any contribution to the aims pursued by the society including as one of its principal elements (in the context of trade practices legislation) the achievement of the economic goals of efficiency and progress". Accordingly, authorization has been granted not only where there is market failure in the economist's technical sense (stemming from economies of scale and scope, transaction costs, externalities and public goods) but also where there is some wider inadequacy of market functioning in the specific case to address the values of society. Those values might be found in the very nature of the conduct for which authorization is sought (e.g. "professional" standards of work and acceptance of fiduciary responsibility);[30] in the use of a non-market process to organize an activity (e.g. co-operative enterprise);[31] or in dimensions of market performance extending beyond static and dynamic efficiency (e.g. the protection of children from some kinds of advertisements).[32]

Thus the public-private dichotomy – public benefit as against private profit – focuses attention upon the exceptional circumstances in which private business motivation responding to market forces is unlikely to register the public interest in the delivery of the efficiencies and other important values that are the ultimate ends of our enterprise system.

That said, it has become undoubtedly the case that the most usual claim for authorization is upon grounds of enhanced efficiency, especially in the context of mergers and acquisitions. The recent Hilmer inquiry has recommended (*Report*, p. 121) that "the authorization provisions should be amended to confirm that economic efficiency is the primary consideration in assessing public benefits". At the same time it noted the relevance of "other valued social objectives" (p. 88) and concluded (p. 97) that parties should not "be denied the opportunity to demonstrate other dimensions of community welfare."

Issues have arisen regarding the authorization test, the scope of its application, and the role of the Tribunal. There is first the issue pressed by the economist R.R. Officer in an influential paper (1987). He has criticised any approach to public benefit that would require the benefit to be passed on to consumers in the form of lower prices or improved quality or service. The essential test, he has written, should be whether there is an improvement in the use of society's resources. If, for instance, a prospective merger would result in efficiencies, reflected in lower costs and higher profits, that is sufficient to establish the existence of public benefit. "Insofar as the producer is better off and the consumers are no worse off we have a Pareto improvement" (p. 8). He suggests that in such a case no distinction should be drawn between private benefit, in the sense of benefit to the companies concerned, and public benefit. He has criticised Commission practice, saying that it discounts or disregards benefits to the companies concerned.

Certainly in the Commission's latest pronouncement, the draft *Merger Guidelines* (1992), there is this paragraph:

> 5.16 "The benefit must accrue to the community at large and not purely to the parties to the merger. Private benefits that accrue to the applicant or some other limited group are not ruled out as long as they clearly have a beneficial impact on the public at large."

It is not altogether clear what the Commission means by such a statement, whether it is valuing "consumers" over "producers", as Officer suggests; or whether it is valuing a widespread distribution of benefits; or whether it is looking for competitive processes of value to the community.

The present writer would agree with the proposition that there must be public benefit in saving resources but would advance a third view, that it is not the immediate distribution of benefits that is important but their durability. If a merger, for example, gives rise to rationalization economies and higher profits that are not "passed on to the consumer", one needs to ask why this is so. It may well reflect enhanced market power which would need to enter the benefit-cost equation; and there may well be a question of whether the lack of competitive pressure will allow productivity gains to be lost – "benefit" to be dissipated – in slackness and rent-seeking activities.[33]

Another issue concerns the scope for authorization exemption. Currently the practices that cannot be subject to authorization are: price fixing for goods (*not* services); misuse of market power (monopolization); RPM (both individual and collective); and "third line forcing" by one corporation of another's products. The Hilmer inquiry provided an opportunity for review of these exemptions. A number of submissions favoured widening the scope for authorization. The *Report* recommends that authorization be extended to third line forcing and RPM, but not to the remainder.

In the case of third line forcing, currently banned per se in the courts but capable of authorization, the recommendation is to remove both elements of this harsh treatment on the ground that it is anomalous to treat third line forcing any differently from other forms of tying (pp. 49–54). In the case of RPM, banned per se overall, the recommendation is that it would be in accordance with modern thinking to permit authorization. However removal of the per se ban in the courts is not favoured in view of the technicality of the economic arguments that may be used to justify RPM (pp. 54–58). There is another consideration that would support the *Report's* recommendation for RPM. This is that, in Australian experience, vertical and horizontal price-fixing have often been intertwined: there is a need to be wary of any treatment that might put too much strain upon a court's capacity to deal with collusion ("arrangements and understandings"). The RPM element might survive the competition test and facilitate horizontal collusion.

In the case of submissions that it is anomalous to permit authorization of price fixing for services but not for goods, and that therefore authorization should be extended to price fixing for goods, the *Report* concluded (p. 38):

> "The status quo is inconsistent in the treatment of goods and services, is not supported in principle, sends conflicting messages to businesses about the acceptability of price fixing and unnecessarily increases the complexity of the law."

Its recommendation is not to widen the scope for authorization but to narrow it: authorization should not generally be permitted for horizontal price fixing, whether goods or services: "It will ... underline the message that price competition is central to effective competition ..." (p. 39).

The *Report* also rejected submissions favoring the extension of authorization to conduct that might be vulnerable to a charge of "misuse of market power" as making for too much "regulatory intrusion into daily business activities", e.g. the introduction of a "new and better product" or "an aggressive marketing campaign" (pp. 72–73).

However there is much to be said in favor of allowing applications for authorization for all practices. In some instances it may not be appropriate for the business strategy concerned but that can be left to the companies themselves to determine: application for authorization is a voluntary option. With all types of practice there is the possibility that a practice or policy gives rise to efficiencies, and efficiency considerations are especially suited to administrative investigation and determination. In the case of price-fixing, the unavailability of authorization would likely tempt the courts to develop some concept of ancillary restraints in the American manner, lengthen the trial and complicate the analysis. Undoubtedly, too, the availability of authorization does permit the statute and the courts to fashion rules that have a sharp cutting edge in the knowledge than an authorization escape hatch is available. And finally, the availability of authorization for conduct that is claimed to constitute misuse of market power would be an especially useful option for the privatized, deregulated utilities that it is now hoped to expose to the Act. Consider, for instance, the prices that might be charged for access to a natural monopoly such as may occur in gas or electricity grids or telephone networks: while they might have an efficiency justification, they might look like exploitation (Ramsey pricing?), price discrimination, or predatory pricing to a court of law.

The third issue is related to the second. This is the question of whether it might be possible to make relatively greater use of such administrative bodies as the Commission or Tribunal, or even of arbitration, and less of the courts. We will return to that issue in the next Section. Meantime it might be appropriate to label such a move as "back to Barwick" – albeit only in terms of general direction, not the whole way. In Barwick's scheme, only collusive bidding and tendering were prohibited per se and subject to court enforcement. The rest were to be assessed in the specially created body, the Trade Practices Tribunal, described in his Parliamentary Statement (Barwick (1962)) as "one which has a minimum of legalism, both in its attitude and approach and in its procedures, and a maximum of business knowledge and understanding." Barwick had been the foremost Q.C. in commercial work prior to his appointment as Attorney-General (and later, Chief Justice of the High

Court).[34] It is of peculiar interest, in view of current controversies, to note what he had to say at the 13th Australian Legal Convention of 1961 (Barwick (1961, p. 379)):

> "... one would aim to remove as much as possible of what you might call the curial – the tactical aspects of a hearing, and the pushing and shoving that sometimes goes on in court proceedings.
>
> One should hope to devise a simple business-like procedure – with a minimum of orally given evidence. In such a course the tribunal needs the co-operation of a great profession such as this."

VI.3. A Pure Market Power Standard?

In this part we explore the question of how far, in logic, it is possible to remove efficiency considerations from the standard of liability used by Australian courts and remit them to the administrative bodies. The more general question is whether, in principle, it is possible to design an antitrust system that partitions the standard of liability between positive and normative elements, with the courts confined to a pure or positive market power standard and some other body addressing efficiencies and other values.

As has been said, in the design of the Australian Act it is certainly assumed that this is possible. Take, for instance, the merger law that came into operation in 1993. Section 50 prohibits an acquisition "if the acquisition would have the effect, or be likely to have the effect, of substantially lessening competition in a market". It supplies a list of factors that must be taken into account:

> "(a) the actual and potential level of import competition in the market;
> (b) the height of barriers to entry to the market;
> (c) the level of concentration in the market;
> (d) the degree of countervailing power in the market;
> (e) the likelihood that the acquisition would result in the acquirer being able to significantly and sustainably increase prices or profit margins;
> (f) the extent to which substitutes are available in the market or are likely to be available in the market;
> (g) the dynamic characteristics of the market, including growth, innovation and product differentiation;
> (h) the likelihood that the acquisition would result in the removal from the market of a vigorous and effective competitor;
> (i) the nature and extent of vertical integration in the market."

Unlike the Canadian statute, there is no mention of efficiency. It seems clear that if a Williamson (1968, 1977) trade-off analysis is to be performed, that will be in the Commission/Tribunal.

But perhaps the matter is not as straightforward as this? One remembers the pronouncement of Mr Justice Harlan in *Clorox*[35] where the charge was that Procter

& Gamble's acquisition of Clorox "might substantially lessen competition or tend to create a monopoly ..." (pp. 597–598):

> "The problem of efficiencies ... must ... be faced. The Court attempts to brush the question aside by asserting that Congress preferred competition to economies, but neglects to determine whether certain economies are inherent in the idea of competition. If it is conceded, as it must be, that Congress had reasons for favoring competition, then more efficient operation must have been among them. It is of course true that a firm's ability to achieve economies enhances its competitive position, but adverse effects on competitors must be distinguished from adverse effects on competition ... Economies achieved by one firm may stimulate matching innovation by others, the very essence of competition. They always allow the total output to be delivered to the consumer with an expenditure of fewer resources."

Yet we are here concerned not with what might be the ultimate goal in enacting an antitrust statute (efficiency and/or other values) but rather with the standard of liability used by the courts. Another relevant distinction is that between the standard of liability (market power) and the evidence that might be judged relevant in asserting market power as in *Pioneer Concrete* previously considered. Recall too, that great reliance is placed upon the condition of entry (which will require consideration of economies of scale and scope etc.). The most that can be said, as a general proposition, is that the adoption of a pure market power standard in the courts assumes that a correlation between market power and efficiency is somewhat exceptional.[36] That, one would think, is precisely the assumption that Senator Murphy was prepared to make when he designed our present law to replace the ambivalent 1965 Act.

It is true that efficiency considerations are nowadays much more prominent in Australian thinking about competition law. The sources of efficiency are understood to extend beyond simple horizontal economies of scale to economies of scale and scope, in both horizontal and vertical dimensions; to transaction costs; to externalities and public goods (giving rise to "free riding" problems). Yet provided the law uses a positive "effects" test in determining liability in the courts, the normative efficiency considerations can be remitted to the administrative forum. This is true, even in the case of vertical practices, where one would wish to recognize that there can be efficient forms of contractual integration that would give rise to sufficient public benefit to outweigh the detriment from enhanced market power.

Nevertheless as our Act is drafted, it seems to this observer that there are two places in the Part IV prohibitions for which efficiency considerations are inherent and should enter as an element of a court's standard of liability. The first of these is in the application of s. 46: misuse of market power. There are here three elements to be satisfied before a court can make a finding of breach: the market power threshold; taking advantage of market power; and for the purpose of eliminating or substantially damaging a competitor, preventing entry into a market, or deterring or preventing a person from engaging in competitive conduct.

Two principles to guide the application of s. 46 were stated in the High Court in *QWI*: first, to "take advantage" of market power is to undertake conduct that is only possible, or would make commercial sense, in a non-competitive market; and two, the role of the purpose requirement is to cut back the categories of monopolistic conduct subject to the Act: "it is these purpose provisions which define what uses of market power constitute misuses." (Mason C.J. and Wilson J. at p.50,010).

Frances Hanks and Philip Williams (1990, p. 446), in a seminal analysis of *QWI*, argue that:

> "The effect of the decision of the High Court in QWI is to encourage parties to argue efficiencies before the courts. Far from introducing value judgments into the section, the construction places economic efficiency at the heart of Section 46."

Hanks and Williams base their contention upon a careful analysis of the "take advantage" test. In any event, one would think from a commonsense viewpoint that to interpret "taking advantage" as conduct that would not be possible or commercially sensible under competitive conditions would point directly to the relevance of evidence on efficiencies likely to result from the conduct at issue. Alternatively, one might point to the "purpose" element of the "offence", and seek to claim that the purpose of the conduct was but to obtain access to efficiencies.

There are other sections in Part IV of the Act that refer to "purpose": ss. 45, 45A, 47 all express the prohibition in terms of "purpose" or "likely effect". The courts have been cautious in their approach to "purpose", seeking to specify a concept that would be both consistent with traditional usages and appropriate to this new subject matter.[37] This may turn out to be a sleeper (defined by Webster as "anything unpromising or unnoticed that attains a startling value or importance"). There has been discussion in the cases as to whether "purpose" is "subjective" or "objective." It has been said that it goes to motivation and reasons; that it might constitute "the result aimed at": what a transaction "was designed to achieve." In *General Newspapers* the Full Court of the Federal Court rejected a claim of exclusive dealing, saying that the contractual terms were explained by "ordinary factors to which a firm would have regard when developing a new product" (p. 41,701).

"Legitimate business justification", for which read production efficiency, may well have a role in Australian antitrust, despite the presence of authorization.

VI.4. THE TREATMENT OF VERTICALS[38]

The control of vertical practices has played an unusually prominent role in Australian antitrust, especially in its early enforcement history.

The current statutory position is as follows. RPM is banned (other than in response to loss leader selling), with authorization unavailable. The practice is defined very comprehensively in the Act, and extends to inducing, or attempting to induce, a person not to sell the supplier's products at less than a price specified by the supplier (with "price specified" held to comprehend an element of approximation in appropriate circumstances). There is no requirement that there be an element of agreement (as in the American manner). While the prohibition applies only to goods, the Hilmer *Report* has recommended that anomaly be corrected. The Hilmer *Report* also recommends (pp. 54–59) that authorization be available for RPM generally. Non-price vertical restraints are for the most part subject to a competition test in the courts, with authorization available. Again, there is no element of agreement, whether vertical or horizontal, required to offend.

A number of the important early authorization cases in both the Commission and the Tribunal concerned vertical practices, e.g. tied outlets (solus trading) in beer, petrol and motor vehicles. They were all denied authorization. The Commission has waged a continuing offensive against RPM in the courts. The statistics on the restrictive practices actions instituted by the Commission in the Federal Court tell the story (Brunt (1990, pp. 595–596)): of 75 causes of action instituted from 1974 to 1989, 27 concerned an allegation of RPM. Of 40 causes of action won, 21 concerned RPM.

The Australian treatment of vertical practices is explained largely by two factors, the early pattern of restrictive practices in Australia and the continuing small size of our economy. Section III described the interlocking pattern of horizontal and vertical restrictions that, in mid-century, frequently blanketed whole industries. There existed what the first Chairman of the Commission referred to as industry-wide "systems" or, in another vivid phrase, "clamps across an industry" (Bannerman 1987, pp. 408, 411). There would likely be non-price vertical restraints and price restraints used in conjunction. The price restraints would be both horizontal and vertical. Often all this would be by overt agreement, as for example between two trade associations; but sometimes there would be sufficiently few suppliers, as in the *Tooth and Tooheys* breweries case described above, for the suppliers simply to adopt parallel practices – in that instance, parallel systems of tied houses.

In some ways the initial problem was analogous to that currently experienced by the centrally planned economies of Eastern Europe, now in transition.[39] In these economies, State monopolies with a high degree of vertical integration, are seen to be ripe for horizontal and vertical separation, since much of the structure cannot be justified by efficiencies. There is a need to "loosen up" the tightly integrated organization – to divest, to foster entry, to prevent not only the horizontal cartelization that might ensue but also vertical foreclosure. Somewhat analogously, the early task in Australian antitrust was to "loosen up" systems of integration by overt and tacit agreement, given that so many of them could not be justified by efficiencies.

The second factor forming our policy towards vertical practices is the relatively small size of the Australian economy. While overt cartelization has been destroyed, high concentration and significant barriers to entry from economies of scale and scope remain routine features. In consequence we often find present the bilateral conditions that are the necessary, albeit not sufficient, conditions for vertical non-price restraints to give rise to market foreclosure and/or to promote collusion.

The current Australian policy stance to vertical practices can be summarized as follows:

(1) Our history makes us wary. While fully aware that vertical practices cannot, of themselves, create market power, we are aware of the manner in which verticals can build upon pre-existing horizontal market power to facilitate collusion and/or foreclose entry. Some of this horizontal market power is the product of efficiencies that we would not wish to destroy; some is the product of tacit arrangements that are difficult to attack.

(2) The Hilmer inquiry gave careful consideration to RPM, summarizing the standard efficiency-reducing and efficiency-enhancing arguments. Its recommendation to maintain the prohibition in the courts but permit authorization is based, in part, upon the technicality of the economic arguments. But the Committee also noted the historical "link" with horizontal agreements to fix prices. It concluded that the current per se provision "has helped to eliminate many inefficient trade practices, has simplified the task of enforcing the prohibition against such undesirable activities and does not prevent recommended retail prices." It was not persuaded that "efficiency-enhancing RPM occurs with such frequency that the per se prohibition should be relaxed" (1993, pp. 57–58).

(3) Much American discussion of vertical practices has stressed the importance of interbrand competition in distribution, as distinct from intrabrand competition. The distinction has not been found helpful in Australia. I would judge this to be for essentially two reasons: first, there may often be a limited number of brands on the Australian market; and second, there has been found to be value in competition between a diversity of retail outlets, including those dealing in the same product. Chairman Bannerman's words on his retirement in 1984 are worth quoting (1984, pp. 193–4):

> "The central vice of resale price maintenance is that it operates as if there were an agreement between resellers not to compete on price, notwithstanding the different package of services they may be providing with the goods and notwithstanding the different costs they may be incurring because of volume, location, hours of trading etc. Indeed, the notion of implicit agreement surfaces from time to time, when resellers ask their suppliers to stop other resellers from price-cutting. The fact that this is now illegal has greatly encouraged price competition in many trades, from petrol distribution to whitegoods and domestic appliances. It has been one of the factors working towards structural changes in retailing. Those changes have been notably in the growth of buying groups in response to the continued growth of the chains and in the restructuring of wholesaling and distribution to meet a more competitive environment where the straight out price competition directly benefits the consumer, e.g. in liquor retailing."

It is accepted, again in Bannerman's words (1987, p. 410) that "dealers are not simply extensions of their suppliers; competition at the dealer level is important too."

(4) At the same time we have become increasingly aware of the potential efficiencies that may be associated with vertical practices. This is partly in response to the overseas antitrust literature but also in response to the diversity of experience thrown up by Australian industry structure. Much of American antitrust analysis of verticals focuses upon distribution restraints. There is also a literature associated with intellectual property restraints. Presumably this narrow focus is explained by the perceived location of a possible "monopoly problem" in the American economy. In Australia, we have a richer set of possibilities, given the incidence of high market concentration and significant barriers to entry. Potential efficiencies extend beyond minimization of free rider problems to those customarily associated with vertical integration – economies of linked processing, economies in transaction costs, greater certainty in quantities/qualities of inputs, etc. There is therefore a diversity in the trade-offs that may need to be contemplated when weighing public benefit against anti-competitive detriment. This Australian experience suggests, too, that there may be a diversity of considerations and trade-offs in different economies when dealing with verticals, and that it may be a mistake to export American doctrines and experience without modification.

(5) It is perhaps in this area of Australian trade practices law that we are most aware that the values fostered by competition extend beyond efficiency to economic opportunity and commercial freedom.

VII. The Challenge of the '90s and the Limits of Australian Antitrust

It is plain that we are now entering a new phase in the development of Australian antitrust law, a phase that will explore the limits of this element of competition policy and the role for alternative mechanisms. The limits are of two kinds.

There is first the political and constitutional limits of our Federal system. There are constitutional restrictions upon Commonwealth legislation to control business enterprises other than "trading and financial corporations" (unless they can be brought under some other head of power such as the interstate trade and commerce power). There must therefore be resort to "co-operative federalism", especially as regards the treatment of unincorporated enterprises, such as the professions. Moreover, the Commonwealth has chosen in s. 51(1)(b) of the Act to exercise unnecessary restraint (unnecessary from a constitutional viewpoint) by granting to the States a power of exemption "to any act or thing ... specifically authorized or approved."

At one time it was thought that the Commonwealth lacked power to bind State Government owned businesses, so it legislated (s. 2A) to extend the operation of the Act to bind the Crown in so far as it "carries on a business" only in right of the

Commonwealth. These days it is apparent that a "shield of the Crown" doctrine is not automatically applicable to State enterprises, whatever their business autonomy; but so far the Commonwealth has not sought to test the limits of its powers over State public utilities. This restraint has been an important limitation on the coverage of the Act, since public utilities such as gas, electricity, water and transport are usually organized on a State basis; for instance in electricity there is a series of regional and local monopolies in generation and distribution with transmission interconnected in limited fashion.

The second limit goes to the intrinsic nature of antitrust law, i.e. the use of a court-centered process to establish rules for enterprise behavior. Putting to one side exemptions from the law, it can be said that we have now achieved much that can be readily accomplished by the enactment of an antitrust statute: the self-enforcing bite of the per se prohibitions and the simpler rule of reason prohibitions has done and continues to do its work. We are now encountering the challenge of the more complex rule of reason territory associated with control of misuse of market power, merger, and sub rosa collusion. Australia is not unique in this, but the problems are exacerbated by the small size of the Australian economy and by certain characteristics of the Australian legal system.

The small size of the economy implies that we cannot place reliance on any simple "numbers doctrine" in fashioning presumptions or weights for the courts (as in the manner of *Philadelphia National Bank* in US merger law).[40] For, to speak loosely, in the domestic market sector small numbers are everywhere! Turning to the legal system, the traditional focus of the civil law is upon the settlement of private disputes through a largely oral adversary process. There is no way that courts with such an undiluted orientation could cope with complex rule of reason litigation with a large "public" element. Fortunately there is change afoot, with much discussion of desirable changes to court "practice and procedure", and a realization that greater economy and relevance can be achieved by – somehow! – getting more economic content into the court process.

The systematic consideration of the limits of such court-centered competition law, and how these limits may be expanded to a degree, is facilitated by contemplating the fundamental character of the Trade Practices Act as economic law. It has three dimensions or, perhaps, levels – statutory interpretation encompassing generally expressed standards of liability, the court process in the reception and evaluation of evidence, and the design and application of penalties and remedies. We are now starting to recognize that we have concentrated rather excessively upon the first of these. We are beginning to shift attention to the court process and the remedial outcome, and to recognize the mixed economic-legal content of both.

At the level of the court process, it is true that fundamentally this is a legal process. But there are choices to be made that can be informed by knowledge of the economic subject-matter and by economic processes of reasoning; for instance, in the formulation of detailed standards of liability. Edward S. Mason once wrote (1956, p. 398) that the justification for use of the courts to implement competition policy "depends upon the possibility of valid inferences from relatively simple statements of fact." And again (p. 394): "An attempt to push enquiry into effects very far is clearly an invitation to non-enforcement." As I said in my 1975 Monash lecture, "The legal process places particular reliance upon certain techniques for establishing breach of the law – the use of per se rules, rebuttable presumptions, and short chains of reasoning stemming from the evidence." Contemplation of the Australian economy suggests that for many problems the core of evidence before the courts can be directed to barriers to entry and the pattern and dynamism of market shares, with appropriate regard to the international setting; and there are indications that the courts are moving in this direction.[41]

Further, so-called "legal" issues of practice and procedure assume great importance, for these can be used as the vehicle for achieving economic relevance. There are important procedural developments under way in the Federal Court – more emphasis upon the pre-trial clarification of issues, greater use of written materials, greater judicial control of the discovery process, discussion of the scope for referral of questions to arbitration or expert report or to the Tribunal, and relaxation of the traditional formal rules governing opinion evidence such as the evidence of economists. This last is important. In the past counsel in hotly contested litigation have been able to hamstring their opponents' economic testimony by relying upon two traditional rules of evidence: the factual basis rule (requiring the expert to confine his opinion to explicitly assumed facts) and the ultimate issue rule (denying the expert the possibility of giving an opinion on the ultimate issue.)[42] A new Rule of the Federal Court (commencing in November 1993) states that the court may:

> 3.1(2)(j) "in proceedings in which a party seeks to rely on the opinion of a person involving a subject in which the person has specialist qualifications, direct that all or part of such opinion be received by way of submission in such manner and form as the Court may think fit, whether or not the opinion would be admissible as evidence."

The rule is cast in very wide terms. At its most obvious, the rule will permit economists, subject to the direction of the court, to submit written material that does not strictly conform to the rules of evidence. But it could also enable the economist-expert to assist the court in whatever capacity might prove useful to resolution of the issues. The rule would appear to give scope for a written submission at any stage in the proceedings, including the pre-trial stage, and thus to widen the opportunity for economists to contribute to clarification of the issues and the assessment of the relevance of evidence.

The structure of remedies and penalties is also being addressed, with a recent substantial increase in pecuniary penalties: for a body corporate up to A$10 million (approximately US$7 million) for each act or omission and, for a person, up to A$500,000 (US$350,000) for each act or omission. In public debate much attention has been given to the limitations of injunctions and divestiture in antitrust law, especially in the context of merger and misuse of market power. Certainly, with treble damages and class actions unavailable, injunctions and related orders have proved to be of vital importance to the private litigant; but there is no private right to injunctive relief in the case of merger; and there is an increasing awareness that the role of s. 46, governing misuse of market power, is restricted by reason of the courts' inability to play an on-going regulatory role. The Act provides for divestiture only in the case of mergers and acquisitions. While there has been some debate as to whether divestiture should be available as a remedy for breach of s. 46, the Commonwealth Attorney-General's Department has argued convincingly that "courts are ill-equipped to decide which elements of a cohesive corporation should be separated." The Department has also submitted that "it is not possible to recreate from one merged entity two effectively competitive organizations for a number of reasons."[43]

In sum, the intrinsic limits of our court-centred competition law are found in these considerations: that the core should consist of rules governing business conduct of a largely self-enforcing character, possessed of reasonable certainty and compliability; that the matters to be litigated are justiciable in the sense that they give rise to articulated and economically relevant issues that can be tested in an adversary setting and evaluated by the court; and that there be available effective remedies of a dispositive and non-regulatory kind.

It was to a consciousness of some of these limits to the court process that we owe our authorization procedure. But now there is a discernible shift in the focus of competition policy to encompass what the Hilmer *Report* refers to as "additional policy elements." The Commission has been taking a lead in this wider orientation.[44]

It is appropriate to conclude this Section with a short account of the import of the Hilmer *Report* released in August 1993. The *Report* clearly constitutes a watershed in the development of Australian competition law. The terms of reference required the Committee to appraise not only the coverage and effectiveness of the Act but also "alternative means for addressing market behavior and structure currently outside the scope of the Trade Practices Act 1974" and "the best structure for regulation including price regulation in support of [inter alia]: ... pro-competitive conduct by government business and trading enterprises and in areas currently outside the scope of the Trade Practices Act 1974" (1993, p.362).

A very brief summary of the contents of this *Report* will serve to indicate the agenda for future competition policy in Australia. The Committee's *Report* has been given initial consideration (February 1994) by the appropriate Federal body, the Council of Australian Governments. The Council has agreed "in principle" to the Hilmer reform agenda. Implementation is to be considered at its next meeting in August 1994.

The perspective permeating the whole *Report* has two characteristics. There is first the recognition of the wide scope of competition policy to extend beyond the provisions of Part IV of the Act to encompass (p. xvi) "all policy dealing with the extent and nature of competition in the economy;" and second, the judgment that reform should be achieved by cooperative federalism rather than by reliance upon the Commonwealth Government's constitutional powers.

One part of the *Report* carries to completion the lines of development of trade practices law of the previous 20 years: it makes recommendations for fine-tuning of the existing "competitive conduct rules" contained within the Act, as already mentioned in earlier Sections of this article, and for universal coverage of the Act accompanied by a rigorous and transparent exemption process. The second, pathbreaking part – a segment that accounts for around two-thirds of the Report's length – breaks entirely new ground. It is designed to meet the two main challenges of the '90s, so far as competition policy in Australia is concerned: first, how the structure and conduct of government business enterprises ("GBEs"), many of them in the process of privatization, can be made compatible with competition goals; and second, how effective competition policy can be formulated and implemented in a Federal system consisting of the Commonwealth, six States and two Territories. The two concerns overlap. In the event, many of the recommendations are to be explained by considerations of politics, rather than by law and economics; and by emphasis upon institutions and decision processes rather than upon economic criteria, such as efficiency. It is plainly hoped to disarm the States. The interest of the States (and Territories) in retaining ownership and control of their utilities can be summed up under three heads: the revenue from monopoly returns, community service obligations, and State sovereignty concerns (including related vested interests).

Of particular interest to economists will be the approach to the regulation of GBEs – the statutory monopolies and privatized utilities – and the interface envisaged with the Act. The *Report* puts forward an elaborate scheme, too elaborate for this paper to attempt to describe.[45] Nevertheless one can indicate the Committee's conclusions on some important points of principle:

(1) Basic restructuring should be accomplished at an initial stage of privatization and/or deregulation. The several governments should adopt a set of principles directed to separating natural monopoly elements from those that are potentially competitive. Both vertical and horizontal separation is envisaged. Regulatory functions should be removed from the commercial entities.

(2) All governments should pursue policies of "competitive neutrality" when GBEs compete with private firms.

(3) It is anticipated that there will be key facilities characterized by "natural monopoly". Accordingly there will be an "essential facilities problem", with a need to ensure access to the facility to permit effective competition in a downstream or upstream activity.

(4) Reliance cannot be placed upon the Act, specifically s. 46 governing misuse of market power, to establish an appropriate access regime. There would be "difficulties", both in "demonstrating a proscribed purpose" and in the court process in "determining terms and conditions" (p. 243), although s. 46 could be used in a supplementary way for on-going problems. Accordingly there is a need for a special legal regime, with principles governing access to each designated essential facility declared by the relevant Commonwealth Minister, on the recommendation of an independent and expert body. These principles can be expected to vary as between facilities.

(5) The Committee opts for "light-handed regulation" by a new generalist regulatory body (the "National Competition Council") appointed jointly by the Commonwealth, States and Territories. This would have the responsibility of advising on restructuring, the declaration of access rights, and the general principles to govern access for each essential facility (crucially, the "access price"). There may be a role for a "prices oversight mechanism" but it should be limited to "monitoring and surveillance" rather than "regulation" or "control" (chapter 12).

(6) The Committee concludes that "neither the application of economic theory nor general notions of fairness provide a clear answer as to the appropriate access fee in all circumstances" (p. 253), other than that there be a requirement that access be on "fair and reasonable" terms to protect the "legitimate interests of the owner of the facility" (p. 252). "No single principle or rule of any degree of specificity is likely to meet the policy concerns of every market" (p. 255). Efficiency is not highlighted as a fundamental criterion. Rather the main considerations are seen to be the promotion of "competition" and the protection of the "legitimate interests" of owners.[46]

(7) Where parties in an access negotiation cannot agree on specific terms, "binding arbitration" would be available under the auspices of the competition authority, a new body to be formed from the existing Trade Practices Commission and Prices Surveillance Authority, to be known as the Australian Competition Commission.

In sum, and from the viewpoint of this paper, the Committee's recommendations regarding the GBEs amount to a decisive rejection of the Act and its institutions as controlling mechanisms in the deregulation and privatization process. This may be the appropriate stance. Nevertheless we would be left, when all is said and done, with a challenging "interface problem," i.e. the interface between this new regime and our antitrust law. Universal and consistent standards as between the two regimes will be desirable if economic distortions are to be avoided. There also needs to be linkages between the various institutions in furtherance of this objective. And finally there needs to be recognition that the "access problem" is not readily separable from much "routine" business conduct in buying and selling in markets, conduct with exclusionary implications that would be subject to the Act.

VIII. Recapitulation and Conclusion

We have travelled a long way since 1974. Those of us who can remember the Australia of the 1950s and '60s have a sense of wonderment at the transformation of the economy and business attitudes that has been achieved in such a short space of time – the abandonment of cartelization as the norm and of the laissez faire philosophy that permitted this to occur. The Australian experience is testimony to the surgical power of antitrust in eliminating overt price-fixing, both horizontal and vertical, and trade boycotts provided there is primary reliance upon per se prohibitions.

Over the period surveyed, there has been a transformation in the approach of the courts to this subject matter – a willingness to go beyond the "ordinary English words", in which a statute is written, to an acceptance that the Act constitutes economic law, and a realization that the phrase "economic law" requires that attention be given to both words. Yet there exists a tension between law and economics which is still in the process of being worked through – in modification of traditional court procedures in reception of evidence, in traditional categories of legal reasoning, and in the traditional approach to penalties and remedies. We have not yet achieved an appropriate concept of regulatory law, one that will require both a higher policy content and a greater inquisitorial element, though we are moving to it.

At the same time, we observe the achievement of a coherent body of antitrust jurisprudence that has relevance not just to the terms of the statute but to the nature of the economy and the characteristics of the legal system. As we have seen, it is understood that there is a fundamental unity in the subject matter of the Act: the Act seeks to control the creation, the extension and the use of market power. The evolving Australian approach is to identify "competition" with constraints upon market power and, in rule of reason cases, to use a "truncated" structure-conduct-performance approach.

There are three major challenges remaining:

- to eliminate unjustified exemptions from the Act that arise merely from legal status (the unincorporated enterprises) and discredited State regulation (such as licensing and arbitrary standards);
- to implement some half-way house of "managed competition" for GBEs and privatized utilities that will combine initial restructuring, "light-handed regulation", and exposure to the Act in a compatible system; and
- to develop operational tests, i.e. detailed standards of liability as to what constitutes "lessening of competition" and "substantial market power" for the different categories of conduct falling under the Act.

These are the kinds of problems that are found in other antitrust systems but, as has been explained, they have been exacerbated in the Australian case by the small size of the economy, our Federal system, and the nature of the legal system.

We have identified some distinctive features of Australian antitrust law: the approach to market definition; the dual adjudication system and the related development of the pure market power standard; and the treatment of verticals. Much of what is distinctive in Australian law today can be explained by three factors: the small size of the economy, the limitations of our courts in performing economic regulatory functions, and history. "History" is a convenient term to refer to the not readily reversible processes in time that have their beginning in the circumstances of an earlier day and the visions of earlier "great men" such as Barwick and Murphy.

We return to the questions posed at the beginning of this paper inspired by a reading of Klaus Hopt. Australian experience does attest to the existence of certain inevitable stages in the development of antitrust law, culminating in a final stage where antitrust reaches its "limits" in the "abuse control of market-dominating companies". There is much detail in Hopt's article that, in uncanny fashion, describes Australian experience. Hopt does recognize that there "remain countless possibilities of divergence in terms of system decisions and rules" (p. 300). But might it not be concluded that Australian experience attests to more than this, namely to the possibility of significant intercountry differences in the structure and impact of antitrust law?

Notes

* An early version of this paper was presented at the Trade Practices & Consumer Law Conference, Terrigal, October 1991. I thank the convenor and participants for their stimulus. It is a pleasure to acknowledge the helpful discussions I have had with David Merrett on historical aspects. He will see that there is plenty left for him to do! I thank Frances Hanks and Philip Williams for helpful comments on the draft of this paper, and I should particularly like to thank the Special Editor for his detailed and constructive comments.

1 See the paper in this issue by Round and Siegfried, for discussion of this issue with respect to price-fixing.

2 The Act encompasses consumer protection as well as the control of restrictive practices, though only the latter are the subject-matter of this article.

3 See Brunt (1990). Statistics are presented in this article for the first 15 years of litigation in the courts (pp. 587–596). From 1975–1989, private parties brought 70 reported cases that generated a judgment at least to the stage of interim or interlocutory injunction; the Commission brought 43 (p. 593). If we exclude the actions relating to secondary boycotts (ss. 45D, 45E), the figures become 37 (private parties) and 43 (Commission). A case may be concerned with more than one cause of action (e.g. s. 46 and s. 47). Excluding cases concerned with secondary boycotts, private parties brought 50 causes of action (of which the largest category is misuse of market power: 15 instances); the Commission brought 45 (of which the largest category is RPM: 21 instances). In the last two years, the Commission has been initiating more actions, and more actions of precedential value, as may be seen by an inspection of its recent *Annual Reports*.

4 The Western Australian Government Railways, for instance, gave evidence that for 46 listed articles (including such diverse items as cement, electrical cables, nails, string, tyres and tubes, toilet rolls, spark plugs and fly wire) whenever tenders are called "the prices offered are identical" (p. 15).

[5] The comparison was particularly appropriate for competition analysis since it was based upon the industry concept espoused and applied in Kaysen and Turner's *Antitrust Policy* (1959, pp. 26–37, 295–331). For each economy an industry classification was drawn up based upon the same principle, viz that it should reflect moderately long-run competitive possibilities as revealed by judgments regarding both cross-elasticity of demand and cross-elasticity of supply for products of the industry.

[6] There is some difference of opinion as to whether the 1965 Act can be truly regarded as Barwick's creation. Barwick himself is said by his biographer to have referred to the Act as "milk and water" (Marr (1992, p. 206)). Certainly the legislation that was enacted was, in J.E. Richardson's words (1967, p. 4), "considerably less ambitious than the initial proposals" of December 1962. However, in my view, what was enacted contained the practical essentials of the Barwick scheme. (See Richardson (1967, pp. 3–4, 11–14) for a convenient short account of the differences between the Act and the initial proposals).

Moreover, the Cabinet Papers (1963) recently released under the 30 year secrecy rule reveal that Barwick himself formulated significant modifications to his initial proposals in light of public discussion (and prior to a somewhat famous meeting with representatives of the Manufacturing Industries Advisory Council in September 1963). He submitted a modified scheme to Cabinet in October 1963 but the submission lapsed because of the General Election held in November 1963. The Cabinet Papers indicate that some amendment is required to Marr's account (1992, chapter 15) of this phase of Barwick's career.

[7] See the speeches listed in the References (Barwick (1961, 1962, 1963a, 1963b)) and Marr (1992, pp. 184–191).

[8] It is significant that in the consumer protection field there has been a similar success with the enactment in Part V of the Act of per se prohibitions of various forms of misleading and deceptive conduct.

[9] See especially *Quadramain Pty Limited v. Sevastapol Investments Pty Limited* (1976) ATPR 40–013; *Top Performance Motors Pty Ltd v. Ira Berk (Queensland) Pty Ltd.* (1975) ATPR 40–004.

[10] *Queensland Wire Industries Pty Ltd v. The Broken Hill Proprietary Company Ltd.* (1989) ATPR 40–925.

[11] See Department of the Treasury (1993, pp. 13–19); Industry Commission (1992, pp. 75–82).

[12] The Hilmer *Report* (National Competition Policy Review (1993)) and its implications will be discussed in Section VII.

[13] Until recent amendments, there was a third variant for mergers, "market dominance."

[14] *Re Media Council of Australia (No. 2).* (1987) ATPR 40–774.

[15] *Re Queensland Co-operative Milling Association Ltd, Defiance Holdings Ltd (Proposed Mergers with Barnes Milling Ltd.).* (1976) ATPR 40–012.

[16] Interestingly, the same passage was quoted by Garfield Barwick in his G.L. Wood Memorial Lecture (1963a, p. 6) at the time he was endeavoring to popularize his proposals.

[17] See Brunt (1993, pp. 155–159).

[18] *Trade Practices Commission v. Ansett Transport Industries (Operations) Pty Ltd.* (1978) ATPR 40–071.

[19] *Arnotts Ltd v. Trade Practices Commission.* (1990) ATPR 41–061.

[20] *Gallagher v. Pioneer Concrete (NSW) Pty Ltd.* (1993) ATPR 41–216.

[21] A recent example is the exclusive dealing case, *Stationers Supply*. Here the relevant market was defined by reference to the parties' business rather than the actual and potential outlets for stationery. See *Stationers Supply Pty Ltd v. The Victorian Authorised Newsagents Association Ltd.* (1993) ATPR 41–255.

[22] *Re News Ltd* (1987) 1 NZBLC (Com) at p. 104,051; *Re Weddel Crown Corporation Ltd* (1987) 1 NZBLC (Com), pp. 104,212–3.

[23] Cf the discussion by Round and Siegfried in this issue.

[24] See *Trade Practices Commission v. Nicholas Enterprises Pty Ltd.* (1979) ATPR 40–126; *Morphett Arms Hotel Pty Ltd v. Trade Practices Commission.* (1980) ATPR 40–157; *Trade Practices Commission v. David Jones (Australia) Pty Ltd.* (1986) ATPR 40–671; and *Trade Practices Commission v. Allied Mills Industries Pty Ltd.* (1981) ATPR 40–237.

[25] *The New Zealand Co-Operative Dairy Company Ltd v. Commerce Commission.* (1991) 3 NZBLC 99–219, p. 102,071.

[26] *Top Performance Motors*, *supra* n.9, pp. 17,114–17,115.
[27] *Re Howard Smith Industries Pty Ltd and Adelaide Steamship Industries Pty Ltd.* (1977) ATPR 40–023.
[28] *Application by Tooth & Co. Ltd; Application by Tooheys Ltd.* (1979) ATPR 40–113.
[29] *Re John Dee (Export) Pty Ltd.* (1989) ATPR 40–938. The approach was initiated in *QCMA* (*supra* n. 15, p. 17,244).
[30] *Re Association of Consulting Engineers, Australia.* (1981) ATPR 40–202.
[31] *In re Rural Traders Co-operative (W.A.) Ltd.* (1979) ATPR 40–110.
[32] *Re Media Council of Australia (No. 2)*, *supra* n. 14.
[33] Cf Fisher (1987), pp. 38–39.
[34] See Marr (1992, chapters 6–9).
[35] *Federal Trade Commission v. Proctor & Gamble Co.* 386 U.S. 568 (1967).
[36] Cf Comanor and White (1992, p. 114). The Australian standard of liability discussed in the text to this point is equivalent (in logic) to a court-based system (such as the US) using a pure market power presumption with an efficiency defense.
[37] *General Newspapers Pty Ltd v. Telstra (Hannanprint).* (1993) ATPR 41–274, pp. 41,696–41,702, where Davies and Einfeld JJ review and discuss the relevant cases.
[38] See also Ian McEwin's paper in this issue.
[39] Fornalczyk (1993), writing of the Polish antitrust scene, gives an entertaining and instructive account of the difficulty of explaining to "people in the United States" that there are real vertical problems in "an economy in transition".
[40] *United States v. Philadelphia National Bank* 374 U.S. 321 (1963).
[41] See the judgment of the Full Court of the Federal Court in *Arnotts*, *supra* n.19.
[42] Yeung (1992) has a very full discussion of both the actual and potential roles of economists in Australian antitrust litigation.
[43] Submission by Officers of the Commonwealth Attorney-General's Department to the Senate Standing Committee on Legal and Constitutional Affairs (the Cooney Committee) reported in (1991) ATPR 30–164, pp. 32,831–2.
[44] See the *Annual Reports* of the Commission. The shift of emphasis is discussed in chapter 1 of the most recent *Annual Report* (1992–93).
[45] See chapters 8, 10 and 11–14 of the *Report*, especially chapters 8 and 11.
[46] See chapter 11 of the *Report* for the main discussion of access issues.

References

Areeda, Phillip E., and Herbert Hovenkamp (1993) *Antitrust Law* (Supplement), Boston, Little, Brown.

Australia, Statements by Prime Minister, Treasurer and Industry Minister (1991) *Building a Competitive Australia*, Canberra, Australian Government Publishing Service.

Australia, Submissions to Australian Cabinet on Restrictive Trade Practices and Monopolies (1963), Submission 994, Vol. 26, Canberra, Australian Archives Office.

Australian Proposals for Legislation for the Control of Restrictive Trade Practices and Monopolies (1963) "Tables of Trade Practices", Canberra, Commonwealth Government Printer.

Bannerman, R.M. (1984) 'Points from Experience 1967–1984', in Trade Practices Commission, *Annual Report 1983–84*, Canberra, Australian Government Publishing Service.

Bannerman, R.M. (1987) 'The Importance of the Trade Practices Tribunal: Does It Have a Future?' *Australian Business Law Review*, **15**, 383–437.

Barwick, Sir Garfield (1961) 'Some Aspects of Australian Proposals for Legislation for the Control of Restrictive Trade Practices and Monopolies,' 13th Legal Convention of the Law Council of Australia, *Australian Law Journal*, **36**, 363–384.

Barwick, Sir Garfield (1962) Speech to the Australian Parliament, delivered by the Acting Attorney General, the Hon. G. Freeth, *Parliamentary Debates*, 6 December 1962.

Barwick, Sir Garfield (1963a) 'Trade Practices in a Developing Economy', The G.L. Wood Memorial Lecture for 1963, Canberra, Commonwealth Government Printer.

Barwick, Sir Garfield (1963b) 'Administrative Features of Legislation on Restrictive Trade Practices', The Sir Robert Garran Oration for 1963, Mimeo.
Brunt, Maureen (1965) 'Legislation in Search of an Objective', *Economic Record*, **41**, 357–386.
Brunt, Maureen (1975) 'Economic Overview,' mimeo, Lecture Number 11 in *Monash Trade Practices Lectures*, Melbourne, copy held in Monash University Law Library.
Brunt, Maureen (1990) 'The Role of Private Actions in Australian Restrictive Practices Enforcement', *Melbourne University Law Review*, **17**, 582–613.
Brunt, Maureen (1993) 'Australian and New Zealand Competition Law and Policy', in Barry Hawk (ed.), *1992 Fordham Corporate Law Institute*, Irvington-on-Hudson, NY, Transnational Juris Publications/GA Deventer, The Netherlands, Kluwer.
Caves, R.E., and M.E. Porter (1977) 'From Entry Barriers to Mobility Barriers', *Quarterly Journal of Economics*, **91**, 241–261.
Comanor, William S., and Lawrence J. White (1992) 'Market Power or Efficiency: A Review of Antitrust Standards', *Review of Industrial Organization*, **7**, 105–116.
Department of the Treasury (1993) *Treasury Submission to the National Competition Policy Review*, Treasury Economic Paper Number 16, Canberra, Commonwealth Government Printer.
Easterbrook, F.H. (1984) 'The Limits of Antitrust', *Texas Law Review*, **63**, 1–40.
Fisher, Franklin M. (1987) 'Horizontal Mergers: Triage and Treatment,' *Journal of Economic Perspectives*, **1**, 23–40.
Fornalczyk, Anna (1993) 'Competition Policy During Transformation of a Centrally Planned Economy' in Barry Hawk (ed.) *1992 Fordham Corporate Law Institute*, Irvington-on-Hudson, NY, Transnational Juris Publications/GA Deventer, The Netherlands, Kluwer.
Freeman, R.D. (1965) 'Trade Associations in the Australian Economy', *Public Administration*, **23**, 329–343.
Hanks, Frances, and Philip L. Williams (1990) 'Implications of the Decision of the High Court in *Queensland Wire*,' *Melbourne University Law Review*, **17**, 437–461.
Hopt, Klaus J. (1987) 'Restrictive Trade Practices and Juridification: A Comparative Law Study', in Gunther Teubner (ed.) *Juridication of Social Spheres: A Comparative Analysis in the Areas of Labor, Corporate, Antitrust and Social Welfare Law*, Berlin, Walter de Gruyter.
Hunter, A. (1961) 'Restrictive Practices and Monopolies in Australia', *Economic Record*, **37**, 25–52.
Hunter, A., and D. Simons (1963) 'Collusive or Level Tendering and Public Authorities', *Australian Quarterly*, **35**, 17–35.
Industry Commission (1992) *Pro-competitive Regulation*, Discussion Paper, Fyshwick, ACT, CPN Publications.
Joint Committee on Constitutional Review (1959) *Report*, Canberra, Australian Government Publishing Service.
Karmel, P.H., and Maureen Brunt (1962) *The Structure of the Australian Economy*, revised edition, Melbourne, F.W. Cheshire Pty. Ltd.
Kaysen, Carl, and Donald F. Turner (1959) *Antitrust Policy*, Cambridge Mass., Harvard University Press.
Marr, David (1992) *Barwick*, second edition, North Sydney, Allen & Unwin.
Mason, Edward S. (1939) 'Price and Production Policies of Large-Scale Enterprise', reprinted in Mason, Edward S. (1957) *Economic Concentration and the Monopoly Problem*, Cambridge Mass., Harvard University Press.
Mason, Edward S. (1956) 'Market Power and Business Conduct: Some Comments on the Report of the Attorney-General's Committee on Antitrust Policy', reprinted in Mason, Edward S. (1957) *Economic Concentration and the Monopoly Problem*, Cambridge Mass., Harvard University Press.
Masterman, George G., and Ezekiel Solomon (1967) *Australian Trade Practices Law*, Sydney, Butterworths.
National Competition Policy Review (F.G. Hilmer, Chairman) (1993) *National Competition Policy*, Canberra, Australian Government Publishing Service.
Officer, R.R. (1987) 'The Public Benefit Test in an Authorization Decision', mimeo.
Richardson, J.E. (1967) *Introduction to the Australian Trade Practices Act*, Sydney, Hicks Smith & Sons.

Tasmania, Royal Commissioner on Prices and Restrictive Trade Practices (1965) *Report*, Hobart, Government Printer.
Trade Practices Commission (1992) *Merger Guidelines*, Draft for Comment, Canberra, Trade Practices Commission.
Trade Practices Commission (1993) *Annual Report 1992–93*, Canberra, Australian Government Publishing Service.
US Attorney-General's National Commmittee to Study the Antitrust Laws (1955) *Report*, Washington DC, US Government Printing Office.
US Department of Justice and Federal Trade Commission (1992), *Horizontal Merger Guidelines*, Washington DC, Department of Justice and Federal Trade Commission.
Walker, Geoffrey de Q. (1967) *Australian Monopoly Law: Issues of Law, Fact and Policy*, Melbourne, F.W. Cheshire Pty. Ltd.
Western Australia, Royal Commission on Restrictive Trade Practices and Legislation (1958) *Report*, Perth, Government Printer.
Williamson, Oliver E. (1968) "Economies as an Antitrust Defense: The Welfare Tradeoffs", *American Economic Review*, **58**, 18–36.
Williamson, Oliver E. (1977) "Economies as an Antitrust Defense Revisited," *University of Pennsylvania Law Review*, **125**, 699–736.
Yeung, Karen (1992) "The Court-room Economist in Australian Antitrust Litigation: An Underutilized Resource?" *Australian Business Law Review*, **20**, 461–515.

Review of Industrial Organization **9:** 527–545, 1994.

Progress Under Pressure: The Evolution of Antitrust Policy in Australia

NEVILLE R. NORMAN*
Department of Economics, University of Melbourne, Parkville Victoria 3052, Australia

Abstract. Australia has developed a balanced and comprehensive antitrust policy. But the process of evolution has seen conflict, misunderstanding and error in applying the relevant economic concepts. Whether antitrust legislation is needed, and in what form, is still debated, as are ways of incorporating new approaches in economics. This is a documented account and commentary on the twenty years of evolution, designed especially for non-Australian readers seeking to gain advantage and avoid error by studying the experience of another country.

Key words: Australian antitrust, economic concepts, competition controversies.

I. Overview

Australia is recognised, along with the United States, Canada and New Zealand, as one of the few countries to have developed a comprehensive competition law.[1] But this development was relatively late in Australia's case; it now celebrates just twenty years of effective antitrust. The process of evolution has also been painful. While the American Sherman Act was in place by 1890 and was actively used soon thereafter, and Britain and several European countries had competition policies in force shortly after the Second World War, Australia lacked a comprehensive antitrust statute until 1974.

This paper presents both an overview and an economist's assessment of the first twenty years of the operation of the Trade Practices Act 1974 (TPA hereafter). It is directed especially to non-Australian readers with a professional interest in antitrust policies and the controversies played out within them, especially on the incorporation of economic concepts into legislation and antitrust practice. The process and its resolution are relevant to almost any country adopting such laws. The aim is to record the context into which Australian antitrust laws were introduced, and to chart the use and evolution of the economic concepts of "market" and "competition".

I.1. Antitrust in Australia and Other Countries

It may be useful briefly to explain, compare and differentiate the Australian approach and institutions in an international setting. In Australia, the law is more fully specified in legislation than it is in the United States. However, the Australian antitrust authority, the Trade Practices Commission (TPC), plays a similar role to the American FTC, and a device known as "authorization" gives effect to something akin to 'reasonableness' in the American sense. As in the United States, there is more lenient treatment of vertical than of horizontal arrangements and similar price-fixing provisions;[2] but by contrast the remedies and enforcement procedures differ. Treble damage provisions and more stringent criminal penalties are missing from the Australian scene. Few antitrust matters receive the lengthy consideration given by the British Monopolies and Mergers Commission, though court cases can become long and involved.

On a higher philosophical plane, Australia has sought neither to attack larger corporations in the spirit of the Sherman Act,[3] nor has it reversed the thrust of antitrust philosophy with the force of the American deregulationist movement of the Reagan years. [4] The TPA which governs Australian antitrust enforcement has evolved towards a balanced and responsive device for promoting and enforcing market competition, in the modern economic sense, while eschewing ideological extremes. Turbulence has occurred mainly in the process of creating and amending legislation and on points of substance within individual cases.

I.2. The Legal-Economic Interchange and the TPA's Development

Part IV of the of the TPA (Sections 45 to 50) concerns horizontal and vertical price and non-price agreements between corporations, abuse of market power, price discrimination and mergers. These sections reflect and demand a close interplay between law and economics and have, in the TPA's first twenty years of life, also been the battlefield for the professions as well as the litigants. The evolution of antitrust legislation in Australia is the story of law and economics being forced to work together, often reluctantly. The process was always bound to be difficult, because (a) the economics of industry behavior was not primarily devised for application in antitrust cases; (b) economists' use of language is often less precise than that of lawyers; (c) economists' reformist zeal needs to be tempered in the hearing of any specific matter; and (d) the economics of industry behavior is often too difficult to be adequately deposed into evidence in legal proceedings. From the other side of this partnership, the Australian legal profession was similarly at first inexperienced in handling economic concepts and economists. [5]

Legal advisers, advocates and judges had to contend with a new vocabulary (dominated by such terms as "substitutability", "market", "competition" and the "public interest"), while economists had to learn the legal way of things, and to avoid discussing the policy content or reform of the TPA while operating within it in individual cases. Many errors have been made in the use of economic concepts, both in principle and in application. Lawyers, economists and industry people came slowly to understand the point and practicalities of this new law; but experience was a faithful teacher, mistakes were progressively erased, and the TPA became better understood, better interpreted and ultimately more settled. After twenty years, Australia has now reached a stage of considerable maturity in the major mechanism through which it exercises competition law, even by comparison with the United States. It is argued as a central theme of this paper that the Australian approach has been more balanced than in most other countries applying antitrust regulations; it has responded, but cautiously, to new initiatives in economic analysis, such as the so-called Chicago school doctrines of policy and analysis.

Overall the TPA has served the Australian people well. Price-fixing agreements, once rife, have been effectively banned, although not entirely eliminated; other corporate practices have come under close public scrutiny; sources of competitive threat are now more commonly present across industry generally; and firms in rivalry with each other take exceptional care to avoid collusion. Moreover, the success or failure of firms and products is now far more than ever before dependent on their actual market performance. This is the essence of competition.

II. Origins of the Australian Approach

The Australian TPA has stood relatively unchanged for twenty years, at least with respect to horizontal and vertical arrangements. [6] It is much closer in principle to the American antitrust laws than to the British approach on which the previous, and largely ineffective, Australian legislation was modelled. It was a difficult and tortuous process, even to establish the legislation. The story is given in brief below. It is necessary to set the scene in such an historical perspective, both to understand how fully, firmly and finally the TPA changed the regulatory atmosphere in Australia, and also to have some starting point from which to assess its achievements over the last twenty years.

II.1. The Period of Inaction and Uncertainty

While the Australian authorities moved quickly to place on the statute books in 1906 legislation (known as the Australian Industries Preservation Act) akin to the American Sherman Act, this law foundered for want of subjective interpretation of the purpose or intent associated with alleged breaches, and successive Australian Governments stood by while industry developed, became more highly concentrated, more highly foreign-owned and (as far as can be told) formed a wide range of restrictive agreements within itself.[7] By the middle 1950s it was a favourite pastime of advanced undergraduate economics students to collect information about these agreements, and industry had no real reason to conceal them, for there was no law or effective public or political censure against them.[8] This was the mood of the times before antitrust began effectively to operate.

By the early 1960s, the range and form of restrictive price and other horizontal agreements had become widespread, but concern about them had now begun to grow.[9] It had been reported in the 1950s that "horizontal agreements on conditions of trade were employed in conjunction with horizontal price agreements . . . and such practices (were) a nationwide phenomenon. Agreements of various kinds were found to affect commodities directly in every one of the fifty-six divisions in the Standard International Trade Classification; horizontal agreements directly affected commodities in fifty-two of them, often in a wide range of industries. "[10] The traditionally more anti-industry (pro-labor union, and Leftist) political party, the Australian Labor Party (ALP) had been in the political wilderness since 1949 (and did not regain power until 1972). There was one close election encounter, however, in 1961, which caused the conservative sitting parties (the Liberal Party and its coalition partner, the Country Party[11]) to reconsider its policies. Part of that reconsideration was a series of proposals manifested in a draft Bill for a Restrictive Practices Act, introduced in 1962 by the then Attorney-General, Sir Garfield Barwick. Barwick's proposals, while mildly interventionist as seen from today's perspective, were not met with widespread support either from within his own political party or from the business community. These proposals never became law, and Barwick left the political scene.

A weaker form of Barwick's proposals was proclaimed by his successor in 1965, and took effect in 1967. Modelled on the former British approach, this Act created a "secret register" of restrictive practices and agreements, and a Commissioner of Trade Practices with a small staff was established to scan these documents and make inquiries. If necessary, the Commissioner could call the parties into a conference and, if unsatisfied by their responses, the Commissioner, bearing the onus of proof, could commence an action at the Trade Practices Tribunal (TPT). The TPT sat only as a mechanism of review once the Commissioner felt there were good grounds for taking action against the firms involved for deprivation of the public interest. It still plays a similar role today.

The powers of the Commissioner were particularly weak and limited, in the following senses:

- few specific actions were prohibited outright or scrutinised under the legislation;
- as long as the register was maintained as strictly "secret", the public knowledge and pressure needed to enforce any action was substantially absent;
- the onus of proving that alleged contraventions were against the public interest lay with the Commissioner.[12]

The 1965 legislation made collusive tendering and bidding per se illegal, while other non-excepted contraventions were either "practices", normally undertaken unilaterally or by a combination of firms acting as one, and "agreements", including price-fixing and other horizontal agreements, which were actions in concert. There was a range of exemptions or "gateways", similar to the post-war British approach, for property rights, employment generally, local and regional employment, and (unlike in Britain) for the protection of small business. In addition, a curious pre-condition was also adopted from British procedures; namely, that certain practices deemed monopolisation could not be examined (by the Commissioner or the TPT) unless the perpetrating parties commanded at least a one-third share of the relevant market.[13]

By 1972, the 1965 Act had struggled to make much impact, at least in law.[14] There were constitutional challenges to its very existence, high hopes in industry that the Act would be repealed, and the weaknesses mentioned above. Academic reviewers and others were urging a stronger and more consistent Act, and the sitting Government in its final months of a record span of government was responsive to these, notably by proposing a reversal of the onus of proof, so that the subject practices would be presumed contrary to the public interest unless the corporations involved could demonstrate that they operated clearly in the public interest. With these amendments it was also proposed to create a Monopolies Commission, along British lines. The proposals never had practical effect, as the Government was defeated at the 1972 election. But they illustrate an evolution in thinking, in the direction of placing corporations under greater pressure to justify the potentially anti-competitive practices and agreements that were still rife in the early 1970s.

II.2. Interventionist Pressures of the 1970s

The change of Government in 1972 heralded the new law. By the time this law commenced to operate in 1974, however, some progress had already been made in identifying and curtailing restrictive trade practices, especially horizontal agreements, although almost the only evidence to support this contention lies in the reports of the Commissioner for Trade Practices and anecdotal evidence from industry and journalists at the time, that many practices had ceased.[15] However, a major price-fixing agreement among sellers of frozen peas had been identified, tried and punished. This provided a strong signal from the law and the regulators that the old days of tolerance to almost any agreement had now passed.

The agreement between ten processors of frozen vegetables, designed to curtail a price slide due to over-production relative to demand, came before the TPT in 1971. While it declared the agreement contrary to the public interest, the determination was notable for its concern for preserving the value of smaller operators as going concerns or takeover targets. This approach was thus tantamount to conditional assent to the price-fixing agreements which it did not otherwise favour. Some confusion was thereby caused, as the consistency of the philosophy of regulation being employed came under question.[16] However, the events surrounding the frozen vegetables decision sent clear signals to industry that price-fixing was being treated as a target by the regulators and industry would be taking severe risks in maintaining such practises.

There was a period of hiatus from the general elections of November 1972, with the first change in Government for twenty-three years, until the TPA became law in mid 1974. This was a period of lobbying and frenetic activity among lawyers, economists and industry leaders. The central event was a Bill for Trade Practices initiated by the new Attorney-General, the late Senator Lionel Murphy, in 1973. Both the terms of the Bill and the speeches given by Murphy in promoting it left no doubt that this law was to have the teeth that previous legislation and practice had lacked. Some business groups objected to much of the cut and thrust of the new legislation, and some devoted considerable resources and argument to making firm their objections. These included the Chamber of Commerce and the Australian Industries Development Association (see AIDA (1973)), which later became the Business Council of Australia. These groups warned of dangerous side-effects from this radical new legislation, which they claimed had been inadequately thought through.

II.3. The Structure and Philosophy of the 1974 Act

The Act that eventuated in 1974 stopped short of the 1973 Murphy Bill. It subjected contracts, arrangements or understandings of a horizontal nature to a competition test. Horizontal agreements could be "cleared" on the grounds that the impact on competition was trivial, although public interest arguments could not be used here. They could be advanced in a separate and more long-lasting mechanism called "authorization" (explained below) on the basis that sufficient public interest justification existed so as to excuse the agreement from further scrutiny under the Act. An exception was made for horizontal price-fixing agreements, which could not be authorized, except in connection with certain joint ventures, making them effectively illegal per se. While mergers are treated separately, as in European practise, their consideration is handled by the same law and institutions as are restrictive practises, in contrast to British practise. From 1977 to 1993 mergers were subject to a dominance test, European style, although the interpretation was so close to a competition test (which became the standard in 1993) that we can consider mergers as being subject throughout to much the same competition test as applied to restrictive practises.

In place of the old arrangements, there were also new and stronger administrative procedures. In place of a single Commissioner, a seven-Commissioner Trade Practices Commission (TPC) with a relatively large staff was established; the register became open; new powers of investigation were established; and the onus of proof in authorization matters was reversed. The TPT remained with functions much as before, with final authority vested in the Australian federal court system.

The life of the Labor Government was a dramatic but short one, and it was replaced in 1975 by a more conservative Liberal Government which came with a mandate to remove or soften any business regulations that did not seem necessary. To this end, a review committee was quickly formed, comprising business representatives, government officials and TPA practitioners. The Swanson Committee (named after its chairman) reported six months later in 1976. Proposed changes to amend s. 45 by removing "restraint of trade" and using a consistent "substantial lessening of competition" test were adopted by the Government;[17] as were those proposing the end of the "clearance" mechanism. Few other substantial changes were made to the Act. Thus, Australian antitrust continued after 1974 to evolve in a very gradual manner, despite attempts to increase its effectiveness with forceful public pronouncements. [18] With the clearance provisions removed, only authorization, the exemptions and competition defenses were left as escape routes for practices caught under the TPA.

For practitioners, especially lawyers acting in litigation and providing advice, the TPA was a novel experience. Elevators in the main barrister chamber buildings in Melbourne and Sydney were crammed with practitioners clutching A. D. Neale's *The Antitrust Laws of the U.s. A.* There was much confusion as lawyers and economists and corporate personnel found their way. None of the previous Australian cases meant as much as the American law. Market definition and the concept of competition confused lawyers and constrained economists to a legal mould. The issues for resolution were essentially to work out what precisely the TPA meant, and much of the past twenty years has been involved in doing just that. There was always bound to be trouble when key words used in the TPA, like "market" and "competition", were not used in economic analysis either internally consistently or exactly as in every day parlance.

III. The Main Competition Provisions of the TPA

To avoid constitutional difficulties, s. 45 and the other main competition provisions of the TPA are confined to the actions of corporations. Specifically, the central s. 45 provides for remedies against any actions which are "contracts, arrangements or understandings" of a horizontal nature that either (a) contain either an "exclusionary provision"[19] or which have the purpose, effect or likely effect of substantially lessening competition in a market for goods and services in Australia or (b) result in prices being fixed, maintained or controlled by an agreement involving corporations. The demonstration of a "substantial lessening of competition in a market for goods and services in Australia" is also required to sustain allegations of anti-competitive mergers (s. 50), vertical restrictions (such as requirements contracts and forms of exclusive dealing) (s. 47) and also, in the case of goods, price discrimination (s. 49).

The central phrases "exclusionary provision" and "substantially lessening competition" are partly defined in the TPA and each has been the subject of extended treatment in case law. There is an ordinary usage of these terms that has often been at variance with the economic notion, and much activity has been devoted to sorting out this contradiction. After twenty years the matter is substantially clarified. Plainly the economic notions of market and competition are integrally involved in matters falling within the first provision (a), whereas the economic notions would seem not to be required under (b), as no competition test is available for price-fixing matters.

The main questions thrown up by the competition provisions of the TPA are the following:

1. What does *market* mean in principle, and what tests in practice should be applied to set the boundaries of a market?
2. What is the meaning and measure of *competition* that exists in the context of any such market, and under what conditions (using the words of the sections) will competitionn be "substantially lessened"?
3. What *public benefits* by type and magnitude are sufficient to warrant the immunity from prosecution that authorization grants?[20]

IV. "Market": A Problem in Marketing What It Means

Wherever the state of or effects upon competition are to be assessed in the TPA, or in similar legislation in other countries, it is necessary at an early stage to form at least a provisional view of what constitutes the relevant market. This definition sets the restricted field of products, regions or even firms within which the process of competition takes place, from which market shares can be calculated, and into which the entry of other firms either takes place or can be prevented or limited. In fact, it is logically impossible to consider either competition or its substantial lessening until the field of activity that comprises the market is established. The Australian approach to market definition is very similar in principle to that applying in other countries practising antitrust law, such as the United States. [21] In practise, controversy has reigned over almost every aspect of market definition and its role in case decisions.

IV.1. Is Market Determination the End of the Story?

It seems pointless to debate whether market definition is an exercise logically separate from competition assessment (as presented in one major Australian determination[22]) or is integrated inseparably with it (as argued in another[23]). Competition must be assessed in the context of some notion of market, even though the boundaries of any postulated market can be stated and argued without completing an analysis of the process of or effects upon competition. In practice there will often need to be some revision of the provisional definition of the market, for the competition analysis will in practice frequently identify such traffic across the provisional market border that the boundary will need to be pushed out. We may, for instance, find such substantial interchange between fashion and casual clothing (on either the demand or production side) that it makes no sense for competition analysis to maintain a distinction between them. The reverse can also be true.

IV.2. Demand and/or Supply Conceptions of Market?

One of the many difficulties standing before the consistent application of a notion of market is the tendency in ordinary usage to think of the term as meaning "where the buyers are" and how they may be influenced to choose among the purchasing options facing them. Plainly, the discipline of marketing is directed to precisely this notion. But the habit is then formed of thinking that only the options facing buyers are relevant to market definition. Such a restricted view can be detected in statements that the "substitutability" or "cross-elasticity" of demand should be determined; such statements do not incorporate supply or production mix options. In economic analysis, competitive pressures move through supplier responses just as much as they move through buyer responses. Thus the broader of the two possible conceptions of market must be selected to encapsulate the competitive pressures that are relevant. In the early 1960s Brunt had set this out very clearly by saying ". . . competition proceeds not only through buyers' substitution in their purchases but also through producers' substitution in their output mix."[24]

The inevitable conflict between the "marketing view" and that imported from economic analysis for studying competition was evident from the start in all relevant applications of the TPA. It even caused difficulty for the TPC itself, which narrowly described the market in some of its reports and at first instance in the widely-quoted merger authorization application known as *QCMA*. This case concerned a proposed merger of flour mills in the Australian State of Queensland, for which an application for authorization had been denied by the TPC. Applying only demand-side substitution principles, the TPC produced rather narrow geographical and line-of-commerce markets, within which some of which the applicants held significant market shares. The applicants complained that the TPC had erred in using such narrow markets, and in relying as heavily as was evident on market share indicia to reach its conclusion that the merger would lessen competition substantially.[25]

On appeal to the TPT, on which Brunt sat as a member, the TPC's approach was rejected, and the Tribunal's judgment became the model for nearly all subsequent cases involving market and competition notions. [26] The passages in *QCMA* expounding the TPT's approach to both market and competition have been cited in every significant Australian antitrust case since and have served to bring the treatment of these notions in line with the approach then current in economic literature. It is thus worth reciting, in abbreviated form, the central passage of this seminal determination, in which the following was said about markets:

> " . . . the identification of markets must be the essential first step in assessment of present competition and likely competitive effects . . . [but] mere

specification of markets cannot be determinative by itself of some ultimate issue . . . A market is the area of close competition between firms or . . . the field of rivalry between them . . . Within the bounds of a market there is substitution – substitution between one product and another, and between one source of supply and another, in response to changing prices. So a market is the field of actual and potential transactions between buyers and sellers amongst whom there can be substitution, at least in the long run, if given a sufficient price incentive . . . In the language of economics the question is this: From which products and which activities could we expect a relatively high demand or supply response to price change. i.e. a relatively high cross-elasticity of demand or cross-elasticity of supply?"[27,28]

It was common experience among practitioners and business people to find it uncomfortable that "substitution" involved not only demand or buyer reactions, but also those on the supply side, as economists had long argued. After much confusion, the notion that supply-side considerations must enter the assessment of "market" was driven home firmly in the famous 1985 *Tradestock* judgment.[29] This case covered both the 1974 and 1977 versions of s. 45 and concerned an alleged boycott by most of the larger Australian transport operators on the activities of a small freight broker known as Tradestock. The case stands as the longest-running and most expensive antitrust case in Australian history, spanning some eight years and involving nearly 50 sitting days for just one witness. The judgment reveals a thorough understanding and acceptance of supply-side substitutability notions relevant to market delineation. The judge concluded that:

". . . one looks at substitution and substit tability from both the buyers' side and the sellers' side and, in general, if one gets a clear answer that the test of substitution or substitutability is satisfied *either* on the buyers' or the sellers' side, it is appropriate to conclude that these two products are in the same market . . ."[30]

While the potentiality indicated by the term "substitut*ability*" (my emphasis of the suffix) is probably implied by "substitution", His Honour put the matter beyond doubt by using the former term, as he did in relation to supply aspects by giving them such prominence. It took thus a decade of experience to establish under the law the relevance of supply or production substitutability in making any relevant assessment of the bounds of the market. There is a continuing debate and confusion about the relevance of supply-side substitutability,[31] but no longer can it be held that market boundaries depend on buyer choices and alternatives considered alone.

IV.3. Is There (Antitrust) Life after Market?

There is a further issue concerning the significance of market, once it has been defined. Suppose that the courts or those responsible for case preparation or advise in these matters have already gained some indication of the likely product and geographic dimensions of the market. To what extent could the answer to the central issues in an antitrust matter be determined by reference to these market facts or suppositions, without resort to any further information or argument? For most of the first decade, and in some cases beyond, the emphasis on case preparation was so heavily devoted to market definition matters, almost to the exclusion of all other considerations, that little else seemed to matter. The object was simply to get the "right market". Normally this meant pressing for a market that was narrow enough, within which an offender loomed large enough, to establish a conviction; or, for the defense, it meant making the market broad enough to diminish the apparent relative size and significance of the alleged offending corporation(s). Often legal advisers came quickly to believe that the success or failure of proceedings would turn almost alone on getting the right market (and hence the right market shares). This concentration of litigious effort on "market" has also been encountered in other countries. [32]

It can be argued that the Australian *QCMA* case of the middle 1970s was well ahead of its time, by world standards of antitrust practice, especially in taking emphasis away from purely structural criteria in judging public detriments. By this time the workable competition approach consistent with Australian practice had been seen in economics, but few other countries had come to place such little emphasis on structural indicia of competition, such as market shares and concentration ratios. In the 1980s, other countries were also to move away from structural criteria, notably the United States, as reflected in the strong attack on inferences drawn from firm numbers in the official 1984 *Merger Guidelines*.[33] The Australian approach did not perceptibly move any further away from market share emphasis in the second half of the 1980s, and in this respect it contrasted with the more pronounced anti-structuralist revolt in the United States in the middle of the Reagan period of office.[34]

Looking both from the prospects of success in litigation and from the public interest standpoint, there are points of concern arising from the heavy emphasis upon market definition that characterised the early approach to antitrust in Australia (and many other countries).[35] First, from the private perspective, making successfully a case for "market" leaves under-explored the remaining matters concerning competition, public interest, market power, dominance and related requirements. Market is normally not enough. Second, from the more general standpoint of the public, establishing inferences from the relative size of a corporation within a market (however defined) runs the risk of attacking bigness for its own sake, rather than situations injurious to public welfare. The more recent extensions of workable competition and the evolution of the "contestable market" concepts, however extreme and pretentious they became, were undoubtedly oriented to making this fundamental distinction, and calling into question the primacy of attention given by some practitioners to "getting the market right". Indeed, midway through the period under review Norman and Williams (1983) attacked the primacy of attention given to market, demonstrating that inferences drawn from market analysis alone can be extremely misleading or redundant. If competition analysis is correctly performed, it may not matter that the market is defined too narrowly or too broadly. Suppose that market is defined too narrowly, by region or range of products included. If suppliers with large market shares within this narrow domain are threatened by others technically outside it, then competition analysis would describe this as a threat of entry; if the market had been more broadly defined, it would be substitution pressures within the broader market. In either case, the firms involved are seen to be subject to restraints, should they contemplate acting anti-competitively.

Looking back, Australian antitrust history has been characterized by highs and lows with respect to market definition. The high points of a clear definition of market and its consistent application have been offset by some determinations of earlier days when a very narrow view of the market and its role led to unduly narrow judicial delineations of the market at issue.[36]

V. Competition Tests Under the Australian Act

While agreements which substantially lessening competition are an offense under s. 45 of the Australian TPA, its negation forms a defense for accused parties under this section, and also in relation to asserted anti-competitive vertical agreements (s. 47), price discrimination (s. 49) and mergers (s. 50). In each of these sections the case law in Australia on the meaning of competition effects has now been clearly established. It is clear that competition is a characteristic of the market, and is *not* concerned directly or indirectly with the "competitive ability" of individual market participants. Again, this distinction had to be learned from experience, as the concept of *market* competition was unfamiliar to many practitioners. [37] Nor has it been consistently applied in all court cases. [38]

From 1974 onwards, applications to have allegedly anti-competitive actions "authorized" (on public interest criteria) were subject to close scrutiny by the TPC and rejected where the benefits were declared not public, not substantiated or "otherwise available".[39] Yet a number of such authorizations were granted, even in situations of high market concentration. In a very early determination of the TPT, a quite uncompetitive market situation was granted authorization, not least because to deny it would, in the opinion of the Tribunal, have sanctioned a greater detriment to the public.[40] The matter concerned a horizontal agreement within the highly concentrated cartage industry which imposed substantial uniformity of freight rates. Business returns had been "more than generous"; however, there was some fringe competition that could not be ignored, even though s. 45 refers only "to the direct effect of the conduct".[41] But by 1978 the Tribunal had been forced to apply a much more stringent test of public benefit that made authorization extremely difficult to obtain. To succeed, it proclaimed, it would be necessary to demonstrate that the arrangement for which authorization was sought was the arrangement most conducive to the public interest.[42] Not surprisingly, applications for authorization, and the activities of determination and review, almost entirely ceased. Accordingly, a major source of the development of case law on competition tended to disappear. It was through the Tribunal that the advanced treatment of strategic entry considerations and import competition had been introduced.[43,44] Further development had to rely on Court cases directed to the primary offenses that, by definition, were not protected by any prior authorization.[45]

From 1978 until the middle 1980s there was little further development. Then, in the *Tradestock* case, Franki J. absorbed and extended the principles of *QCMA* and other relevant statements of the competition tests relevant to s. 45 matters, declaring *inter alia* that "The economic meaning (of competition) must be applied in a practical way to accommodate the concern of the Act with business and commerce"; and of the structural tests of competition – market shares (or concentration), product differentiation, entry barriers and corporate relationships – he noted that " . . . the most important factor was said to be the height of barriers to entry, that is the ease with which new firms might enter and secure a viable market"; while " . . . competition must be read as referring to a process or state of affairs in a market."[46]

Since December 1992, some indicia of "competition" have been inserted as a specified list of nine criteria at s. 50(3) of the TPA, as a guide to the assessment of the anti-competitive effects of mergers, with obvious application to all sections in which the competition notion applies. [47] To a large degree, the list formalises the developing approach in the TPA, in economics and in overseas antitrust practice to supplement structural criteria. But beyond this it makes specific mention of the competitive influence of import competition, countervailing power, the impact of the loss or removal of a competitor and the dynamic characteristics of the market. The list imposes a demanding requirement on the regulatory authorities and on practitioners. However, it takes the formal emphasis further from the older reliance on market shares, such as the United States five per cent rule of the 1970s and the structural emphasis of the earlier Australian approach.[48] If the courts make an informed assessment of the role and conduct of any disappearing firm and then draw inferences about its ability to constrain other firms, then the conclusions drawn about competition will be similar to those derived from applying the Norman and Williams (1983) proposal of making inferences about competition effects from the power to constrain.

The thrust of these developments in Australia and other countries has been to adopt a greater technical sophistication in the interpretation of competition effects, but at the expense of losing simplicity. It is plainly easier to count firm numbers or to draw conclusions from information concerning market shares than to delve into the operational and conduct features of a market. But the manner in which a market actually worked began to mean more than its structure and within the structural considerations, market shares, market numbers and concentration ratios (the narrow structural criteria) became less important than behavioral phenomena such as entry barriers and product differentiation. Accordingly, it became necessary for the Federal Court and the TPT to make more thorough studies of the operating conditions in which the firms operated. Highly concentrated market situations can be sufficiently competitive if pressures of potential rivalry are present, at least in the firms' own expectations. This is completely in line with developments in economic analysis.

While the Australian Courts and Tribunal showed little consciousness of the underlying developments in economic theory, their general approach in moving away from the narrow structural criteria for judging competition effects was not inconsistent with them.[49] By contrast, contestable market analysis and the Chicago School (including some of the key proponents in person) gained direct recognition and a substantial following in New Zealand.[50] By international standards the Australian approach could be classed as responsive but balanced in its attitude towards these developments. It does not fully adopt the central message of tolerance in the Chicago approach; equally, it repudiates the older structuralist convenience of relying heavily on market share criteria.[51]

VI. General Judgment and Challenges for the Future

Australian attempts to implement effective antitrust legislation failed in essence until the operation of the Trade Practices Act 1974. There was, before then, neither the widespread concern, nor the will, to control abuses of market power, the unfair accumulation of wealth or the distortions in the operation of markets that had motivated antitrust action in the United States and a handful of other countries. In the decade before 1974 Australia had attempted to bring on effective legislation, though support for it was fragmentary. The antitrust events of that decade, however, laid the necessary groundwork for the 1974 Act. Antitrust in Australia has considerably matured over the last twenty years. From one-sided approaches to market definition and crude conceptions of competition based almost entirely on conditions of market structure, more consistent and advanced economic concepts have gradually been incorporated, often in the face of controversy.

Australian antitrust has not to this stage embraced the extreme (anti-structural ist) strictures of contestable market analysis, sunk cost entry criteria, and notions drawn from strategic oligopoly and game theory analysis of modern microeconomic theory. In this respect it differs from New Zealand and American practise. Yet it has captured the essence of them, and in this sense remains relatively balanced. It may be true, as Alfred Kahn argues, that "The evolution of regulatory policy will never come to an end".[52] But it is important that it does not run in circles or swing as a pendulum. As it has mostly avoided this, Australian antitrust can be declared to have achieved a balanced progression, both generally and in comparison with the antitrust legal and regulatory systems of other countries.

Further balanced progress will require the joint venture of law and economics of which antitrust is comprised to become more efficient, and perhaps a little less "competitive".

Notes

* I dedicate this piece to John Nieuwenhuysen, who inspired my interest and involvement in antitrust in Australia and who was among the leading independent commentators of the legislation as it evolved. I thank Alan Hughes, Cliff Pratten and Alistair Sutherland of Cambridge, England for helpful comments as non-Australian practitioners, but most especially David Round, the Special Editor for this issue, for his general encouragement and detailed comments on earlier drafts.

[1] *Notice*: All Australian case references are to the CCH (Australia) *Australian Trade Practices Reporter* (ATPR), designated by case number (eg 40–042) and page references where appropriate. International readers should note that this CCH series is distinct from the United States antitrust case references. Burgess (1992, p. xvi).

[2] As in *US v Sealy Incorporated* (1961) 388 US 350.

[3] And its use with related legislation against Standard Oil in 1911 and Alcoa in 1945, for instance.

[4] See United States Department of Justice (1984) and commentary upon this in Shepherd (1985, p. 382).

[5] An inside account of some of the early professional tribulations is offered in Norman (1993).

[6] Major amendments to the TPA occurred with respect to controlling the misuse of market power in 1986 and to restraining mergers in both 1977 and 1993.

[7] Accounts of this period which provide greater detail may be found in Nieuwenhuysen (1970) and Nieuwenhuysen and Norman (1976).

[8] Some record of these practices is found in Karmel and Brunt (1962, pp. 95–97). Perhaps the most widely-quoted account of these practices arose in an unpublished dissertation by Richard Freeman, which was widely quoted in texts and more general accounts of the Australian economy. Freeman found a widespread incidence of horizontal agreements, especially price-fixing agreements, among employer associations in Victoria, and Cook and others found similarly for other states, including direct evidence of collusive tendering and bidding.

[9] See Karmel and Brunt (1962, Ch. 3).

[10] A mid-fifties assessment quoted some time later in Nieuwenhuysen (1976, Ch. 2).

[11] Now known as the Liberal-National coalition, and since 1983 the political opposition in Australia.

[12] A full account of this period and its institutional features and economic consequences is given in Nieuwenhuysen and Norman (1976, Ch. 1 especially).

[13] See the paper by Norman in Nieuwenhuysen (1970, Ch. 3). Note that the British trigger share was later moved to one-quarter.

[14] See Nieuwenhuysen and Norman (1976, Ch. 1).

[15] *Ibid.*, Chs. 1–2.

[16] For an account of the decision, its origins and aftermath, see the paper by Davey in Nieuwenhuysen (1976, Ch. 3).

[17] The original terms of s. 45 were stated as subjecting to law any (non-exempt) "contract, arrangement or understanding" of a horizontal nature, unless it had only an insignificant effect on competition. Initially a "restraint of trade" provision borrowed from common law was adopted, but this had to be abandoned when a contradictory interpretation made that provision unworkable. See *Quadramain Pty. Limited v Sebastapol Investments Pty. Limited (Howie and Anor.)* (1976) ATPR 40–013.

[18] One of the Commissioners of the new TPC warned the business community that it faced significant risks if it persisted with horizontal practices against the thrust and practice of the TPA, noting that agreements did not have to be enforceable at law, and that it would be sufficient if one party communicated with another. Hence, his advise was ". . . if you are at a meeting with competitors and one of them suggests a discussion on pricing practices, head for the nearest door, fire escape, laundry chute or window. Even if the window is on the second floor, your company could find it cheaper to pay your workers' compensation than face the penalties contained in the

Trade Practices Act." (Pengilley (1978, p. 12) Plainly, the law had more teeth, and statements like this from senior officers of the TPC were designed to gain attention and force compliance.
[19] This was further defined to mean contracts, arrangements or understandings between competitors that amounted to preventing, limiting or restricting competition.
[20] The Australian concept of "authorization" was devised to prevent the TPA applying to business practices, takeovers or agreements to which it might otherwise apply, but which were excepted on the grounds of carrying some "public benefit", such as industry rationalization, securing technological advance, or assisting particular regions or groups when other means of doing so were unavailable. Authorization is not available for price-fixing agreements or for price discrimination or for other matters such as abuse of market power (s. 46) or resale price maintenance (s. 48).
[21] See Erickson et al.(1977, pp. 99–103).
[22] *Trade Practices Commission v T.N.T. Management Pty. Ltd. & Ors* (1985) ATPR 40–512. See also *Application by Broken Hill Pty. Co. Ltd. & Anor. pursuant to sec. 101A for review of notice by the Commission re purchasing agreement with Koppers Pty. Ltd.* (1981) ATPR 40–203.
[23] *Queensland Wire Industries Pty. Limited v The Broken Hill Proprietary Co. Limited* & Anor (1988) ATPR 40–841, pp. 49,074–75. See also *Applications of Southern Cross Beverages Pty. Ltd., Cadbury Schweppes Pty. Ltd. and Amatil Ltd. for review of Commission notice under sec. 93(3)* (1981) ATPR 40–200 where at p. 42,757 the Tribunal objected to a "forced and somewhat artificial process" of distinguishing between market and competition.
[24] Karmel and Brunt (1962, p. 77).
[25] It was at this time that American debates were shifting the emphasis away from both demand substitutability and market share criteria, but the TPC remained unmoved.
[26] *Re Queensland Co-operative Milling Association Ltd., Defiance Holdings* Ltd. *(Proposed Mergers with Barnes Milling Ltd.)* (1976) ATPR 40–012.
[27] Note how closely and faithfully this section mirrors the famous Stigler definition which Brunt had quoted earlier and approvingly in Karmel and Brunt (1962, p. 77).
[28] *Supra* n. 25 at pp. 17,246–47. A source listing of over twenty important Australian trade practices cases that followed the *QCMA* principles explicitly is given in Norman and Cornwell (1990), pp. 1723–31.
[29] *Supra* n. 21.
[30] *Ibid.*, p. 46,139, emphasis added.
[31] This was fuelled by the High Court appeal determination in the Queensland Wire case under which some primacy was given to "demand" rather than "supply" factors in market delineation, although supply factors were not excluded or ignored. See *Queensland Wire Industries Pty. Ltd. v The Broken Hill Proprietary Company Limited* & Anor (1989) ATPR 40–925, at p. 50, 014 and p. 50,021.
[32] See Maitland-Walker (1984).
[33] Issued by Attorney General William F. Smith, as U. s. Department of Justice (1984).
[34] For instance, the 1984 *Merger Guidelines* (United States Department of Justice (1984)) which "incorporated the latest legal and economic learning [that] most merger activity does not threaten competition" (p. 1, Release), carried the following strong statements against heavy into some magical formula and wait for a computer to decide " (p. 3), and "While market definition has historically played a crucial role in merger activity...the Department will consider a number of other factors" (pp. 3, 9), including "the explicit recognition of foreign competition and world markets" (p. 12) and "the probable demand responses of consumers and the probable supply responses of other firms". The *Guidelines* went on to say "Market share and concentration data provide only the starting point for analyzing the competitive impact..." (p. 22). Far more important were "the likelihood and probable magnitude of entry" (p. 28) and various aspects of the conduct of firms.
[35] This observation is made by the present writer as a participant in over 100 antitrust cases or potential cases in preparation in Australia over the period. There is judicial support for it in strong terms in *In re Tooth & Co. Ltd; In re Tooheys Ltd.* (1979) ATPR 40–113 at pp. 18,193–94.
[36] The clearest definitions are given in the *QCMA* case (*supra* n. 25); in the *Tooth/Tooheys* case (*supra* n. 34); a very clear statement of principle and application is made in *Trade Practices Commission v Ansett Transport Industries (Operations) Pty. Ltd. & Ors* (1978) ATPR 40–071, at p. 17,710; in *Trade Practices Commission v Nicholas Enterprises Pty. Ltd.* (1979) ATPR 40–126;

in the *BHP/Koppers* case (*supra* n. 21); and in the *Tradestock* case (*supra* n. 21) at pp. 46,137–46. Examples of questionable and usually narrow market definitions being found are in the otherwise professionally-drafted Swanson Committee (1976) at para 4.22; in *Top Performance Motors Pty. Limited v Ira Berk (Queensland) Pty. Limited* (1975) ATPR 40–004 (where a single brand of motor vehicle in a small region was held to constitute the market); in *The Victorian Egg Marketing Board v Parkwood Eggs Pty. Ltd.* (1978) ATPR 40–081; in *J. Ah Toy Pty. Ltd. v Thiess Toyota Pty. Ltd.* (1980) ATPR 40–155, where at p. 42,218 the Court found two different markets in successive paragraphs without any apparent support for either, or recognition of its confusion; in the *Southern Cross Beverages* matter (*supra* n. 22) at p. 42,758; in *Hecar Investments No. 6 Pty. Ltd. v Outboard Marine Australia Pty. Ltd.* (1982) ATPR 40–298; and possibly in *Arnotts Limited & Ors v Trade Practices Commission* (1990) ATPR 41–061, at p. 51, 786.

37 Especially as evidenced in the *Hecar* case (*supra* n. 35), where a marketing expert's evidence on outboard marine markets based on buyer substitutability alone was favoured in the trial at first instance and consciously advanced, by the respondents, in effect against their own interests. (An approach adopting the economist's notions of competition was preferred in the Full Court appeal. See *Outboard Marine Australia Pty. Ltd. v Hecar Investments (No. 6) Pty. Ltd.* (1982) ATPR 40–327).

38 The impact of competition in the individual sense seems to have concerned the Court in *Cool & Sons Pty. Ltd. v O'Brien Glass Industries Ltd.* (1981) ATPR 40–220, where the detriment suffered by an individual competitor was equated with a substantial lessening of competition. This was corrected on appeal in *O'Brien Glass Industries Ltd. v Cool & Sons Pty. Ltd.* (1983) ATPR 40–376.

39 See Norman and Cornwell (1990).

40 *Application of G. and M. Stephens Cartage Contractors Pty. Ltd. on behalf of the Members of the Concrete Carters Association (Victoria)* (1977) ATPR 40–042.

41 *Ibid.*, at pp. 17471–73.

42 *A. C. Hatrick Chemicals Pty. Ltd.* (1978) ATPR 40–057.

43 Among the outstanding statements of principle of world best-practice quality coming from the Tribunal are the following: (i) a clear distinction of sub-markets from markets, and the role and relevance of each, in *QCMA* (*supra* n. 25 at p. 17,247) and in *Tooth/Tooheys* (*supra* n. 34 at p. 18,197); (ii) the role of strategic entry barriers in assessing competition in *QCMA* at p. 17,246; and (iii) the advanced treatment of integrated market sequences in *BHP/Koppers* (*supra* n. 21).

44 Some evidence of a continued stringent approach by the Tribunal to applications for authorization is found in recent rejections, such as *Re John Dee (Export) Pty. Ltd. & Ors* (1989) ATPR 40–938.

45 Throughout the twenty years of experience with the TPA, and in relation to horizontal competition matters especially, there has been ambiguity and uncertainty over what set of circumstances fall within and without the boundary between "substantial" and "insubstantial" effects on competition. See, for example, *Tillmanns Butcheries Pty. Ltd. v The Australasian Meat Industry Employees' Union & Ors.* (1979) ATPR 40–138, *Cool & Sons Pty. Ltd. v O'Brien Glass Industries Ltd.* (1981) 40–220, at p. 43,003, and *Radio 2UE Sydney Pty. Ltd. v Stereo F.M. Pty. Ltd. & Anor.* (1982) ATPR 40–318, p. 43,918.

46 *Supra* n. 21 at p. 46,142. These statements were in fact adopted from the *Outboard Marine/Hecar* appeal judgment (*supra* n. 36) and from the case *Dandy Power Equipment Pty. Ltd. & Anor v Mercury Marine Pty. Ltd.* (1982) ATPR 40–315.

47 The nine matters are "(a) the actual and potential level of import competition in the market; (b) the height of barriers to entry to the market; (c) the level of concentration in the market; (d) the degree of countervailing power in the market; (e) the likelihood that the acquisition would result in the acquirer being able to significantly and sustainably increase prices or profit margins; (f) the extent to which substitutes are available in the market or are likely to be available in the market; (g) the dynamic characteristics of the market, including growth, innovation and product differentiation; (h) the likelihood that the acquisition would result in the removal from the market of a vigorous and effective competitor; (i) the nature and extent of vertical integration in the market".

48 See Shepherd (1985, p. 378) who comments that "most [American] observers [before 1945] took it for granted that market share was a key element [of competition analysis in the U.s. A.]".

[49] At the same time as the Australian Courts were evolving the Australian antitrust approach, economic analysis was itself progressing beyond the notion of "workable competition", towards newer work involving contestable market analysis and the strategic interaction among firms, some of it based on game theory. (See Bailey and Baumol (1984); for a critical appraisal and review of this doctrine with reference to antitrust matters, see Shepherd (1984)). In yet another direction, the so-called Chicago school was drawing upon both these developments and any other development in economic analysis that seemed to justify actions taken by firms to promote or protect themselves, including the defence of horizontal and vertical agreements. In strategic analysis and game theory, the behavior of firms is said to be dominated by their attitude to risk, their consciousness of rivals and views they might take about likely rival reactions, potential entry, product competition and technological competition. (See Tirole (1988) and Gee & Norman (1992), especially chapter 18 by Dixit which gives a good short summary of recent strategic oligopoly theory relevant to antitrust).

[50] See Farmer (1993) and the paper by Bollard in this special issue.

[51] That the approach of many practitioners was overly reliant on market shares in making competition assessments, and that this might be misleading, is stated directly in Donald and Heydon (1978, at p. 212). The evolution of thinking in American academic and antitrust circles is reflected in the increasing sophistication of explanatory accounts, such as the three editions of the excellent work by Shepherd (1979, 1985 and 1990).

[52] Cited and discussed in Burgess (1992, p. 503).

References

AIDA (1973) (Australian Industries Development Association) *The Australian Trade Practices Bill*. Canberra: Halstead.

Bailey, Elizabeth E. and William J. Baumol (1984) 'Deregulation and the Theory of Contestable Markets', *Yale Journal of Regulation*, **1**, 111–137.

Burgess, Giles H., Jr, ed, (1992) *Antitrust and Regulation*. Vermont: Elgar.

Donald, B.G. and J.D. Heydon (1978) *Trade Practices Law*. Sydney: The Law Book Company Limited.

Erickson, Myron L. et al. (1977) *Antitrust and Trade Regulation*. New York: Wiley.

Farmer, James M. (1993) 'Recent Developments in Trade Practices in New Zealand', forthcoming in *Competition and Consumer Law Journal* (Butterworths).

Gee, J.M.A. and George Norman, eds, (1992) *Market Strategy and Structure*. London: Harvester Wheatsheaf.

Karmel, P.H. and M. Brunt (1962) *The Structure of the Australian Economy*. Melbourne: F.W. Cheshire Pty. Ltd.

Maitland-Walker, Julian, ed, (1984) *International Anti-trust Law*, volume 1: *A Review of National Laws*. Oxford: ESC.

Neale, A.D. (1967) *The Antitrust Laws of the U.s. A.*. London: NIESR.

Nieuwenhuysen, John P., ed, (1970) *Australian Trade Practices: Readings*. Melbourne: F.W. Cheshire Publishing Pty. Ltd.

Nieuwenhuysen, John P., ed, (1976) *Australian Trade Practices: Readings*, second edition. London: Croom-Helm Ltd.

Nieuwenhuysen, John P., and Neville R. Norman (1976) *Australian Competition and Prices Policy*. London: Croom-Helm Ltd.

Norman, Neville R. (1993) "Economists in the (Trade Practices) Act", *Competition and Consumer Law Journal*, **1**, 1–19.

Norman, Neville R, and Philip L. Williams (1983) 'The Analysis of Market and Competition under the Trade Practices Act: Towards the Resolution of some Hitherto Unresolved Issues', *Australian Business Law Review*, **11**, 396–419.

Norman, Neville R, and Phillip J. Cornwell (1990) 'Markets and Competition: A Note on Economic Concepts Imported from Economic Analysis', in CCH Inc., *Australian Trade Practices Reporter*, volume 1, 1711–1852. Sydney: CCH Australia Limited.

Pengilley, Warren J. (1978) *Collusion, Trade Practices and Risk Taking*. Sydney: CCH Australia Limited.

Shepherd, William G. (1979) *The Economics of Industrial Organization.* Englewood Cliffs, N.J.: Prentice-Hall.

Shepherd, William G. (1984) '"Contestability" versus Competition', *American Economic Review*, **74**, 572–87.

Shepherd, William G. (1985) *The Economics of Industrial Organization*, second edition. Englewood Cliffs, N.J.: Prentice-Hall.

Shepherd, William G. (1990) *The Economics of Industrial Organization*, third edition. Englewood Cliffs, N.J.: Prentice-Hall.

Swanson Committee (1976) *Trade Practices Act Review Committee.* Canberra: Australian Government Publishing Service.

Tirole, Jean (1988) *The Theory of Industrial Organisation.* Cambridge, Mass. : M.I.T. Press.

United States Department of Justice (1984) *Merger Guidelines – 1984*, text issued June 14, 1984, Washington.

Review of Industrial Organization **9:** 547–568, 1994.

Judicial Approaches to Economic Analysis in Australia

JUSTICE R.S. FRENCH
Federal Court of Australia, Perth, Western Australia 6000, Australia

Abstract. Although Australia has had State and Federal antitrust laws for most of the twentieth century, its antitrust jurisprudence has only developed significantly since the enactment of the *Trade Practices Act* 1974. Judges have had to come to grips with economic concepts not readily amenable to syllogistic reasoning and traditional fact finding processes. There has been increasing sophistication in judicial reasoning in the area of competition law. However restrictions placed by the rules of evidence upon the role of expert economists have attracted criticism. A new rule of court enables such testimony to be received by way of argument or submission rather than as evidence. This reflects the evaluative and normative nature of many of the judgments required under competition laws. It also provides an opportunity for a more fruitful and constructive interaction between economists and the judiciary in the application of such laws.

Key words: Antitrust law, economic analysis, judicial method, antitrust history, market definition, economic evidence

I. Introduction

Australia is a Federation of 17 million people in which both State and Federal legal systems are well supplied with courts and judges. As in the United States, there is, in each of the States of Australia, a hierarchy of courts administering the general run of civil and criminal litigation under State law and some Federal laws.[1] The Federal Court of Australia, established in 1976, exercises jurisdiction in civil matters under a variety of Federal laws including, in particular, the antitrust provisions of the *Trade Practices Act* 1974.[2] The ultimate court of appeal for both the State and Federal judicial systems is the High Court of Australia which occupies a position under the Australian Constitution broadly similar to that of the United States Supreme Court.

In recent times there has been public comment and debate about the way in which Australia's judges discharge their functions.[3] The Federal Court has been the subject of criticism in some economic and legal circles concerning the way in which it deals with economic evidence and issues in antitrust cases. In the short term of its existence, the Court has built up a substantial jurisprudence in its application of antitrust laws. Recently it has enacted a new rule of court permitting the reception of economic testimony as a species of argument rather than evidence. The rule provides for a flexible approach to deciding economic issues and an opportunity to adjust judicial methods and economic analysis more comfortably to each other.

The logical process of syllogism provides a model of judicial reasoning that is attractive by virtue of its simplicity. There is a major premise, the relevant rule of law which is to be ascertained. There are relevant facts to be found as the minor premise. Apply the law to the facts and there emerges a conclusion by way of a declaration or distribution of rights or liabilities. That model may be valid in limiting cases involving the trial of undeniably factual questions according to rules of law expressed in words which bear their ordinary English meaning and have concrete factual referents. Outside that safe and tiny harbour however questions of construction arise in relation to rules of law, whether derived from statute or precedent, which involve evaluative and sometimes normative judgments. At the interface of law and economics the judges are well clear of their syllogistic haven. The boundary between fact and law becomes blurred and so too the judicial function which takes on creative elements outside the framework of logical reasoning. That is not new to the law. Oliver Wendel Holmes made similar points about aspects of legal reasoning nearly one hundred years ago when discussing the general tension between logic and other processes in the life of the law:

> "Behind the logical form lies a judgment as to the relative worth and importance of competing legislative grounds, often an inarticulate and unconscious judgment, it is true, and yet the very root and nerve of the whole proceeding. You can give any conclusion a logical form."[4]

II. Application of Economic Laws

Statutes which embody normative or evaluative concepts of which economic laws are a paradigm require for their construction more than the mere discovery of preexisting meaning. Their application approaches a legislative function. The concept of "reasonableness" involves mental processes of this kind. But it has its roots deep in the common law.[5] It reflects what the late Professor Julius Stone called a "legal standard" as opposed to a "legal rule":

> "When courts are required to apply such standards as fairness, reasonableness and non-arbitrariness, conscionableness, clean hands, just cause or excuse, sufficient cause, due care, adequacy or hardship, then judgment cannot turn on logical formulation and deduction but must include a decision as to what justice requires in the context of the instant case. This is recognised, indeed, as to many equitable standards, and also as to such notorious common law standards as "reasonableness". They are predicated on fact-value complexes, not on mere facts."[6]

In the context of economic legislation specific examples footnoted by Stone are the rule of reason in US antitrust law and the words "detriment of the public" and "advantageous to the Commonwealth" which appeared in the first Australian federal antitrust law, the *Australian Industries Preservation Act* 1906. In classifying the form and origins of what he loosely called "judicial law-making in relation to statutes", Stone took as his second category the situation:

> "... where for some reason the legislator has (in effect) consciously delegated norm-creation to the judiciary, whether because flexibility of administration is required as in the Sherman Antitrust Law, or because conflicting views and interests within the legislature prevent agreement on anything but vague expression."[7]

Competition law embodies rules of a general kind which require normative and evaluative judgments in particular cases. The statutory language is derived in part from economic ideas some of which are expressed in terms of metaphor. The concept of market is a leading example. It is a metaphor which, for the mathematically minded, may evoke the image of a sphere in some imaginary space whose orthogonal axes measure geography, product range and function. And all three are embedded in a barely visible fourth dimension of economic policy judgment.

In Australian antitrust law there are a number of key economic concepts reflected in statutory language. This is exemplified by such established terms as "substantially lessening competition", "a substantial degree of power in a market", "take advantage of ... power", "eliminating or substantially damaging a competitor", "preventing the entry of a person into (a) market". More recently with the amendment to s. 50 of the *Trade Practices Act* relating to mergers, a new litany of economic terms and metaphors is explicitly acknowledged as affecting the question whether an acquisition would have the effect or be likely to have the effect of substantially lessening competition in a market. That litany includes references to "height of barriers to entry to the market", "the level of concentration in the market", "the degree of countervailing power in the market", "the dynamic characteristics of the market, including growth innovation and product differentiation" and "the nature and extent of vertical integration in the market". Some of these factors may be familiar to readers of the 1992 US *Horizontal Merger Guidelines*.[8] Each has to be considered in the antitrust economist's metaphorical workplace which is the market. Some of them add metaphor to metaphor.

Australia does not have a long history of serious judicial involvement in the application of economic statutes. The learning curve is gradual and questions have arisen about the involvement of economists in the decision-making process whether as witnesses or as tribunal or court members. Although Australian antitrust law goes back to 1906, a review of its history demonstrates that it did not require close judicial attention until after the enactment of the current legislation in 1974. The growth of case law has been gradual but appears to have been accelerating. Associated with that growth the development of notions of market definition is but one example of the increasing economic sophistication being demanded of the Australian courts.

The question has arisen of the suitability of the judicial system as a vehicle for determining economic questions. The question is not new. Nearly twenty five years ago Hunter said in respect of all jurisdictions that a reading of some reports suggests that frequently judges and commissioners are not masters of the materials they examine. While some judgments might be correct and often are in law, it is not entirely clear on what economic grounds they are right. It is perhaps encouraging, however, that Hunter was able to conclude of judgments in cases involving restrictive and monopoly practices thus:

> "The decisions reached are not always what an economist would wish for. However, we should be surprised that any sensible judgments are found from the chaos of facts and argument presented to a court on issues of monopoly and competition; and pleasantly surprised that they bear a definable relationship to the economic ideas buried in the words of the relevant statute."[9]

It is to be noted in further mitigation of the sins of judges and commissioners, that even economists do not share universal satisfaction about the state of economic theory in relation to antitrust. Consider the centrality of the concept of substantial lessening of competition in a number of the provisions of the *Trade Practices Act* 1974 and the observation by Demsetz that:

> "The proper issue for antitrust, then, is not the degree to which a market descriptively diverges from perfect competition but the degree to which it diverges in either direction from that intensity of competition which takes account of the real social costs of competing. No one yet has successfully tackled this problem, so central to antitrust policy, although the unsuccessful effort by Clark to define workable competition represents an important attempt to do so."[10]

There is in Australia today, a need for constructive dialogue between professional economists and the legal and judicial professions to enable a greater understanding and accommodation of their respective functions where they interact particularly in the enforcement of antitrust law. It is when the economist moves into areas of evaluative and normative judgment that the traditional distinctions between evidence and argument generate tension in terms of role definition. It is useful in this context to again bring to bear some minatory but encouraging words from Hunter:

> "The economist is more-than-average competent in the handling of value judgments, and distinguishing them for other people, since he is trained to segregate the economic from the non-economic not only in terms of objectives but also of language, data and technique. On the other hand, he has no special authority in this area. He cannot validly speak for others – only try to interpret what they may want. Summarising these facts: he may be a guide, but he should not be a mentor."[11]

The question of the suitability of the judicial system as a vehicle for determining economic questions requires careful consideration in terms of the accountability of the enforcement process whether it be in public or private party litigation. Importantly, in Australia, there is an irreducible core of judicial constitutional jurisdiction (enhanced by wide statutory jurisdictions relating to the judicial review of decisions of Commonwealth officials). No administrative tribunal set up under Commonwealth law can escape that jurisdiction while the Constitution remains in its present form. The possibility therefore remains open that any decision taken under an economic statute by any administrative official will be reviewed in the High Court or Federal Court. Such review can involve interpretation and construction of the relevant law, including its economic concepts, the logic of its application in a particular case, and the procedures attending that application.[12]

III. Antitrust Law in Australia – a Potted History

III.1. The Australian Industries Preservation Act 1906

Australia's competition laws before the *Trade Practices Act* 1974 had little impact on the trade and commerce of the nation. They generated only a limited and fragmentary jurisprudence. The first such law was the *Australian Industries Preservation Act* 1906 with the long title "An Act for the Preservation of Australian Industries and for the Repression of Destructive Monopolies". It was based upon the Sherman Act but as originally enacted conditioned its principal prohibitions upon the existence of an intent to cause a detriment to the public. The monopolization provision, s. 7, provided:

> "7(1) Any person, who, monopolizes or attempts to monopolize, or combines or conspires with any other person to monopolize, any part of the trade or commerce with other countries or among the States with intent to control, to the detriment of the public, the supply or price of any service, merchandise or commodity is guilty of an offence.
>
> (2) Every contract made or entered into in contravention of this section shall be absolutely illegal and void."

The *Sherman Act* 1890 s. 2 provides:

> "Every person who shall monopolize or attempt to monopolize or combine or conspire with any other person or persons to monopolize any part of the trade or commerce among the several States or with foreign nations, shall be deemed guilty of a misdemeanor."

Sections of the *Australian Industries Preservation Act* which were expressly directed to anti-competitive conduct by corporations were held in 1908 to be beyond the legislative power of the Commonwealth with respect to corporations.[13] A first test of the legislation which went to trial on the merits was the so called Coal Vend case.[14] That case involved the laying of charges against the proprietors of coalmines in New South Wales and various shipping companies. The allegations in substance were of agreements and combinations between colliery owners and between colliery owners and ship owners which involved price fixing and production quotas and regulated entry to the market. The trial lasted 73 days and was heard in the original jurisdiction of the High Court. The trial judge, Isaacs

J, described it as "... exceptional in its character, partaking necessarily to a great extent of the nature of an investigation" (p. 399). There were forty defendants of whom sixteen were individuals, twenty two corporations and two named as commercial trusts under the Act. The detriment to the public alleged "... the practical and persistent annihilation of competition on land and sea, excessive, arbitrary and capricious prices charged to consumers, restriction of their opportunities of choice, difficulties in obtaining particular classes or grades of coal desired, substitution really compulsory of other coal for coal preferred, and delays in obtaining delivery" (p. 399). The 270 page judgment has been described as "an analytical tour de force which displays an understanding of the economics of monopoly which is creditable by any standards"[15] and as "one of the finest antitrust judgments ever written".[16] It does not appear that Isaacs J had the advantage of expert testimony from any economists. He did, however, express the opinion that "... the prevention or destruction of all reasonable and effective competition – the natural commercial safeguard of the public – is at the root of the conception of monopoly within the meaning of the statute".[17] The defendants he found "intended to grasp into one huge hand, the whole inter-State supply of Newcastle coal".[18] Some of his language suggests an anticipation of the concept of workable or effective competition developed decades later by Clark and others.[19]

Isaacs J was reversed on appeal upon grounds that the evidence neither established detriment to the public nor intent to cause such detriment.[20] The notion of public detriment was seen in the Full High Court as requiring consideration of a public inclusive of consumers and producers:

> "It may be that the detriment, if it be one, of enhancement of price to the consumer is compensated for by other advantages to other members of the community, which may, indeed, include the establishment or continuance of an industry which otherwise could not be established or would come to an end."[21]

A philosophical predisposition to regard competition as a somewhat disorderly and, to a degree, undesirable process was revealed in the language of the judgment:

> "Cut throat competition is not now regarded by a large portion of the public as necessarily beneficial to the public."[22]

The combination of colliery owners known as the Vend was said to have had as one of its purposes the prevention of "unlimited and ruinous competition" (p. 82). The intention of the parties was:

> "... to put the Newcastle coal trade on a satisfactory basis, which would enable them to pay adequate wages to their men and to sell their coal at a price remunerative to themselves having regard to the capital and risk involved in the enterprise."[23]

These and like observations were said to make it clear that the judges reviewed the evidence before them in the light of prejudices inherited from the common law.[24] The judgment of the High Court on appeal from Isaacs J was affirmed by the

Privy Council.[25] There was little significant recorded judicial activity thereafter under Commonwealth law until the enactment of the *Trade Practices Act* 1974.[26]

III.2. State Antitrust Laws

There were a number of State antitrust acts which pre-dated the *Trade Practices Act* 1974. These included the *Profiteering Prevention Act* 1920 (Qld) which was invoked in a case which considered whether vertical price fixing agreements between a soap manufacturer and retailers indicated the existence of a commercial trust for the purposes of that Act.[27] The answer was in the negative on principles of statutory construction that did not involve any overt economic content in the reasoning.

Other State legislation included the *Monopolies Act* 1923 (NSW), the *Fair Prices Act* 1924 (SA) and the *Prices Act* 1963 (SA), the *Profiteering Prevention Act* 1948 (Qld), the *Unfair Trading and Profit Control Act* 1956 (WA) and the *Trade Associations Registration Act* 1959 (WA). In *Attorney-General v. Brickwork Pty Ltd*,[28] proceedings were taken for breaches of the *Monopolies Act* 1923 (NSW). That Act, in the provisions relating to monopolisation, reflected the terms of the *Australian Industries Preservation Act* prior to the amendments of 1910. Nicholas CJ referred to the reasoning of the Courts in the Coal Vend case as throwing light on the meaning of the term "reasonable" in its application to prices, the term "public" in the *Monopolies Act* and the nature of the intent, the detriment and the monopoly against which the Act was directed. He observed that a number of decisions had established that agreements for the purpose of maintaining or raising prices are not ex facie illegal or detrimental to the public.[29] Walker has commented that there were thus imported into the Act "... all the preconceived policy notions of the 19th century English judges".[30] It is fair to say that against traditional approaches to statutory construction the notion of public detriment invited a conclusion that there were good monopolies and good restrictive practices as well as bad. The comparatively benign attitude of the Australian courts towards monopoly and restraints of trade in the statutory context predating the 1974 Act appear to have reflected attitudes derived from the common law in relation to agreements in restraint of trade.

The concept of monopolization under the *Unfair Trading and Profit Control Act* 1956 (WA) was considered in a series of connected decisions in the late 1950s related to action taken by the Commissioner for the Prevention of Unfair Trading against two cement producers. An inquiry and charges instituted by him concerned an agreement between Swan Portland Cement Ltd and Cockburn Cement Pty Ltd which between them were said to control all known raw materials in Western Australia for the production of portland cement. Their combined production potential far exceeded the requirements of the State. On 1 November 1956, Swan agreed to sell its entire production to Cockburn for a period of twenty years. Cockburn formed a marketing company to sell cement provided by both Swan and Cockburn. Proceeding under his statute, the Commissioner found Cockburn to be a monopoly and therefore an unfair trader under the Act and declared it as such. In appeal proceedings in the Supreme Court, Wolff SPJ held that, in view of the Commissioner's findings that the company was facing competition and that there was a fall in the demand for cement by reason of substitute products, his conclusion that Cockburn had "complete control" of the market was not warranted and it could not be said to be "using monopolising" under the Act.[31] The relevant market was not the subject of analysis in the case. It seems to have been assumed that the market was for the sale of cement to retailers in Western Australia. Emphasis was placed upon substitute products. The word "monopoly" had been said by Wolff SPJ in the Full Court in earlier cognate prohibition proceedings against the Commissioner "to import the sole power to control the sale and/or distribution of goods and services in an area or field of operations".[32] This did not reflect any statutory definition but what Wolff SPJ called "a well recognised meaning". Monopolizing was the act of getting such power or control. Jackson J, also sitting in the Full Court, saw the term as referring to the acquisition and exercise of a monopoly.[33] In the appeal proceedings which followed the prohibition proceedings, Wolff SPJ, sitting alone, referred[34] to the American Cellophane case,[35] and the competition from substitute products that undercut Cockburn's market position:

> "Glass, aluminium, plastics and wood are all playing their part in reducing the demand for cement. The falling off in demand has been serious and comparatively rapid... and for this reason [Cockburn] urges that it is not in a position to dictate price because it must always keep itself in a position to meet the competition of these other materials."[36]

Walker considers that the judgment was remarkable for not attempting to read the statute subject to the common law.[37] In 1959 the *Unfair Trading and Profit Control Act* 1956 (WA) was replaced by the *Trade Associations Registration Act* 1959 (WA), a registration statute which did however attack collusive tendering. Despite the interesting analysis in *Cockburn Cement* which showed an implicit sensitivity to product market definition by reference to substitutes, the overall record of State statutes in this area has not been impressive. As Walker has said:

> "Like the Federal statute of 1906 these have remained largely unenforced owing to restrictive interpretation, apathy in government and ignorance among the people."[38]

III.3. The Trade Practices Act 1965

The *Australian Industries Preservation Act* 1906 was supplanted by the *Trade Practices Act* 1965. The latter Act provided for registration, on a secret register, of various classes of agreements between competitors. A number of examinable practices were also defined being price discrimination, third line forcing, inducing refusal to deal and monopolization. These matters could be taken by the Commissioner of Trade Practices before a Trade Practices Tribunal established by the Act and he could argue that the agreement or practice was contrary to the public interest according to criteria set out in s. 50 of the Act. The Tribunal was empowered to make restraining orders. The term "monopolisation" was defined in s. 37(1). A person engaged in monopolisation if being in a dominant position in the trade in goods of a particular description or in the supply of services of a particular description in Australia or a part of Australia he took advantage of that position so as to induce another to refuse to deal with a third person, or engaged in price cutting with the object of substantially damaging the business of a competitor or imposed prices or other terms on conditions of dealing that he would not be able to impose but for his dominant position. The word "market" appeared in sub-s. 37(2) but only in a geographical context. The notion of substitutability which is now regarded as a critical element of market definition was implicit in s. 37(3). Geographical extent and product substitutability, elements necessary to market definition were recognised in this statute but not brought together conceptually.

The Act was amended in May 1971 to introduce a new Part IVA prohibiting resale price maintenance. In September 1971, the High Court held that, to the extent that they relied upon the corporation's power, provisions of the Act requiring particulars of restrictive agreements to be supplied to the Commissioner of Trade Practices went beyond the legislative powers of the Commonwealth.[39] The invalidity thus disclosed was not terminal as it turned upon the failure of a particular section of the Act to limit the general provisions to circumstances within Heads of Commonwealth power. Subsequently, the 1965 Act was repealed and the *Restrictive Trade Practices Act* 1971 was enacted. The model of examinable agreements and practices was continued but on the narrower basis of agreements and practices involving corporations. The Act had only a short life and was supplanted by the *Trade Practices Act* 1974.

III.4. THE TRADE PRACTICES ACT 1974

In his second reading speech on the bill which became the *Trade Practices Act* 1974 the Minister for Manufacturing Industry criticised the Restrictive Trade Practices Act as "one of the most ineffectual pieces of legislation ever passed by the Parliament". Referring to the drafting of the proposed bill he said:

> "Legislation of this kind is concerned with economic considerations. There is a limit to the extent to which such considerations can be treated in legislation as legal concepts capable of being expressed with absolute precision. Such an approach leads to provisions which are complex in the extreme and gives rise to more problems then they remove (sic). The present bill recognises the futility of such drafting. Many matters have, of course, had to be stated in detail. But other provisions, particularly those describing the prohibited restrictive trade practices have been drafted along general lines using, wherever possible, well understood expressions. I am confident that this will be more satisfactory. The courts will be afforded an opportunity to apply the law in a realistic manner in the exercise of their traditional judicial role."[40]

What the Minister had in mind when he spoke of the courts applying the law "in a realistic manner in the exercise of their traditional judicial role" is not clear. It can be said, however, that the approach of the courts has evolved from a fairly traditional judicial approach exemplified in some of the pre-1974 cases to one more sensitive to the economic questions that arise generally under the legislation and in particular cases.

In this evolution the role of the Trade Practices Tribunal established under the Act to review determinations of the Trade Practices Commission on authorisation applications has been of significance. The function of the Tribunal has been enhanced by its hybrid constitution which requires it to sit with a presidential member who is a judge of a Federal Court and two members qualified for appointment by virtue of their knowledge of, or experience in, industry, commerce, economics, law or public administration. In practice, the Presidential member of the Tribunal, who has always been a member of the Federal Court, sits with at least one member who is a leading economist. Although it is not a court, the decisions produced by the Tribunal form part of Australia's jurisprudence of competition law.[41]

While the scope of this paper does not extend to a general review of judicial approaches to economic analysis, the development of the concept of market and the process of market definition can be traced through some of the Tribunal decisions in which members of the Court have participated and through decisions of the Court itself. Much of that development is set out in the judgment of the Full Court in *Singapore Airlines Ltd v. Taprobane Tours WA Pty Ltd.*[42] It is useful however to revisit some of the history and aspects of the market concept which require the normative and evaluative judgments referred to earlier.

IV. Market Definition in Australia

IV.1. The Search for Methodology

Prior to the creation of the Federal Court of Australia in 1976 jurisdiction in respect of proceedings under Part IV of the *Trade Practices Act* 1974 was conferred upon that Court's predecessor, the Australian Industrial Court. As its name indicates the principal jurisdiction of that Court lay in the area of industrial law. In one of the first reported cases under Part IV of the new Act, the Court was concerned with an application by a retail car dealer to stop its wholesale distributor from terminating the dealer's franchise.[43] The action was brought, inter alia, under s. 46 of the Act which then provided that:

> "A corporation that is in a position substantially to control a market for goods or services shall not take advantage of the power in relation to that market that it has by virtue of being in that position –
>
> (a) to eliminate or substantially damage a competitor in that market or any other market..."

The applicant submitted that there was a retail market for the sale of Datsun cars in the City of Gold Coast and Southport in Queensland. This contention was accepted. In accepting it, Joske J said:

> "In my opinion whether there is a market and what that market consists of and what area it covers must be a question of fact in any particular case. In determining this question of fact it must be borne in mind that market means trade or traffic, especially as regards a particular commodity... and that s. 46 is aimed at preventing the control of a market for goods as provided by that section. In my opinion the offering for sale of goods under their trade name may constitute trade or traffic in a particular commodity."[44]

His Honor concluded that there was a market for the sale of Datsun cars on the Gold Coast. There was no analysis of product substitutability. Smithers J said he agreed with Joske J but seems to have regarded the relevant market as the wholesale market for Datsun cars of which the respondent had "total control". Evatt J agreed with both. The narrow brand market adopted by Joske J favored the applicant in establishing the requisite level of market power. But the applicant failed on the question of taking advantage of market power. The court held that the exercise of the contractual power to terminate the dealership agreement was not an exercise of market power. It may be said at this point that the characterisation of market definition as a question of fact allows it to fit neatly into the syllogistic model of judicial reasoning. It does not, however, reflect the nature of the reasoning process involved in determining the market. It has subsequently been accepted, as will appear below, that the process of market definition requires purposive and normative evaluation which cannot be characterised as mere fact finding.

An authoritative exposition of the market concept was essayed by the Trade Practices Tribunal in the *QCMA* case. The Tribunal which decided that case comprised Woodward J of the Federal Court, Mr J. Shipton, a business executive, and Professor Maureen Brunt, a distinguished economist. In a well known and much cited passage, which no doubt owed much to Professor Brunt, the Tribunal said:

> "We take the concept of market to be basically a very simple idea. A market is the area of close competition between firms or, putting it a little differently, the field of rivalry between them. (If there is no close competition there is of course a monopolistic market). Within the bounds of a market there is substitution – substitution between one product and another, and between one source of supply and another, in response to changing prices. So a market is the field of actual and potential transactions between buyers and sellers amongst whom there can be strong substitution, at least in the long run, if given a sufficient price incentive. Let us suppose that the price of one supplier goes up. Then on the demand side buyers may switch their patronage from this firm's product to another, or from this geographic source of supply to another. As well, on the supply side, sellers can adjust their production plans, substituting one product for another in their output mix, or substituting one

geographic source of supply for another. Whether such substitution is feasible or likely depends ultimately on customer attitudes, technology, distance, and cost and price incentives.

It is the possibilities of such substitution which set the limits upon a firm's ability to "give less and charge more". Accordingly, in determining the outer boundaries of the market we ask a quite simple but fundamental question: If the firm were to "give less and charge more" would there be, to put the matter colloquially, much of a reaction? And if so, from whom? In the language of economics the question is this: from which products and which activities could we expect a relatively high demand or supply response to price change i.e. a relatively high cross-elasticity of demand or cross-elasticity of supply?"[45]

The evaluative aspects of the judgment involved in market definition were not made express in that passage although it can be said they are a necessary incident of the reasoning processes necessary to arrive at the judgment which is required to be made. The purposive nature of the process however was not expressly addressed and does not arise as an incident of the observations in *QCMA*. The case seems to proceed on the assumption that the exercise of market definition is to a large extent a matter of quantitative fact finding.[46] In *G. & M. Stephens Cartage Contractors Pty Ltd*, Deane J, then of the Federal Court, now a member of the High Court of Australia, presided on the Tribunal with Mr Walker and Professor Brunt.[47] The Tribunal recognised the significance of market definition in the following terms:

"The identification of relevant markets must be the essential first step in the assessment both of present competition in existing circumstances and likely competition in postulated future circumstances. Competition is an active process rather than a passive situation. Nevertheless, the existence and extent of competition or likely competition between those competing within a market will depend, to a large extent, upon the distinctive, albeit evolving, structure of that market."[48]

It is important to note that from the outset the Tribunal has drawn a distinction between markets and sub-markets, regarding the latter as tools for analysis rather than as defining long run competitive effects.[49]

Shortly after the *QCMA* decision, the Trade Practices Review Committee (the Swanson Committee) published its report to the Minister of Business and Consumer Affairs on the operation and effect of the Act.[50] It referred to the concept of market as involving the performance of a function in relation to a product being goods or services within a geographical area. The boundaries of product and geographic markets were seen as "necessarily flexible" because of their dependence upon the relationship between such factors as price, product substitutability, desired use and distance from supply. The Committee said:

"The Committee considers that no advantage would be gained by attempting to define exhaustively the term 'market'. No definition could produce a formula capable of certainty, having regard to the variable nature of the factors discussed in the paragraph above. Importantly also, the Committee has regard to the fact that persons involved with particular cases wish the matters in dispute to be judged on the particular facts, as they may present them, and not by artificial rules designed to achieve what we would suggest is an illusory certainty."[51]

The Committee did however consider that the Act could give useful legislative guidance in relation to product substitution and recommended that it require that in the determination of a "market" for particular purposes, regard should be had to substitute products, being products which have a reasonable interchangeability of use and which have high cross-elasticity of demand. It seems that this may have in part been a response to the brand market definition adopted in the *Top Performance* case. That recommendation of the Committee led to the enactment of s. 4E of the Act in the 1977 amendments. That section provides:

> "For the purposes of this Act, unless the contrary intention appears, "market" means a market in Australia and, when used in relation to any goods or services, includes a market for those goods or services and other goods or services that are substitutable for, or otherwise competitive with, the first mentioned goods or services."

As Wilcox J observed in *Mark Lyons Pty Ltd v. Bursill Sportsgear Pty Ltd*,[52] the enactment of s. 4E cast doubt upon the continued application of the *Top Performance* case unless it could first be found that no other brands would have been substitutable for Datsun products. His Honor noted that the new definition was not inconsistent with the continued application of the *QCMA* case which had been cited and relied upon by the Court in two earlier cases.[53]

In *Re Tooth & Co. Ltd; Re Tooheys Ltd*,[54] the Tribunal comprised Keely J of the Federal Court sitting with Mr J. Shipton and Professor Brunt. The Tribunal there saw the task of a complex market analysis as involving:

1. Identification of the relevant area or areas of close competition.
2. Application of the principle that competition may proceed through substitution of supply source as well as product.
3. Delineation of a market which comprehends the maximum range of business activities and the widest geographic area within which, if given a sufficient economic incentive, buyers can switch to a substantial extent from one source of supply to another and sellers can switch to a substantial extent from one production plan to another.
4. Consideration of long-run substitution possibilities rather than short-run and transitory situations recognising that the market is the field of actual or potential rivalry between firms.
5. Selection of market boundaries as a matter of degree by identification of such a break in substitution possibilities that firms within the boundary would collectively possess substantial market power so that if operating as a

cartel they could raise prices or offer lesser terms without being substantially undermined by the incursions of rivals.

6. Acceptance of the proposition that the field of substitution is not necessarily homogeneous but may contain sub-markets in which competition is especially close or especially immediate. This is subject to the qualification that competitive relationships in key sub-markets may have a wider effect upon the functioning of the market as a whole.

7. Identification of the market as multi-dimensional involving product, functional level, space and time.[55]

The various Tribunal decisions to which reference has been made and others which have not been cited, involved the input of a combination of judges and economists. They evidence a continuing and constructive dialogue between those members of the judiciary who sat on the Tribunal and experts in the field of the economics of competition who sat with them. There is little doubt that the input of economists through the Tribunal has, at the very least, provided those judges who constituted the Tribunal from time to time and other judges who have followed its decisions, with some of the vocabulary and methodology which is necessary to the proper application of competition law.

IV.2. Market Definition by the Federal Court

In the *Mark Lyons* case, Wilcox J rejected a propounded market in ski boots of a particular brand. The relevant market, he held, should be described as the Australian ski boot market. In doing so his Honor also rejected a hopelessly broad product market defined by reference to "sportsgear". He left open the possibility of a brand name market, however, for a sufficiently distinctive brand. His Honor's view was that the best evidence of the dimensions of the relevant market is the behavior of people in the trade. He adopted a passage from a leading Australian antitrust law text in relation to evidence from those in the trade:[56]

> "Their records will establish the dimensions of the market; they will show the figures being kept of competitors' and customers' behaviour and the particular products being followed. They will show the potential customers whom salesmen are visiting, the suppliers whom purchasing officers regularly contact, products against which advertising is directed, the price movements of other suppliers which give rise to intra-corporate memoranda, the process by which products are bought, what buyers must seek in terms of quantities, delivery schedules, price flexibility, why accounts are won and lost."

Wilcox J returned to the question of market definition in *Trade Practices Commission v. Australia Meat Holdings Ltd.*[57] Whereas in *Mark Lyons* he had been concerned with a market in which the relevant company was a vendor of goods to the public, the case before him was one in which the company acted as a purchaser of cattle from a wide variety of vendors. Nonetheless, the *QCMA* concept of market held. Based upon evidence given by an academic economist and submissions of the parties, his Honor accepted a redefinition in the following terms:

> "A market is the field of activity in which buyers and sellers interact, and the identification of market boundaries requires consideration of both the demand and supply side. The ideal definition of a market must take into account substitution possibilities in both consumption and production. The existence of price differentials between different products, reflecting differences in quality or other characteristics of the products, does not by itself place the products in different markets. The test of whether or not there are different markets is based on what happens (or would happen) on either the demand or the supply side in response to a change in relative price."[58]

In that case there was both trade and economists' evidence as to the proper product and geographical market. As to the latter, his Honor observed that "[q]uestions of degree are involved which, in the end, require an exercise of judgment."[59] He expressed concern that the curial determination of the limits of a market about which he assumed commercial people frequently make almost intuitive judgments, should be seen as requiring the time, effort and expense involved in that case. While he supposed that the very flexibility of the concept of market necessarily casts a wide evidentiary net there was a particular need for rigorous consideration of the probative value of potential items of evidence given the urgency of such proceedings. His Honor went on to say:

> "In particular I deprecate the course... of supplying to economists proofs of the evidence to be given by other witnesses and then eliciting from those economists opinions as to the proper conclusion upon the definition of the market. Economists are able to assist the court in relation to economic principles. But, once the relevant principles are expounded, their application to the facts of the case is a matter for the court. The proper definition of a market is entirely a matter of fact, the determination of which ought not to be made more protracted and expensive by the adduction of unnecessary expert evidence."[60]

Between the first instance decision in *Australia Meat Holdings*, which was delivered on 15 July 1988, and the decision of the Full Court in that case which was given on 3 March 1989, the High Court delivered its important judgment on misuse of market power in *Queensland Wire Industries Pty Ltd v. BHP*.[61] The joint judgment of Mason CJ and Wilson J identified the purposive character of the process of market definition in the context of misuse of market power:

> "In identifying the relevant market, it must be borne in mind that the object is to discover the degree of the defendant's market power. Defining the market and evaluating the degree of power in that market are part of the same process, and it is for the sake of simplicity of analysis that the two are separated."[62]

The passage cited makes explicit the linkage between the process of market definition and the determination of market power. In this context the characterisation of market definition as a fact finding process seems incomplete. It may be that some analogy can be drawn with the notion of "proximity" in the common law of negligence. Like "market" it is a multi-dimensional abstraction which involves the making of value judgments. Deane J made this point in *Queensland Wire*. After observing that the word "market" is not susceptible of precise comprehensive definition when used as an abstract noun in an economic context, his Honor said:

> "The identification of relevant markets and the definition of market structures and boundaries for the purpose of determining whether BHP's refusal to supply Y-bar to Q.W.I. contravened s. 46(1) *involves value judgments about which there is some room for legitimate differences of opinion*. The economy is not divided into an identifiable number of discrete markets into one or other of which all trading activities can be neatly fitted. One overall market may overlap other markets and contain more narrowly defined markets which may, in their turn, overlap, the one with one or more others. The outer limits (including geographic confines) of a particular market are likely to be blurred: their definition will commonly involve assessment of the relative weight to be given to competing considerations in relation to questions such as the extent of product substitutability and the significance of competition between traders at different stages of distribution."[63] (emphasis added)

Dawson J who generally agreed with Deane J, also said:

> "A question of degree is involved – at what point do different goods become closely enough linked in supply or demand to be included in the one market – which precludes any dogmatic answer... The process is an inexact one as may be illustrated by reference to the concept of a sub-market which has been employed from time to time."[64]

In the decision of the Full Court in *Australia Meat Holdings Pty Ltd v. Trade Practices Commission*,[65] reference was of course made to the judgments in *Queensland Wire*. Davies J accepted that the relevant principles were correctly understood and applied at first instance. There was, however, a caution, consistent with the approach taken by Wilcox J, about the necessity to relate the process of market definition to commercial realities. Davies J said:

> "The existence of a market, a concept of economics and commerce, ought not to be determined by reference to theoretical possibilities."[66]

His Honor quoted with approval a passage from a leading antitrust text:

> "Any geographic market... must be one that both corresponds to the commercial realities of the industry and represents an economically significant trade area. Because a geographic market determination looks to actual trade patterns, it is not required that geographical boundaries be drawn with exactitude; some amount of "fuzziness" is inevitable."[67]

Sheppard J agreed with both Davies and Pincus JJ in the *Australia Meat Holdings* appeal. He accepted that the drawing of any line to define the geographic market is an arbitrary exercise which would never be completely correct, as "[t]here will always be a certain fuzziness about it."[68] The purposive nature of market definition was acknowledged by Pincus J saying that:

> "The process of identification of the relevant market must be carried out keeping in mind the object of doing so; in the instant case that is to determine whether the appellant was at the relevant time in a position to dominate the market, or was by the acquisition placed in such position."[69]

It is against the background of these developments that it was said in *Singapore Airlines v. Taprobane Tours*:

> "There is necessarily a close relationship between the delineation of a market and description of the distribution of power within it. The first process is logically anterior to the second and is frequently so expressed ... But that does not mean that market definition may be settled without resort to a consideration of structure and power distribution. It is a focussing process and the Court must select what emerges as the clearest picture of the relevant competitive process in the light of commercial reality and the purposes of the law. There is a feedback between any proposed market and the structure and power distribution which that proposal throws up."[70]

The vexed question of the kinds of economic evidence that might be received in relation to market definition and other economic issues fell for consideration by the Full Federal Court in *Arnotts Ltd v. Trade Practices Commission*.[71] The Court referred to what was said in Queensland Wire, particularly the passages already mentioned from the joint judgment of Mason CJ and Wilson J and the judgments of Deane and Dawson JJ. The *QCMA* definition was cited again with approval. The evaluative nature of judgments on the question of product substitutability was acknowledged.[72] In relation to the use which might be made of expert economists in such cases the Court said after discussing principles generally governing the admissibility of expert evidence:

> "Applying those principles to a case such as the present, it seems to us that an expert economist may legitimately give an opinion, for example, as to the proper method of defining a market. The economist may go further, rendering that opinion more apposite to the case by proffering a definition relevant to the particular case. ... It does not matter whether ... the issue is one upon which the Court has to reach a finding. What does matter ... is that the assumptions upon which the opinion is based are identified and articulated."[73]

The Court stigmatised as illegitimate the use of expert witnesses "to filter the facts" where the witness is asked to hear or read all the evidence and then express factual conclusions. Counsel had submitted that the Court should permit the admission of expert economic evidence without requiring disclosure of the assumptions upon which the evidence was based. The proposal was rejected as "mischievous". The Court said:

> "There are two reasons why we are of that opinion. The first is the very justification advanced by counsel, the difficulty in predicting "the permutations

> and combinations necessary to cover all possible findings by the Court." If an economist were permitted to express opinions upon the effect of the evidence given, without identifying the facts which he or she assumed for the purpose of those opinions, it would be impossible for the Court to know how to apply that evidence. One of the permutations or combinations may have rendered the opinion inapplicable, in the expert's eyes, but the Court would never know."[74]

The approach taken by the Full Court in *Arnotts* to the use of economic evidence has been the subject of criticism as imposing an unnecessarily restrictive approach to the way in which economists can be used in antitrust cases. I do not propose to engage those criticisms. The Full Court has given a decision and the working out of that decision and its practical application in the context of pending changes in the statute law relating to evidence is a matter for the future. It is important, however, to recognise the nature of the tasks set for courts and judges in the area of competition law. The approach to market definition is but one limited example. As decisions of the Trade Practices Tribunal have demonstrated, there is room for fruitful and constructive co-operation between judges and economists in this area. And there is scope for optimism in this respect. A recent important change to the Federal Court Rules provides a framework within which economists can act as guides to the Court in the difficult judgments required by this area of the law without being unnecessarily hampered by restrictive rules of evidence.

V. Economic Testimony as Argument

In recent times there has been debate about the operation of restrictions imposed by rules of evidence on the reception of expert evidence in the Federal Court. The emphasis of that discussion has been on the use of economic evidence in cases brought under Part IV of the *Trade Practices Act* 1974. It has, however, also been applied to the reception of expert evidence in intellectual property litigation. In August 1993, the report of an independent committee of inquiry, the Hilmer Committee, concerning a national competition policy, was delivered to the Heads of the Federal, State and Territory Governments in Australia.[75] The Committee observed that competitive conduct rules require a number of judgments to be made about various economic facts such as market definition, levels of market power and the extent to which particular conduct lessens competition. Submissions to the inquiry had suggested a degree of dissatisfaction with current court procedures for the utilisation of economic material in the process of making such judgments. The committee, however, was not satisfied that any perceived difficulties peculiar to competition law were of sufficient magnitude to warrant major departures from current practices and procedures. It recommended the establishment of an appropriate consultative process to consider proposals for refinement of current court procedures including relaxation of the rules of evidence.[76] In the event, the Judges of the Federal Court have enacted a new rule of court taking effect from 1 January 1994. The rule provides that the Court may:

> "in proceedings in which a party seeks to rely on the opinion of a person involving a subject in which the person has specialist qualifications, direct that all or part of such opinion be received by way of submission in such manner and form as the Court may think fit, whether or not the opinion would be admissible as evidence."[77]

The rule recognises that expert testimony adduced from economists and some other experts may be characterised less as evidence than as argument. This is particularly so where the Court is concerned with the application to evidence of statutory terms involving economic concepts. Judgments about such questions as whether and in what circumstances one product is substitutable for another and within what geographic range products compete and at what functional levels they compete, are matters of fact. The question where a line should be drawn along the spectrum of substitutable products in order to define a product market boundary may be, in essence, one of argument and submission. Similar examples may occur in determining whether evidence reflects a situation properly described as a lessening of competition and whether such lessening is "substantial" or not. So too, there is room for debate and submission on the question of market power. Economic "evidence" so called may at times be argument about the significance of evidence as distinct from opinions fairly based on proven facts. Similar situations can occur in intellectual property litigation where it is sought, for example, to adduce testimony relating to infringements of claims made in a patent, reproduction of a substantial part of a copyright work, or imitation of a registered design. In the circumstances, there is no relaxation of the rules of evidence if the Court receives such material as argument. So characterised, some of what an economist has to say can be received by way of written brief or oral submission or both. Cross-examination may not be appropriate in such a case but the procedure for receiving such submissions can be flexible. It can, for example, extend to a panel arrangement under which opposing economists or other experts put views and engage in an exchange controlled by the Court. On this basis, what now passes for expert evidence might be put in its proper place at the bar table. This is not to be taken as understating the benefit that can flow from the insights to be derived from economic and other expert testimony in these areas. But the new procedure can be accommodated within the existing framework of rules of evidence.

VI. Conclusion

From time to time the question is raised of the suitability of the judicial system as a vehicle for determining the kinds of issues that arise under competition law. Some will go so far as to say that the courts are not properly adapted to handle this class of decision-making. There have been calls for the establishment of a specialist competition tribunal or the extension of the powers of the Trade Practices Tribunal. The nature of the reasoning process and the evaluative and normative judgments which are involved in the application of competition law lie well outside the realms of syllogistic judicial reasoning readily capable of characterisation as rulings of law or findings of fact. But there are many examples in other areas of the law which fall well outside what I called in opening, that safe and tiny harbour. Whatever institutional choices are made in the future about the administration of competition law, the fact remains that in Australia there is an irreducible core of judicial review jurisdiction vested originally in the High Court and by statute in the Federal Court. Different institutional arrangements may be made for the future but, short of some apocalyptic constitutional change, the judicial system will continue to be involved in the administration of competition law.

By way of peroration, there is at the interface of economics and law challenge and opportunity for the courts and the community to develop a more sophisticated response to the problems of maintaining competition in Australian markets. The development of our jurisprudence has been enhanced by the contributions of the Trade Practices Tribunal which has involved economists directly in its work. Under the recent change to the Federal Court Rules, coupled with an increasing appreciation of economic issues by Judges of the Court, there is room for a fruitful interaction between judges and economists in the development of Australia's competition law.

Notes

[1] State judicial hierarchies comprise Magistrates Courts which deal with minor civil and criminal cases, intermediate District or County Courts which deal with most serious crime and middle-ranging contract and tort cases and a Supreme Court to deal with major civil litigation and the most serious criminal cases. The Supreme Courts exercise original and appellate jurisdiction, the latter by way of a Full Court or Court of Appeal usually comprising three judges.
[2] The Federal Court is both a trial and appellate court. Trials are conducted by single judges sitting without a jury. Any three judges of the Federal Court may constitute a Full Court with jurisdiction to hear appeals from the judgments of single judges. Other national courts are the Family Court of Australia and the newly created Industrial Relations Court.
[3] The political dimensions of recent decisions of the High Court giving rise to a theory of implied constitutional rights and a recent decision affirming the existence of a common law native title for Australia's indigenous peoples, have excited unprecedented debate about its composition and the way in which its members are appointed. The issue of systemic gender bias in all courts has also stimulated wide debate.
[4] 'Path of the Law', (1897) 10 *Harvard Law Review*, pp. 457–466.
[5] *Giris v. Federal Commissioner of Taxation* (1969) 119 Commonwealth Law Reports 365, p. 383, Windeyer J.
[6] Stone, Julius (1968) *Legal Systems and Lawyers Reasonings*, Maitland, pp. 263–264.
[7] *Ibid*, p. 353.
[8] US Department of Justice and Federal Trade Commission (1992) *Horizontal Merger Guidelines*, reprinted in 4 Trade Regulation Reporter (CCH) 13,104. For a comparison of the *Guidelines* with section 50 of the *Trade Practices Act* 1974 see Round, D.K. and R.A. Miller (1993) 'The Australian Merger Guidelines: A Comparison with the U.S. Merger Guidelines', *Review of Industrial Organisation*, **8**, 211–229.
[9] Hunter A. (ed.) (1969) *Monopoly and Competition*, Ringwood, Penguin, p. 15.
[10] Demsetz, Harold (1989) 'Economics as a Guide to Anti-Trust' in Demsetz, Harold (1989) *Efficiency, Competition and Policy*, London, Blackwell. Volume 2, p. 198.
[11] *Supra* n. 9, p. 14.

[12] For a general discussion of the history and nature of the constitutional jurisdiction of the High Court and the associated statutory jurisdiction of the Federal Court in judicial review see *David Jones Finance and Investments Pty Ltd v. Federal Commissioner of Taxation* (1991) 99 Australian Law Reports 447, pp. 454–460.
[13] *Huddart Parker & Co. Pty Ltd v. Moorehead* (1909) 8 Commonwealth Law Reports 330.
[14] *Attorney General (Cwth) v. Associated Northern Collieries* (1911) 14 Commonwealth Law Reports 387.
[15] Walker G. de Q. (1967) *Australian Monopoly Law: Issues of Law, Fact and Policy*, Melbourne, F.W. Cheshire Pty. Ltd., p. 32.
[16] Ransom, A.A. and W. Pengilly (1985) *Restrictive Trade Practices: Judgments, Materials and Policy*, Sydney, Legal Books, p. 163.
[17] *Supra* n. 14, p. 654.
[18] *Loc. cit.*
[19] See generally Nieuwenhuysen, J. P. (1976) 'The Theory of Competition Policy' in Nieuwenhuysen, J.P. (ed.) (1976) *Australian Trade Practices: Readings*, 2nd Edition, London, Croom Helm Ltd., pp. 270 ff.
[20] *Adelaide Steamship Co. Ltd v. The King and the Attorney-General* (1912) 15 Commonwealth Law Reports 65.
[21] *Ibid*, p. 77.
[22] *Ibid*, p. 76.
[23] *Ibid*, p. 91.
[24] Walker, *supra* n. 15, p. 33.
[25] *The Attorney-General of the Commonwealth v. The Adelaide Steamship Company Limited* (1913) 18 Commonwealth Law Reports 30. At that time it was possible to bring an appeal from the High Court to the Privy Council constituted by a Judicial Committee of the House of Lords. Appeals to the Privy Council were abolished in Australia in the 1980's.
[26] Principal antitrust judgments of the High Court between 1913 and 1973 can be shortly listed. They are: *Redfern v. Dunlop Rubber Australia Ltd* (1964) 110 Commonwealth Law Reports 194; *Johnston v. Egg Marketing Board of New South Wales* (1965) 112 Commonwealth Law Reports 343; *Meyer Heine Pty Ltd v. China Navigation Co. Ltd* (1966) 115 Commonwealth Law Reports 10; *Attorney-General v. Dalgety Trading Co. Ltd* (1966) Argus Law Reports 194; *John Robertson and Co. Ltd (In liquidation) v. Ferguson Transformers Pty Ltd* (1973) 129 Commonwealth Law Reports 65.
[27] *J. Kitchener & Sons Pty Ltd v. Stewarts Cash & Carry Stores* (1942) 66 Commonwealth Law Reports 116.
[28] (1941) 41 State Reports (New South Wales) 72.
[29] *Ibid*, p. 84. Nicholas J referred, with approval, to a New Zealand judgment in *Kerridge v. Rotorua Theatres Ltd* (1937) New Zealand Law Reports 156 in which an agreement involving the closure of several cinemas in the North Island of New Zealand was upheld. The case decided that "The law enforces restrictions arranged between traders for the purpose of regulating their business arrangements when to obtain or to submit to such restrictions is necessary to preserve stability of trade and adequate profit."
[30] *Supra* n. 15, p. 36.
[31] *Cockburn Cement Pty Ltd v. Wallwork* (1958) 59 Western Australian Law Reports 75.
[32] *R v. Wallwork; Ex parte Cockburn Cement Ltd* (1957) 59 Western Australian Law Reports 49 p. 61.
[33] *Ibid*, p. 66.
[34] *Supra* n. 31, p. 103.
[35] *USA v. E.I. Dupont de Nemours & Co.* 100 US 751.
[36] *Supra* n. 31, p. 103.
[37] *Supra* n. 15, p. 35.
[38] *Loc. cit.*
[39] *Strickland v. Rocla Concrete Pipes Ltd* (1971) 124 Commonwealth Law Reports 468.
[40] Parliamentary Debates House of Representatives 16.7.74, pp. 227–228.

[41] A leading and frequently cited exposition of the market concept referred to later in this paper is taken from the decision of the Tribunal in *Queensland Co-operative Milling Association Ltd; Re Defiance Holdings Ltd* (1976) 25 Federal Law Reports 169 (the *QCMA* case).
[42] (1991) 33 Federal Court Reports 158.
[43] *Top Performance Motors Pty Ltd v. Ira Berk (Qld) Pty Ltd* (1975) 24 Federal Law Reports 286.
[44] *Ibid*, p. 289.
[45] *Supra* n. 41, p. 190.
[46] The approach to market definition adopted by the Tribunal was followed by the Tribunal differently constituted in *Re Howard Smith Industries Pty Ltd and Adelaide Steamship Industries Pty Ltd* (1977) 28 Federal Law Reports 385.
[47] (1977) Australian Trade Practices Reports 40–042.
[48] *Ibid*, p. 17,460.
[49] In the *QCMA* case the Tribunal accepted that the distinction between markets and sub-markets can be merely one of degree. It saw sub-markets as more narrowly defined and typically registering discontinuity in substitution possibilities. While sub-markets might be especially useful in registering the short-run effects of change, they were regarded by the Tribunal as misleading if used uncritically to assess long-run competitive effects.
[50] Trade Practices Review Committee (1976) *Report to Minister of Business and Consumer Affairs*, Canberra, Australian Government Publishing Service.
[51] *Ibid*, para 4.21.
[52] (1987) 75 Australian Law Reports 581.
[53] *Trade Practices Commission v. Ansett Transport Industries (Operation) Pty Ltd* (1978) 20 Australian Law Reports 31; *Adamson v. West Perth Football Club* (1979) 27 Australian Law Reports 475.
[54] (1979) 39 Federal Law Reports 1.
[55] *Ibid*, p. 38.
[56] Donald, B.G. and J.D. Heydon (1978) *Trade Practices Law*, Volume 1, Sydney, The Law Book Company Limited, p. 92.
[57] (1988) 83 Australian Law Reports 299.
[58] *Ibid*, p. 317.
[59] *Ibid*, p. 336.
[60] *Ibid*, p. 316.
[61] (1989) 167 Commonwealth Law Reports 177.
[62] *Ibid*, p. 187.
[63] *Ibid*, p. 195.
[64] *Ibid*, p. 199.
[65] (1989) Australian Trade Practices Reports 40–932.
[66] *Ibid*, p. 50,092.
[67] Von Kalinosski, J.O. (1971) *Anti Trust Laws and Trade Regulations*, Vol.3, para. 18–96.
[68] *Supra* n. 65, p. 50,097.
[69] *Ibid*, p. 50,104.
[70] *Supra* n. 42, p. 177.
[71] (1990) 24 Federal Court Reports 313.
[72] *Ibid*, p. 331.
[73] *Ibid*, p. 351.
[74] *Ibid*, p. 352.
[75] National Competition Policy Review (F.G. Hilmer, Chairman) (August 1993) *National Competition Policy*, Canberra, Australian Government Publishing Service.
[76] *Ibid*, p. 179, para. 7.3.
[77] *Federal Court Rules* Order 10 rule 1(2)(j).

Review of Industrial Organization **9:** 569–606, 1994.

Horizontal Price Agreements in Australian Antitrust: Combatting Anti-Competitive Corporate Conspiracies of Complicity and Connivance

DAVID K. ROUND and JOHN J. SIEGFRIED*
Department of Economics, University of Adelaide, Adelaide, South Australia 5005, Australia
Department of Economics, Vanderbilt University, Nashville, Tennessee, 37235, U.S.A.

Abstract. When the Trade Practices Act came into operation in 1974, Australian executives, for whom price-fixing had previously been commonplace, faced the prospect of having to abandon their usual methods of doing business. However, with no criminal penalties and a maximum monetary penalty of $250,000 (changed to $10m only in 1993), and with little social antagonism towards cartels, there were no significant incentives for firms to act independently. Yet while relatively few major price-fixing cases have been instituted, and no defendant has paid a major monetary penalty, there nevertheless has been a change in business attitudes towards price-fixing. It is not easy to provide a systematic characterization of either the products, firms, markets or justifications which have featured in these cases. To avoid being found guilty in the absence of "smoking gun" evidence, the courts have established that firms need only show that their behavior was consistent with ordinary commercial conduct.

Key words: Collusion, price-fixing, authorization, exemptions, principles, penalties

I. Introduction

In 1963 Karmel and Brunt (1963, pp. 94–5) argued that:

> "Restrictive practices have a long history in Australia and have come to be regarded by businessmen and consumers alike as normal business behaviour. Indeed, certainly until very recently, the average businessman would have been rather hurt to hear his trade agreements described as restrictive ... While just about every restrietive practice known to man is used in Australia (other than those subject to common law restraints), price agreements, both horizontal and vertical, are undoubtedly the most common."

Given that the Australian tradition of "mateship" applied to the business sector as much as it did to personal relationships, this statement came as no surprise to Australians interested in the conduct of firms. After the Commonwealth of Australia's loss, in 1913 (on appeal to the Privy Council in the UK, at that time the final court of appeal for Australian cases), of Australia's first price-fixing case (the *Coal Vend* case, discussed below), there had been virtually no attempt to enforce the legislation which covered inter-firm agreements. As a result, tacit and overt collusive agreements, especially on price, flourished and Australian consumers suffered.[1]

But such a concerted effort was not to come until 1962, when the Attorney General decided to take a close legislative look at business practices. The idea that they should act independently shocked many Australian executives, and great pressure was brought to bear on the government of the day to stifle this initiative. Yet having had a small promise of the benefits of competitive markets, others lobbied for legislation to curtail at least the worst types of corporate behavior. Finally, in 1967 there began a limited antitrust statute which signalled the beginning of the end of cosy corporate conspiracies among Australian businesses. An enthusiastic regulator managed, with limited resources and considerable legal opposition, to stop a number of restrictive practices, including some significant price-fixing agreements. By the early 1970's, there was growing consensus in Australian political, legal and economic circles, as well as in many parts of the business community, that it was time for a direct prohibition on price-fixing. A newly elected reformist Labor Government hastened the process.[2] Since 1974 price-fixing for goods has been virtually illegal per se (even more so since 1977) under the Trade Practices Act ('the Act' hereafter).

This paper takes both an historical and an analytical look at horizontal price agreements in Australia, concentrating mainly on the post-1974 period. In Section II we briefly discuss the economic rationale for proscribing price co-ordination. Section III presents a short history of the Australian legislation, and the Australian enforcement framework is discussed in Section IV. Section V analyzes the major Australian price-fixing cases, both judicial and administrative, and assesses the penalties which have been imposed. We then derive the key principles which have characterized the judicial treatment of price-fixing, and assess whether the Australian cases fit the traditional cartel model which underlies legislation against price-fixing agreements around the world. Finally in Section VI we evaluate the success of the Act in eliminating price-fixing, and offer some suggestions for reform.

II. Economic and Legal Considerations of Price Fixing

The strength of a competitive economy emanates from its ability to disseminate information about opportunity costs to individual decision makers at low cost. Price is the vehicle for conveying this information. Consumers naturally compare the value they would receive from a purchase to the price they must pay for it. If price reflects opportunity cost, consumers indirectly weigh the benefit they would receive from consuming an item against the greatest benefit that could otherwise be created with the resources that are required to make it. Competition among sellers ensures that price reflects opportunity costs.

Profit maximizing sellers, however, prefer not to sell in competitive markets. They prefer, instead, to charge prices which exceed marginal cost, as higher prices yield greater profits. Thus sellers have an incentive to collude to create a monopoly and elevate price above the competitive level. It is in their joint interest to conspire not to cut price below the agreed level, even though a modestly lower price for one firm would still exceed marginal cost and would generate more very profitable sales for that seller. In successful conspiracies, the elevated price exaggerates opportunity costs and misleads consumers into refraining from purchases that are actually worth more to them than to anyone else. For a free market economy to work efficiently, it is essential that conspiracies be eliminated and prices be determined competitively, which is why price-fixing prohibitions commonly form the foundation of competition policy in developed free market economies.

While profit maximizing incentives encourage the formation of cartels, incentives that emerge from the quest for profits tend to undermine price-fixing agreements. First, competing sellers may find it difficult to agree among themselves on a price if their costs differ because of varying prices of essential inputs, diverging production methods, or differing business acumen. Second, each seller prefers that price be elevated by means of *its rivals'* output restriction, since as prices rise, expanded sales become even more attractive. This tempts individual sellers to shade their price below the agreed price. If all succumb to the temptation, more substantial price cuts than simply "shading" are required to expand sales. Sufficiently large price cuts, however, destroy the cartel. Third, a successful cartel must decide how to allocate profits, not a trivial problem when the co-operation of each (greedy) rival is essential to its success. Since each seller can reasonably ascribe *all* of the cartel profits to its co-operation (after all, if it expands production sufficiently, the remaining conspirators cannot maintain a price above the competitive level), the demands for shares of the loot can easily exceed available cartel profits, and the cartel may collapse. Finally, even if the conspirators can solve all their internal problems, they must develop a method to restrain new entrants attracted by the prospect of sharing in the cartel's spoils. Some observers (for example, Armentano (1982)) believe that one or more of these problems will inevitably destroy any cartel.

Others, however, like Qualls (1974), who are sceptical of the speed at which natural forces operate, see a role for government policy to discourage the formation of cartels and speed the demise of those that do evolve. When this view has prevailed, horizontal pricing agreements among competitors have generally been prohibited. A per se prohibition against conspiracies in restraint of trade has served as the foundation of American competition policy since it was first ruled constitutional almost a century ago.[3] A per se ban minimizes the judicial costs of sorting good from bad conspiracies, and strengthens the deterrent effect of the policy, as fewer prospective conspirators will be tempted in the belief that their attorneys will later be able to "get them off the hook". If there are few benefits from conspiracies, unambiguous prohibition can improve social welfare.

The law against explicit price-fixing has been enforced vigorously in America, even in supposedly pro-business Republican administrations, as demonstrated by

Gallo, Craycraft and Bush (1987).[4] Prison sentences and large financial damage awards have become common punishment for price-fixing convictions in the US since 1960. In recent years a few general conspiracy defences have emerged, including "the government made me do it"[5] and "the industry will not exist without it".[6] The most important exception in the US, however, deals with price leadership and conscious parallelism. Oligopolists who establish or follow high prices because they recognize the likelihood of rival retaliation for failure to do so escape the law against price-fixing, so long as they make their decisions independently.

Populist views that favor small business and fear centralized economic power mesh well with vigorous prosecution of conspiracies in restraint of trade. Yet there is an irony to this aspect of American competition policy which, on the whole, has relied less on behavioral proscriptions and more on structuralist policies that reduce the need for monitoring and controlling business conduct. Behavioral rules generally play a larger role in smaller economies, where the cost disadvantage of small scale operations provoked by structuralist reforms may have serious consequences for international competitiveness. Behavioral rules are also more common where there is less distrust of central authority than in the US. Thus it is natural that Australian competition policy relies heavily on a price-fixing prohibition. A second reason to expect a strong ban on price-fixing in Australia is the limited number of sellers in most important Australian industries, many of which historically were heavily protected from international competition by substantial trade barriers.

Economic theory predicts that conspiracies will be easier to form and maintain when:[7]

* there are fewer sellers (agreements can be reached more easily and price cutters can be detected);
* there is greater equality of firm size and/or firms enjoy similar cost conditions (less incentive to cheat, or if cheating occurs it will be easier to detect);
* there are impediments to new entry (cartel profits are not shared with opportunists);
* demand is relatively inelastic (buyers have little choice but to pay higher prices);
* the product is homogeneous (facilitating agreement on price) and non-price competition is not a significant aspect of the market (making it easier to detect cheating);[8]
* demand is stable or declining (because profit prospects without conspiracy are less attractive), and the market is not subject to rapid technological change;
* buyer concentration is low, with small, regular and frequent orders (large one-time orders are likely to tempt colluders to cheat, given the gains to be had);
* sales occur via open bids (detecting cheaters is easier than if bids are sealed);
* firms enjoy a low ratio of fixed costs to variable costs (a high ratio provides a powerful incentive to cut prices when demand is slack);

* managers have substantial ownership stakes in their firms (benefits flow to them);
* there is a communication mechanism for information exchanges between rivals, whether it be legitimate industry trade associations, traditional industry social structures, or some other agreed-upon facilitating practices (making it easy to transmit pricing information or co-ordinate decisions, either directly or under some covering cloak of respectability).

Patterns of price-fixing enforcement in the US have been consistent with these predictions. The small number of price-fixing cases in Australia to date precludes conducting a detailed systematic examination of whether its convictions for price-fixing fit the economic model, but we do make a brief tabular assessment of the collusive characteristics of 16 Australian markets in which firms have been charged with price-fixing.

III. History of Anti-Collusion Legislation in Australia

Australian antitrust history has seen three distinct statutes relating to price-fixing agreements among firms. The first and third, modelled on the Sherman Act, prohibited such conduct outright (or close to it), but the second was less specific, reflecting the state of philosophical and ideological maturity, both political and business, which was current at the time.

The first Australian antitrust statute was the Australian Industries Preservation Act ('AIPA' hereafter), passed in 1906. This Act, which could be called "the son of Sherman", contained inter alia in Section 4 of Part II (which was headed "Repression of Monopolies") a per se prohibition on any contract or combination entered into

> "with intent to restrain trade or commerce to the detriment of the public; or ... with intent to destroy or injure by means of unfair competition any Australian industry the preservation of which is advantageous to the Commonwealth, having due regard to the interests of producers, workers and consumers."[9]

Following an unsuccessful prosecution in 1913, the AIPA was not used again against horizontal combinations. It was replaced by the Trade Practices Act 1965, which became effective in 1967. This Act followed the then current British approach to antitrust, rather than the American approach, in so far as it was prescriptive rather than proscriptive.[10] Collusive bidding and tendering were made criminal offenses and were per se illegal. A broad range of restrictive agreements had to be registered on a secret (non-public) register held by the Commissioner of Trade Practices, the newly formed antitrust regulator.[11] Agreements between competitors were examinable if they contained restrictions on prices or other terms or conditions of sale; allowances, rebates, discounts or credit; quantities, qualities, or kinds of goods or services; market areas; or buyers. Mere registration carried with it no assumption of contravention – this could only occur after an investigation and prosecution by the Commissioner before the Trade Practices Tribunal (a quasi-judicial body), which had to decide if the practice was on balance against the public interest.[12] The term public interest was defined to include, inter alia, the needs and interests of producers, distributors, employees, consumers, exporters, importers, owners, investors, and small businesses, and also encompassed the promotion of efficient production and new enterprises. With such a long extensive list of possible defenses, it is not surprising that only two cases were prosecuted through to victory. Like the great majority of the 14,403 agreements which had been registered by June 1974, these successful prosecutions involved price-fixing agreements.[13]

Both the Commissioner's work and the two cases decided by the Tribunal suggested by the early 1970's that a strict rule was needed if price-fixing were to be curtailed in Australia. It was time to force Australian executives to set prices independently, and to face the uncertainties of the market place, rather than to enjoy the quiet life so cherished by price-fixers. The first body blow to price-fixing was delivered by the Trade Practices Act 1974; the knockout punch came with the 1977 Amendments to the Act. With these changes, the slow case-by-case approach under the 1965 Act was replaced by direct prohibitions.

Section 45 of the 1974 Act was expressed simply – a firm should not make a contract or arrangement, or enter into an understanding, in restraint of trade or commerce if the contract had, or would likely have, a significant anti-competitive effect. The Act provided an escape clause through what were known as clearances (given by the Trade Practices Commission (TPC), the newly established antitrust regulator, if it determined that the impact of the agreement was not significantly anti-competitive) and authorizations. An authorization was an administrative decision made by the TPC that the agreement was on balance in the public interest.[14] Section 90(5) of the Act provided that for s. 45 matters authorization could be granted if the agreement resulted, or was likely to result, in a substantial benefit to the public, this benefit could not otherwise be achieved, and in all the circumstances, that result justified the granting of the authorization. Except for some joint ventures, authorization was not available for price-fixing agreements on goods. Price-fixing arrangements also were excused if they had "such a slight effect on competition as to be insignificant".

Following a High Court judgment in 1976,[15] it became evident that s. 45 would be difficult to enforce, because "restraint of trade or commerce" was construed narrowly. A committee (the Swanson Committee) set up to review the Act recommended that "in restraint of trade or commerce" be replaced by a broad prohibition on agreements which prevented or restricted competition in a substantially adverse way between the parties to an agreement.[16] Price-fixing with respect to goods was said to be per se unacceptable. Following these recommendations, the Act was amended in 1977, and has remained largely the same since then.

Section 45 prohibits contracts, arrangements and understandings if they contain an exclusionary provision, or if they contain a provision which has the purpose, effect or likely effect of substantially lessening competition.[17] A separate s. 45A was introduced in 1977 to deal with horizontal price-fixing agreements for goods. It deems them to substantially lessen competition. While s. 45A establishes a per se breach, it still requires a limited competition analysis through its requirement that the parties involved must compete with each other – in other words, there is no need to prove an anti-competitive effect, but there must be some rivalry between the parties. There are, however, three exceptions to this deeming provision:

* recommended price agreements for goods or services between 50 or more independent parties, providing there is no attempt to enforce these "recommendations";
* price agreements for goods or services originating from joint ventures; and
* agreements as to the price for which goods or services are to be collectively acquired, and for the price at which they are to be jointly advertised for resale.[18]

However, if any of these three situations has the purpose, effect or likely effect of substantially lessening competition, an exemption is not possible. Each of these categories of agreements may be authorized,[19] as may the price-fixing of services, effectively making them subject to a rule of reason test, but other agreements fixing the price of goods are per se illegal.[20] The standard to secure an authorization is no longer as strict as it was before the 1977 amendments – all that is now required is that the agreement will result, or will likely result, in a benefit to the public which outweighs any anti-competitive detriment caused by the agreement.[21]

In a recent review of competition policy (National Competition Policy Review (1993)) it was recommended by the Hilmer Committee (named after its chairman) that authorization for price-fixing agreements covering services be no longer possible,[22] and that recommended price agreements among 50 or more parties no longer be automatically exempt from s. 45A, but rather be subject to authorization.[23]

IV. Enforcement Procedures

Under the 1906 AIPA, enforcement reponsibility lay with the Commonwealth Attorney General, and proceedings ran in the High Court of Australia under strictly legal rules. Appeals went to the Full Bench of the High Court and from there to the Privy Council in the UK. Proceedings initiated by the TPC under the 1965 Act went before the Trade Practices Tribunal, whose President had to be a lawyer but whose composition also included lay members.[24] The Tribunal was effectively a trial court – it alone had the power to determine whether a practice was contrary to the public interest. It could issue cease and desist orders. With the implementation of the 1974 Act, the determination and review process changed again. The Tribunal became the review authority for TPC refusals to authorize particular conduct. Enforcement by the TPC is carried out through what is now the Federal Court. Appeals from Federal Court decisions made by a single judge go to a Full Bench of three judges, and the final court of appeal for Australian antitrust matters is the High Court of Australia, which to date has considered very few such cases.

A major concern when authority to determine antitrust liability was transferred from the Trade Practices Tribunal to the judiciary was that Australian judges had little formal training in economics. Prior to 1974 the Tribunal had been the sole authority ascertaining antitrust liability, and its composition ensured that economic and business expertise was on hand to complement judicial input. In the early stages after 1974, some judges floundered with economic issues, with some decisions on market definition and what constituted competition defying economic logic.[25] Other judges, however, grasped the essentials of economic commonsense and have produced well-reasoned decisions. In many cases, Federal Court judges deferred to the analytical structures provided by the Tribunal in its authorization determinations, thus enshrining as precedents the Tribunal's procedures for identifying and evaluating relevant economic phenomena.[26]

V. The Australian Cases

V.1. The Pre-1974 Experience

Australia's first price-fixing trial, the *Coal Vend* case,[27] occurred in 1911. It has been described as one in which "[a] clearer case of a combination with intent to restrain trade to the detriment of the public ... is almost impossible to contemplate" (Pengilley (1983, p. 926)), and as "one of the most far-sighted and enlightened antitrust opinions ever written" (Ransom (1981, p. 331)). Unfortunately, this judicial tour de force, which was adept at applying economic reasoning, did not find favor with the defendant coal mining companies, the firms which shipped their coal, nor with two appeal courts, which both reversed the trial judge's opinion. In the face of a classic horizontal and vertical price fixing arrangement which was found by the trial judge to have caused demonstrable damage to the Australian public, their Lordships in the UK Privy Council were steadfast in their determination to support entrenched corporate positions of power and wealth. Because the cartel did not include all the collieries, they argued, competition was not eliminated. Besides, there was no intention to injure the public, and no satisfactory evidence of injury to the public existed, and prices set were perfectly reasonable, especially in view of the fact that prices prevailing before the agreement were "disastrously low".[28] The result of this decision was that antitrust enforcement virtually disappeared in Australia until 1967.

The 1965 Act finally recognized the need to deal with price-fixing conspiracies. Inspection of the reports issued by the Commissioner of Trade Practices indicates that price agreements were rife throughout Australia. From 1969 to 1974, over 40 horizontal agreements on price were terminated after intervention by the Commissioner – most where the restrictions were lifted after discussion, two after formal proceedings before the Trade Practices Tribunal.[29] Many of the same industries have figured prominently in price-fixing prosecutions in the US. They often involve homogeneous products, few sellers, impediments to entry and inelastic demand. It seems that some industries have structural, technological and behavioral characteristics which render them universally prone to such agreements. The so-called "tyranny of distance" which has characterized Australia's geographic isolation clearly has not immunized it from price-fixing.

The Commissioner's persuasive powers were not sufficient to terminate price agreements in the fibreboard containers and frozen vegetables industries. Thus these agreements went to the Tribunal, which in each case held that they were contrary to the public interest.[30]

In the frozen vegetables matter,[31] ten processors (five of whom accounted for more than 90 per cent of all frozen vegetables produced in Australia) fixed minimum prices and limited discounts. The industry had been rapidly expanding, and unit costs of production were falling, with keen competition causing prices to fall. Then a bumper pea crop led to excessive stocks and a price war, which precipitated the negotiations to fix minimum prices.[32] As with many cartels, the agreement was broken almost immediately by some processors, and breaches continued to occur, even during the Tribunal hearing.

The Tribunal considered ten categories of public benefit put forward by the processors. It accepted as a benefit that the agreement terminated the price war and restored some "sanity" in the industry, but raised the question whether a less offensive agreement could have achieved the same result. The Tribunal did not accept as benefits claims that the agreement provided price stability, allowed for a rational carry-forward of stocks, or encouraged the development of new products. It rejected the argument that the agreement provided any special benefit to growers or distributors, prevented social waste by eliminating price fluctuations, or was necessary to produce a price umbrella to protect small processors from predation by more efficient large rivals. It rejected claims that the agreement was necessary to protect processors from oppression by retail chains, and found that prices fixed by the agreement were higher than would have occurred under free competition. It rejected a claim that prices were reasonable because they were set only at the level which had prevailed in 1964. Since 1964 the unit costs of production had, in fact, fallen. The Tribunal concluded that the anti-competitive detriments of the minimum price agreement outweighed any possible benefits. "Public interest" was interpreted from the consumers' perspective. The Tribunal was unequivocal in its philosophy that most importance had to be accorded to free competition.

The Commissioner may well have won the battle, but in one way he lost the war, as shortly after the Tribunal's decision, some companies in the industry merged, thereby circumventing the price-fixing prohibition. In at least three other industries, mergers similarly occurred after challenges to price-fixing agreements,[33] leading the Commissioner to lament that the 1965 Act, which did not cover mergers at all,

> " ... takes a logically incomplete approach when it leaves such cases free of public interest examination ... it is beyond argument that the merging of competitors, who have previously been parties to restrictive agreements, is the ultimate restriction of competition between them."[34]

The fibreboard containers case of 1973 was different.[35] The producers had agreed to co-operate on the standardization and rationalization of production, in the interest of achieving greater efficiency, but price agreements were tacked on to these accords. The Commissioner argued that these price agreements could hinder standardization and rationalization by relaxing pressure to improve efficiency. The price agreement was only among members of the Australian Fibreboard Container Manufacturers' Association, and not all paperboard converters were members. Competition from non-members had been a restraining factor, at least for some types of container, as was potential competition from other forms of packaging if prices went too high. The Tribunal's main concern was that if a customer got its first price quotation from a high cost supplier, it would be locked in to a high price, as lower cost suppliers were bound by the agreement to charge no less than the first supplier's quoted price. The Tribunal concluded that free competition would reward efficient producers, spurring the search for efficiency and innovation.

This decision led the Commissioner to say, shortly before the 1974 Act began, that price agreements were "very unlikely to be consistent with the public interest",[36] and that it was now apparent that "the climate has changed ... I think business accepts now that price agreements in general must go."[37] It had been a long and winding road in Australia to get to this point, although the task of converting executives to a competitive mindset was still far from over. The 1974 Act, which firmly branded collusive price-fixing as inimical to the public interest, accommodated the Commissioner's wishes. By the time s. 45A was added to the Act in 1977, Australia appeared determined, at least in principle, to eliminate price-fixing for goods, although the paltry maximum penalties of $A250,000 for corporations and $50,000 for individuals did little to deter executives who longed for the good old days.[38] Yet the Tribunal had not completely buried the notion that price-fixing agreements were socially beneficial if instituted to prevent ruinous competition. As we shall see, such attitudes still have not completely disappeared in Australia among some members of the judiciary.

V.2. Tribunal Findings Since 1974

Since the 1977 amendments to the 1974 Act, price-fixing on goods in Australia has been per se illegal. Agreements on prices for services can be authorized, and there exist also the three exceptions to the per se prohibition on price agreements identified earlier. Authorizations which have been granted by the TPC have been concentrated in professional services like architects and consulting engineers, as well as in advertising agencies, road transport, international air transport, motor vehicle repair, real estate, and plumbing, and have related mainly to guideline price scales, with no associated compulsion to charge the guideline price. Agreements on maximum prices for services have been authorized frequently, as have arrangements to assist small service providers, like car repair shops, in determining the appropriate time required to perform certain services.

However, authorization has been denied by the TPC for a number of price agreements on services. Only a few of these denials have been appealed to the Tribunal. In the *Consulting Engineers* case, the Tribunal was asked to authorize a mandatory minimum fee scale established by the Association of Consulting Engineers, together with the Association's ban on fee competition.[39] The Tribunal affirmed the TPC's denial, stating that

> "The Australian community believes that the consequences of competition, including competition on the basis of price, are largely beneficial ... Very powerful reasons indeed would be required before a tribunal such as this would enshrine ... [a] ban on competition on the basis of fees or price."[40]

The Tribunal, however, warned that it did not want to encourage the selection of engineers "more on the basis of fees and less on the basis of merit",[41] as this also could be socially undesirable. Accordingly, it granted authorization for the Association to publish a reference scale of fees, so long as it was clearly indicated that engineers and their clients were free to negotiate fees on any basis.[42]

One of the Tribunal's notable early decisions authorized the Concrete Carters Association (Victoria), a group of truck owner-operators, to jointly negotiate hauling rates with ready-mixed concrete producers.[43] The Tribunal noted the specialized and standardized nature of the trucks used to deliver ready-mixed concrete and that each owner-operator delivered only for one firm. It accepted the wish of owner-operators not to be equated with employees, with the result that they considered it inappropriate to be solely represented in hauling rate negotiations by the Transport Workers Union, an association of employees. It concluded that the concrete delivery market could not be regarded as even moderately competitive and was highly unlikely to become so. Thus, the proposed arrangement would have little adverse effect on competition in the market for hauling concrete, and so the matter of public benefits was irrelevant. Even though there was only a limited possibility of competition between owner-operators as to rates for concrete haulage, this possibility was at least higher than the (zero) probability of competition among company employees who would be represented by the Transport Workers Union in their dealings with firms.[44]

Tribunal hearings are effectively a rehearing of a matter, so that the Tribunal must form its own conclusions on the evidence before it. In doing so over the years, it has established a framework for the economic analysis of competition and public benefit (especially in its deliberations on mergers) which has been followed by the TPC and the courts in their determinations of matters both under ss. 45 and 45A, as well as other sections of the 1974 Act. In relation to authorization of price-fixing for services the Tribunal has stressed the need to keep prices flexible, to avoid high entry barriers and to preserve the competitive process.

V.3. JUDICIAL DETERMINATIONS

V.3.1. Overview of the cases

Given the entrenched attitudes towards price-fixing in Australia, and the legislative determination to stamp it out, at least in markets for goods, it will be somewhat surprising for a non-Australian reader to discover that there have been only twenty horizontal price-fixing cases in Australia since 1974.[45,46] Most cases have involved relatively small firms in local retail markets. Only three cases, either at trial or on appeal, establish important precedent. Only six cases have involved firms which could be described as major Australian corporations. Given the minimally-deterring maximum fine of $250,000 which applied until 1993, and the lack of any real corporate stigma associated with being caught fixing prices, it is surprising that more of these conspiracies have not been uncovered amongst large Australian firms. One possible explanation may be the generally high levels of concentration in Australia, where in many markets only two or three firms dominate production. In such situations, informal agreements, price leadership and "news travels fast" mechanisms might be enough to support an informal industry pricing discipline. The TPC has brought very few cases other than those where formal meetings were held in order to fix prices. It has not persistently attacked parallel pricing and tacit collusion. There are probably three reasons for this: the cost of proceedings in the absence of "smoking gun" evidence; the difficulty of persuading courts to infer price-fixing from circumstantial evidence; and the TPC's loss in an early (poorly presented) case where parallel pricing was the result of a systematic interchange of price lists between the only two Australian suppliers of kilowatt hour meters.[47]

An alternative explanation for the dearth of cases might be that Australian firms have become more competitive in the last twenty years, and have largely eliminated price-fixing from their menus of commercial tactics. Larger firms, in particular, have developed in-house antitrust compliance and education programs. The drive to become more competitive in export markets has pushed Australian firms to a new competitive mindset. Increasing competitive pressures from deregulation and reduced tariff protection have also forced manufacturers to become more effective competitors. The fact that only five price-fixing cases (involving bread, kilowatt hour meters, automotive windshields, liquid glucose and steel products) brought in Australia since 1974 have involved manufacturing industries supports this line of reasoning.

Six cases have involved price-fixing in retail gasoline markets, while two others have involved the wholesale supply of windshields, and one related to an agreement among automotive paint distributors. Thus, almost half the cases have involved various inputs into the operation and maintenance of automobiles – the great majority of whose users are already highly taxed in Australia. The other cases have involved, at the retail level, beer, liquor, barbecue grills, and bed linen; and at the wholesale or manufacturing level, bread,[48] liquid glucose, fruit and vegetables, ready-mixed concrete, steel products, kilowatt hour meters and radio advertising.

Many of the early cases involved lengthy delays as legal challenges slowly ground their way through the courts. It was not until 1979 that the first substantive price-fixing case under the 1974 Act was decided. This is not to suggest that the TPC had been uninvolved in price-fixing matters. Some cases were started quite early but dragged on in preliminary legal skirmishing.[49] The years 1983–1985 were the golden years of price-fixing prosecutions, with seven cases being heard, all of which ultimately resulted in decisions against the defendants, albeit not with substantial penalties.[50] There have been only four cases since 1986. None of these ranks among the major cases, and in two of them the TPC did not prove its case. The small number of recent cases may reflect TPC priorities elsewhere (mergers and misuse of market power), or a decline in violations after two strong price-fixing judgments in 1985 against comparatively large firms in the retailing and ready-mixed concrete markets, or an increasingly sophisticated realisation among those who fix prices that they need to have a plausible commercial justification for their conduct which is judicially acceptable.

V.3.2. Cases won by the TPC

The first price-fixing trial under the 1974 Act occurred in 1978, nearly three years after the agreement at issue was implemented.[51] Like many cases which followed it, the agreement was between relatively small firms (in this case eight merchants operating at the Sydney wholesale fruit and vegetable markets) operating in a narrowly defined market.[52] It was alleged that these companies entered into an understanding to levy farm produce growers with charges for sorting and stacking their produce at the market, in some cases irrespective of whether this work was done. The respondents admitted they had contravened the Act, but they attempted to convince the Court that the agreement was never intended to do more than recognize that economic circumstances warranted each firm independently passing on porterage charges to growers – in other words, that the merchants' behavior "was fully explainable by ordinary commercial considerations".[53] This is the first of many occasions on which this excuse has been offered to a price-fixing charge. Taking all the circumstances into account, including the fact that firms were just learning how to operate under the Act, the judge ordered the defendants each to pay $2500 (which he thought was not a nominal amount) and cease and desist from the agreement.[54]

A theme permeating cases where price fixing occurred after a retail price war is judicial sympathy for the plight of small (and in some cases not-so-small) firms seeking to restore profits to previous levels. These sentiments are especially noticeable in cases relating to price-fixing of gasoline in local retail markets. Discounting of wholesale prices by oil refiners in Australia, together with subsidies provided to meet low prices set by retail independents who own their own sites, has led to chronic intermittent price wars. Thus, for example, in *Culley*,[55] a retail gasoline price war in Perth pushed prices down to the government-approved wholesale price.

At a meeting of about 15 out of 500 Perth retail operators, an informal agreement was made to try to limit discounts to at least two cents above the wholesale price. The two respondents attempted unsuccessfully to persuade another retailer to raise his prices, but took no further action to implement the meeting's decision, and the discount war continued. In fining each respondent a "modest" $500, the judge gave as his reasons

> "... the respondents' conduct was motivated by an understandable desire on their part to achieve a reasonable level of profitability in their businesses without causing harm to the public ... Whilst their conduct was clearly in breach of the Act, it is difficult not to have some sympathy with [them] ... It is a real question whether cut-throat price competition which makes it impossible for retailers to trade economically is in the public interest in the long term, even if there are short term price advantages to consumers."[56]

In a case involving gasoline sales in Adelaide, a meeting of retailers was held with the aim of raising prices after a bout of discounting.[57] Two retailers admitted that they had fixed prices. A third retailer denied the charge, and was found not guilty, despite evidence that he had organized the meeting and had urged his local rivals to raise price, and had organized a higher price to be shown on the price board of another retailer who had not raised his price on the day in question.[58] In setting the penalty, the judge noted that the respondents were small retailers who had followed the lead of some unidentified retailer(s), in the process acting "stupidly but not maliciously ... I have a strong measure of sympathy for them."[59] Counsel for the guilty respondents argued that the judge should follow the principles laid down in *Culley*, but the Court distinguished the case from *Culley*, in which an arrangement had been made, but never implemented. After concluding that the brief rise in prices (discounting broke out again within a few days) occasioned no damage to the public because of the average motorist's mobility and the fact that not all gas stations increased prices, the judge fined the two firms $4000 and $4400, with each owner collecting a personal penalty of $500 and $550 respectively, arguing that "[s]horn of the corporate veils, I am dealing with two young men who are hard workers striving to survive in a very difficult industry... They have admitted their contraventions and that, in my assessment, entitles them to a substantial "discount"."[60]

Similar evidence of judicial compassion for price fixers is found in cases involving Adelaide retailers of barbecue grills, bed linen, and beer, the same judge sitting in each case.[61] Without a doubt, the leading authority on price-fixing is the decision in the beer case, even though one part of the trial court decision was qualified on appeal. In *Nicholas Enterprises*,[62] four Adelaide hotels (bars) were charged with having agreed at an informal luncheon meeting of hoteliers, to reduce the discount on purchases of beer by the dozen, shortly before the peak Christmas period. This was a fortuitous meeting on a social occasion – it had not been planned in order to raise prices. But, given the level of heavy discounting then prevalent, it was natural that talk turned to the problem, and especially to its impact on profits.[63] An executive of the leading discounter had indicated that his hotel would be reducing its discount in two weeks' time. Another hotelier indicated he would go along with this, and subsequently attempted to induce other retailers to do the same, while a third simply said "that's interesting" and a fourth remained silent. While all four raised their prices on the day in question, the latter two operators were found not to have been party to an understanding, as they had not raised any expectations or accepted mutual obligations. One successfully raised the defence that he had driven past rival hotels on the day in question and, having observed from price boards that discounts had fallen, returned to his own hotel and did likewise. The other produced evidence of advertisements prepared prior to the luncheon which indicated that he had planned to reduce discounts. Thus, the Court found that mere parallel action is insufficient if there exists an alternative plausible commercial explanation of the behavior at issue.

In finding the first two hotels guilty, the judge noted that the hotel whose executive made the proposal at the luncheon was the market leader and the largest discounter, and had the most to gain from the arrangement. The other guilty party was a much smaller operator with a local clientele, which did not advertise itself as a discounter of packaged beer. It was difficult to determine the overall impact of the understanding on the market, and it was "easy to envisage other understandings which would be much more pernicious in character and more detrimental to the public interest."[64] With little other discussion, penalties were set at $8,000 and $5,000 respectively, which the judge clearly regarded as significant, saying that the penalty needed to have a deterrent effect. This was the first price-fixing trial of any substance under the Act, and the decision established an important series of precedents for finding that price-fixing had occurred in the absence of direct proof. There has been no basic re-interpretation by the Federal Court of the *Nicholas Enterprises* precedents.

In *Cook-On Gas*,[65] two wholesale suppliers and two retailers of outdoor barbecue equipment sought to end discounting of the Cook-On range by fixing retail prices. Other retailers were invited to contact the wholesaler if they observed further discounting. One retailer had been selling so near cost that other retailers regarded the Cook-On range as unsaleable, limiting its distribution. The respondents claimed the purpose of the agreement was not to increase retailers' profits at the expense of consumers, but rather to ensure that retailers could trade profitably. As no consumers had complained about the increased prices at any time, the judge fined each respondent only $2000.

Heavy discounting of a leading brand of bed linen over a five-month period led to the *David Jones* case.[66] The brand's Adelaide distributor arranged a meeting with several retailers, including national department stores and local specialists, to discuss prices. Shortly thereafter, a price list circulated among retailers, after which retail prices exhibited a uniform 70 per cent markup on the wholesale price. The respondents denied any form of understanding, arguing that the distributor had merely made unilateral exhortations to retailers to lift their prices, the list being designed to provide an aid to retailers to help them calculate retail prices.[67] The judge rejected this reasoning, concluding that an effort to persuade discounters to increase their prices would be ineffective without some form of understanding among the large retailers. Using the methodology developed in *Nicholas Enterprises*, he found that the respondents had both the incentive and opportunity for a meeting of minds on the need to raise prices. While the evidence was circumstantial, the respondents' failure to explain their conduct on oath as a reasonable business practice hurt them. Drawing on language from *Coal Vend*,[68] Judge Fisher found that

> "... these acts exhibit such a concurrence of "time, character, direction and result" that they, taken in conjunction with the meeting and the circumstances in which it was held, encourage the drawing of the inference that the acts were "the outcome of pre-concert"."[69]

The two national retailers were fined $15,000 each, the distributor and a smaller local retailer were fined $6,000 each, and five executives each were ordered to pay $1,000. As in *Cook-On Gas*, the judge thought that the circumstances of the case were exceptional – only three retailers were involved out of a much larger number of bed linen retailers, two large firms were not party to the agreement, and the national retailers continued to compete with each other, notwithstanding the agreement, although consumers had lost the capacity to buy bed linen at exceptionally low prices from the respondents. However, the retailers' conduct had been neither "flagrant nor a deliberate breach of the Act but rather very careless conduct" by executives who were not aware that what they had done was in breach of the Act.[70]

Not long after *Nicholas Enterprises*, the TPC received inside information on price-fixing in the liquid glucose industry. In *Allied Mills*,[71] which involved the five leading Australian flour milling firms, a new entrant had sparked a series of deep price cuts. Futile attempts had been made to lead prices back up. After a few months during which liquid glucose customers experienced almost daily offers of lower prices, there came an abrupt end to the low prices. Substantial price increases (from about $225 to $275 per ton, the approximate price level before the new entrant appeared) took place almost simultaneously, with suppliers quoting on a "take it or leave it" basis. An employee of the largest firm gave evidence that he had been instructed to raise prices as a result of an agreement. The judge found that there were no ordinary commercial explanations for the simultaneous increases, such as price leadership or common input cost increases, and that the evidence was capable of establishing that the respondents were parties to a price-fixing arrangement. During the main trial, the new entrant withdrew its defense and agreed to pay a penalty of $50,000.[72] This turn of events provoked the other respondents to withdraw their defenses too. They faced a judge who believed in equality of treatment – each was fined $50,000,[73] despite considerable differences in corporate size and degree of involvement in the agreement. Thus, a strong precedent was set for leniency for large, profitable Australian firms which fix prices.

In four other price-fixing cases the respondents all pleaded guilty, and so the Court's only task was to set the penalty. In *Tubemakers*,[74] a leading steel fabricator attempted to induce its subsidiary distributor and other steel merchants to reduce discounts. The two executives who had attempted the conspiracy (only one was charged – the other had brought the matter to the attention of the TPC) were reacting to a Tubemakers admonition to its subsidiary to improve profits. The modest corporate penalties of $15,000 and $10,000 were based on the fact that the respondents had a policy of educating executives on trade practices issues, that senior executives were unaware of the conduct, and that no loss or damage had occurred, as it was an unsuccessful attempt at price-fixing with little prospect of success.[75]

Pioneer Concrete was a classic price-fix between the five major producers (their combined market share was about 90 per cent) of ready-mixed concrete in Melbourne.[76] A severe price war (following entry by several new firms) saw prices drop from $40 a cubic meter to $28 over a three month period. Meetings were then convened to try to end to the price war. It was agreed to increase prices up to a range of $41 to $51, and a common pricing formula was adopted. When the plan was implemented, a smaller competitor complained to the TPC, and subsequently the respondents all admitted the agreement. In fixing penalties close to $50,000 for each firm, the judge took into account that the price-fixing occurred after a war which had driven price below costs, that the increases resulted either in only reduced losses or a modest profit, that the respondents co-operated with the TPC and admitted the facts, that steps had been taken to prevent further contraventions and that no customers had complained. He noted the multiplier effect of increased concrete prices, however, and that senior executives were involved in the conspiracy. Yet, allowing for inflation, the penalties were less than those imposed under similar circumstances in *Allied Mills*.

Australian Autoglass has facts similar to *Pioneer Concrete*.[77] Five respondents collectively held about 90 per cent of the Australian motor vehicle replacement windshield market. Regular meetings took place among these manufacturers, as, with about 3,000 windshields on the market, all suppliers had to rely on their rivals for windshield types which they themselves did not make. A price war in southern Queensland led to an agreement to limit discounts offered to body shops, car yards and the like in both southern Queensland and Melbourne. The arrangements apparently had no significant, lasting, commercial effect. The judge found that there was great scope for harm to the public interest in a situation where the three major suppliers held most of the market, and where there were no alternative suppliers of most windshields. However, the attempted conspiracy had met with little success, in the judge's view probably because "the forces of competition proved too strong".[78] The respondents had co-operated with the TPC and had given assurances as to their future good conduct. Yet the contraventions were serious, having been maintained deliberately by senior executives. The judge used *Pioneer Concrete* as the basis for setting penalties, making allowances for inflation and the market shares of each of the three main respondents. The two largest respondents paid a penalty of $65,000, still the largest penalty for price-fixing in Australia; the other two were fined $40,000 and $25,000.

Two years later the TPC successfully charged 12 Melbourne automotive paint distributors with price fixing in *Patterson Cheney*.[79] Following a price war in which prices had fallen to cost, the respondents met and formed a Paint Distributors Advisory Council in an attempt to ensure that members adhered to a recommended price list produced by Dulux, a major paint supplier. To ensure compliance, a $500 membership bond was paid by each member. But by the third meeting of the group, some three months later, discounting was rife again and the PDAC had been unable to curtail it. When charged by the TPC, all the firms admitted having violated the Act. In assessing corporate penalties from $1,000 to $5,000, the judge found that there had been no loss or damage caused by the agreement, especially in view of the fact that many automotive paint suppliers had not been parties to the agreement. He characterized the third meeting of the PDAC as illustrating "the Keystone Cops quality of the whole ill-conceived and amateurishly executed understanding or arrangement",[80] saying it was "bound to fail". The product was only a small part of the business of most of the respondents, and the executives involved were low in the managerial hierarchy.

V.3.3. Penalties

Of the 18 cases initiated by the TPC, it succeeded in 13 against all respondents, and in two others against most of the respondents. It lost outright in only three cases. In 11 of the successful cases all or some of the respondents agreed to the facts. Of the eight cases where at least one respondent denied price-fixing, the TPC was successful against all defendants in three and against at least some of them in two others. Only five trial Court decisions on liability have been appealed, including the two private price-fixing actions. In only one appeal was the original decision overturned, in favor of the TPC. By all accounts, therefore, the TPC's success rate is good. It has lost only one major price-fixing case.

Despite the TPC's success on liability, there has been a judicial reluctance to assess penalties anywhere near the allowable maximum. The highest individual monetary penalty set so far has been only $65,000, in *Australian Autoglass*. Of course, those found guilty of price-fixing had heavy attorney and court costs to meet in many cases, but the fact remains that Australian judges seem unwilling to issue severe fines, being especially sympathetic to colluders who have sought to raise prices after prolonged price wars. Rational business executives, taking this as a guide, may well have concluded that it is not unwise to begin or continue fixing prices with rivals, as the expected present value of the benefits from such conduct has likely outweighed the expected cost of being detected, taken to court, found guilty and receiving a modest fine.

Monetary penalties have been assessed in twelve cases prosecuted by the TPC. The nominal total dollar value collected is a mere $865,950. In five cases individual executives were charged as well as corporations, but the *total* of their assessed penalties was but $10,550, for an average of $754 – not even a slap on the wrist, despite judicial rhetoric to the contrary. The average corporate penalty over all cases was $16,773, also trivial.[81] All but two cases involved price-fixing in local markets. In markets where price-fixing had implications for more than one state of Australia (involving liquid glucose and automotive windshields), and which involved only manufacturers, the average penalties were much higher – $50,000 per firm in the glucose case, and $48,750 for windshields. In addition, the firms involved in these two cases were larger than the typical respondent in most other cases. It remains to be seen whether the new $10 million maximum penalty will induce judges to raise their fines. Considering the number of occasions when guilt has been admitted, and the fact that the earlier maximum of $250,000 was never a binding constraint, one would have to be pessimistic about price-fixers receiving tough treatment.[82]

Because the fines for price-fixing convictions have been relatively low, especially in view of the fact that the respondents confessed in so many cases, it is instructive to consider the Act's guidance regarding monetary penalties. According to s. 76(1), if a contravention has been proved, then the penalty shall be set at a level which

> " ... the Court determines to be appropriate having regard to all relevant matters including the nature and extent of the act or omission and of any loss or damage suffered as a result of the act or omission, the circumstances in which the act or omission took place and whether the person has previously been found by the Court in proceedings under this Part to have engaged in any similar conduct."

From this guide, judges have deduced a number of more specific criteria to use in their assessment of an appropriate dollar penalty. They can be categorised as follows:

1. *Market circumstances*
   * Industry profitability when the contravention occurred, especially if a price war existed.
   * Whether the conduct was "very much out of the ordinary".
   * Whether the firms involved were the only traders in the market, and their market share.
2. *Firm motives*
   * Whether the agreement was flagrant or deliberate, or rather just careless conduct.
3. *Corporate and personal characteristics*
   * The size and financial strength of the firms.
   * The financial circumstances of individuals.

4. *Managerial seniority, involvement, and personal gain*
   * The level of management at which the agreement was orchestrated.
   * Whether individuals stood to gain personally.
   * Whether individuals are still employed by the firm, and their future employment prospects.
5. *Method of implementation and enforcement*
   * Aggressiveness in arranging the agreement, and potential gain from the conduct.
   * Who was the ring leader, and whether any pressure was brought to bear on others to gain their co-operation.
   * Whether the agreement was implemented or not, and its degree of success.
   * Whether there were defections from the agreement.
6. *Impact*
   * Whether any significant or lasting loss or damage was suffered by anyone.
   * Whether there was any potential harm to the general public or the public interest.
   * The duration of the conduct.
7. *Method of discovery*
   * Whether the TPC learned of the agreement from complaints by consumers.
8. *Co-operation with the TPC's investigation*
   * Whether the contraventions were admitted, and the extent of co-operation given to the TPC.
9. *Steps taken to prevent future breaches*
   * Whether corporate education programs have been implemented to ensure future knowledge of and compliance with the Act.
10. *Previous conduct and institutional considerations*
   * Recidivism.
   * The extent of bad publicity relating to the case.
   * Equality with penalty levels in other cases, adjusted for the effects of inflation.
   * The need to deter the respondents and others from repeating such conduct.
   * Whether the parties have accepted restraining orders and injunctions.
   * The level of costs to be paid.
   * The degree of corporate and personal contrition and regret.

There is no American counterpart to this list of factors, given the more prominent role played by prison terms in the US, and the fact that fine levels generally are not argued in American price-fixing cases.

V.3.4. Cases lost by the TPC

In *Leslievale*,[83] the TPC alleged that gasoline retailers and a local representative of a major oil refining firm in a city in Queensland met to fix the retail price of gasoline. While the Court found that such a meeting with the purpose of curtailing price cutting had taken place, there was doubt whether mutual obligations had been entered into, or a sufficient meeting of minds had occurred, to create an agreement. One retailer pledged to sell three cents below what other operators thought was an acceptable price. The Court concluded that it would have made little commercial sense for other sellers to have sold at the suggested price level.

The TPC brought action in the *Service Station Association* case against the Association and its president and executive officer for attempting to induce Sydney gasoline retailers to fix prices.[84] It lost both at trial and on appeal.[85] Profits from gasoline retailing had sunk to a very low level, provoking the SSA to launch a campaign urging retailers to focus on price, and hence profit, rather than on volume. The president of the SSA initiated the message at a meeting of 200 of the Association's 1100 members, and repeated it at some 25 local area meetings. After the first meeting, retail prices rose sharply, compounded by the effects of the Iraqi invasion of Kuwait. The Court was not persuaded that the Act had been breached, however, finding that the SSA instead had promoted the idea that retailers, *as individual traders*, should raise prices in order to become more profitable. Rather than encouraging dealers to fix gasoline prices, the SSA's activities had emphasized the need to compete, and for retailers to make independent decisions on price, volume, service etc, noting that higher prices would naturally be accompanied by lower volume. The recommended retail prices published by the SSA were just recommendations carrying no express or implied obligation. Many dealers did not, in fact, follow the recommended price, indicating that there had been no prior agreement on prices. The judge noted also the mobility of motorists, who could move their purchases in response to small price differentials, and so a price-fixing arrangement would need to cover a very wide geographical area to be effective. To the extent that prices were uniform, there remained alternative plausible explanations, especially recommended retail prices. There was no evidence of mutual promises or undertakings between dealers, or expectations raised and obligations accepted.

It is difficult to argue with this part of the decision. But the judge also concluded that the SSA's urging for dealers to increase margins by the order of 10 per cent lacked "the degree of certainty inherent in the concept of fixing, controlling or maintaining prices".[86] Surely *any* non-incidental arrangement on prices, or on margins, even if it does allow some tolerance, breaches the Act, especially where the breach alleged is a per se one. The effect on retail gasoline prices would hardly have been incidental.[87] After all, the Court had found in *Australian Autoglass* that agreements among rivals setting maximum discount prices which did not require adherence to the maximum were illegal.[88] The Full Bench, however, dismissed the TPC's appeals. It concluded that the SSA's intentions were legal – namely to persuade dealers to examine their individual businesses and to charge a profitable price. It expressed no concern with the trial court's conclusion that ambiguity about the price level implies the absence of fixing or controlling prices. The Full Bench reiterated the trial court's conclusion that the precise price influences consumer behavior in the retail gasoline market, concluding that an agreed-to, vague margin would be of little use to sellers in such a market, as small differences in price could influence at which retail outlet a motorist would buy gasoline.

Perhaps the most controversial Australian price-fixing case has been *Email*,[89] involving the only two Australian suppliers (imports were minimal) of kilowatt hour meters.[90] About 98 percent of all meters were sold to state electricity supply authorities (all of whom bought through a sealed bid tender system, although some made public the prices paid), whose preferred position was that there be two suppliers, even though there was no evidence that the existence of Warburton Franki led to any real price competition. Both manufacturers believed that Email, with about a 70 per cent share of sales, was the low cost market leader. Both respondents regularly issued and exchanged identical price lists; they submitted identical tenders (always in accordance with their respective price lists) to the supply authorities; and they adopted the same price variation clause. Because of the greater size and efficiency of Email, there was a belief on its part that if it priced too close to its costs, it would drive Warburton Franki from the market and could perhaps find itself in breach of s. 46 of the Act which prohibited the misuse of market power (at the time s. 46 of the Act had not been tested in court). There was no direct evidence of communication between the two firms; the TPC relied on the circumstantial evidence of parallel pricing and exchange of price lists to infer an understanding between them. It accepted that Email was a non-collusive price leader. But the TPC argued that the offensive conduct – the exchange of price lists – exceeded independent price leadership.

Email is one of the three major Australian cases identifying criteria sufficient to sustain a charge of price-fixing. The TPC argued that price list exchanges constituted sufficient communication to infer a meeting of minds, and that these exchanges led to mutual expectations that each firm would accept limits on its pricing freedom. The judge, finding in favor of the respondents, argued that the history and nature of the industry could alternately explain the common pricing structures. It was a matter of commercial necessity, recognized by both firms, for Warburton Franki to follow Email. If it tried to price according to its own costs, its product would be priced above that of its rival, and it would be financial suicide for it to charge a lower price. Foremost in the decision was the fact that the exchange of price lists was done "unilaterally for sound commercial reasons".[91] This practice did nothing that was not available through normal market information-gathering processes – the only effect was to speed up the receipt of the information (and indeed there was evidence that Warburton Franki monitored Email's prices by means other than the receipt of the price lists, as it did not altogether trust it).[92] The rivals were under no obligation to do anything upon receipt of the lists. While they may have hoped and predicted that their actions would lead to identical prices, the Court was unwilling to infer that they expected such prices and that each was bound to adopt them. There could be no offense if Warburton Franki chose to accept Email as the price leader. While the course of conduct clearly led to each party forming firm expectations as to how the other would behave, no commitment was established. The judge noted that there was "no point in an arrangement bare of reciprocity",[93] as presumably an arrangement would be concluded only if each party would thereby achieve "some commercial objective beneficial to itself".[94] There was no obligation for Warburton Franki to follow Email's prices, although the judge found that Email was confident that it would in fact follow. But as there were no formalities in the exchange, there was no legal arrangement. Yet, in acknowledging that Email stood to benefit by Warburton Franki's following, the judge acknowledged the commercial advantages stemming from the exchange of lists.

While it is true that no formal commitment was established between the two firms, in a market with the structural features of this one, there was hardly any need for a commitment to be communicated to obtain the necessary meeting of minds.[95] If parallel conduct can be characterized as a "conscious commitment to a common scheme",[96] then surely repeated matching of a rival's price when costs differ indicates that a firm has made a conscious commitment to follow it in a common scheme. Yet the judge looked in vain for something more, some component of a joint commercial decision to push parallel conduct into the realm of an illegal arrangement. He did not, however, believe that parallel conduct could never constitute circumstantial evidence from which an arrangement could be inferred – it simply depended on the facts of the case, such that if "a credible explanation is given by a defendant it may be sufficient to negate the inference of an arrangement or understanding".[97] In saying this, he referred to several US cases which provided "powerful authority" for the proposition that parallel conduct by itself cannot support an allegation of conspiracy, for this could be the result of independent commercial decisions made by competitors in the market.[98]

Yet the reasoning of Judge Lockhart stands in stark contrast to the position of the US courts, where the single most important facilitating practice found in collusion cases has been bilateral information exchanges among rivals or price data and pricing formulae exchanges through trade associations.[99] From a practical viewpoint, no Australian firm should conclude from *Email* that it would be wise to send price lists to a rival, for these reasons:

* the judge's observations on mutuality stand in contrast to the obiter dicta of the Full Court in *Morphett Arms* (see below);

* the judge's inability to grasp why a firm would act in a certain way without reciprocation is answered by the very facts of the case;

* it would be a dubious competition law which justified an exchange of price lists if the parties did so for "sound commercial reasons" as firms likely enter into restrictive arrangements on this basis.

V.3.5. A private price-fixing action

In *Radio 2UE*,[100] heard also by Judge Lockhart, two new FM radio stations joined marketing forces to produce a combined rate card for advertisers, in order more effectively to promote themselves against their entrenched AM rivals. While their rates were jointly advertised in this manner, they were independently determined by each station (one station's rates being higher than the other's), and each station also had its own individual rate card. In addition, the published rates on the individual cards were only a benchmark, from which discounts were negotiated by advertisers. By the date of the hearing, no discounts had been given for business done through the combined card, but little business had in fact been done through the combined card at all. Radio 2UE, a major AM station, alleged price-fixing under s. 45A.

The Court found none of the essential ingredients of price-fixing present, because each FM station determined its own prices independently of the other. Indeed, the Court concluded that the conduct of the entrants actually promoted competition between them and the AM stations. The controversial part of the judgment was contained in the judge's *obiter dicta* on s. 45A. He noted that it was important for the Court "to distinguish between arrangements ... which restrain price competition and arrangements which merely incidentally affect it or have some connection with it. Not every arrangement between competitors which has some possible impact on price is per se unlawful under the section".[101] He then suggested that s. 45A might only apply to arrangements which *directly* affect price. Yet by proscribing arrangements which have the purpose, effect or likely effect of fixing, controlling or maintaining prices, however, the section clearly catches *any* arrangement which has even an incidental effect on price. The judge also argued that

> "sec. 45A [was not] introduced by Parliament to make arrangements unlawful which affect price by improving competition. It is fundamental to both sec. 45A and 45 that the relevant conduct, in purpose or effect, substantially lessens competition or would be likely to do so. If competition is improved by an arrangement I cannot perceive how it could be characterised as a price fixing arrangement within the ambit of those sections."[102]

One cannot fault the actual decision in the case, as the action of the two FM stations did appear to promote competition in the market, but this dicta clearly is inconsistent with a per se treatment of price-fixing.[103] Section 45A clearly and unambiguously deems price-fixing to lessen competition substantially even if any one instance of it happens on balance to be pro-competitive.[104] Such occasional problems are an acknowledged possibility of a per se rule.

The Full Federal Court dismissed 2UE's appeal, on the grounds that the two FM stations were free to change their own individual prices at any time. All the combined rate card offered was convenience, and did not constitute an arrangement under the Act. In coming to this conclusion, the Full Court found that:

> "... not every determination of a price, following discussion between competitors, will amount to a price "fixing". There must ... be an element of intention or likelihood to affect price competition before price "fixing" can be established. This will often be a matter of inference ..."[105]

It declined to comment on Judge Lockhart's suggestion that a price-fixing arrangement which can be shown to have a net advantageous effect on competition cannot be in breach of s. 45 of the Act. It elected to confront the issue "if and when it directly arises for determination."[106] The question has not yet resurfaced.

V.3.6. The economic characteristics of markets involved in price-fixing cases

We turn now to examine whether, collectively or individually, the markets and firms involved in price-fixing in Australia conform to the characteristics which economists have identified as associated with collusive markets. The assessment is displayed in Table 1, for those 16 situations where the case was tried and the courts gave reasons for their decisions.[107]

Some cases fit neatly into the taxonomy of characteristics of collusive markets, while others do not. Price-fixing has occurred in markets where products are homogeneous, demand is inelastic, industry associations promote commercial and social intercourse, fixed costs loom large, buyer concentration is low, orders are small and frequent, sealed tender bids are not usual, technology is stable, and frequently a price war has wreaked havoc on profitability. Yet collusion has largely (but not exclusively) occurred where the transaction costs of sustaining the agreement were high, firm sizes were quite disparate, entry barriers were of no real consequence, and absent the participation of all sellers in the relevant market.

V.4. The Australian Principles

What principles have Australian courts used to decide whether an alleged price-fixing agreement breaches the 1974 Act? Only a few decisions have had to develop such principles, given that most cases have involved admissions. The cases which have created authority are *Nicholas Enterprises*, *Email*, and *Radio 2UE*, together with *Coal Vend* from Australia's antitrust past. What emerges from judicial reasoning is that a price-fixing arrangement does not have to be permanent or of any specific duration to contravene the Act, and the form of the arrangement is not relevant – it is the purpose or the effect which matters. The economic circumstances under which the breach took place seem only to affect the penalty.

The necessary conditions for an arrangement can be traced back to *Coal Vend*, where Judge Isaacs stated that

> "Community of purpose may be proved by independent facts, but it need not be. If the other defendant is shown to be committing other acts, tending to the same end, then though primarily each set of acts is attributable to the person whose acts they are, and to him alone, there may be such a concurrence

Table I. Economic characteristics of collusive industries

Case	Product	No. of firms in industry*	Size similarity	Entry barriers	Inelastic demand	Homo-geneous product	Demand growth	Technogical change	Buyer concen-tration	Order frequency	Sealed tenders	Fixed/ variable cost	Manage-ment stakes	Facilitating practices
Court found collusion														
Bryant	produce	many; 8	U	U	Y	Y	U	L	L	H	N	U	Y	Y
Nicholas	beer	526; 5	D	L	Y	Y(G)	U	L	L	H	N	H	Y	Y
Allied Mills	glucose	5	D	H	Y	Y	L	L	L	H	N	H	N	Y
Cully	gasoline	500; 2	D	L	Y	Y(G)	U	L	L	H	N	H	Y	Y
Tubemakers	steel products	many; 1	U	L	Y	Y	L	U	L	H	N	U	N	Y
David Jones	bed linen	>7; 3	D	L	Y	Y	U	L	L	H	N	H	Y/N	N[†]
Parkfield	gasoline	> 8; 2	D	L	Y	Y	U	L	L	H	N	H	Y	N[†]
Cook-on Gas	barbecue grills	many; 2	D	L	U	N	U	U	L	H	N	U	U	N[†]
Pioneer	ready mixed concrete	>5; 5	D	L	Y	Y	U	L	L	H	U	H	N	N[†]
Autoglass	automotive windshields	5; 3	D	L	Y	Y	U	U	L	H	U	U	U	Y
Patterson Cheney	automotive paint	>35; 12	D	L	Y	N	U	U	L	N	N	U	Y/N	N[†]
Russell	gasoline	many; 2	D	L	Y	Y(G)	U	L	L	H	N	H	Y	Y
Court found no collusion														
Email	meters	2	D	H	Y	Y	U	L	H	L	Y	H	N	Y
2UE	radio advertising	many; 2	D	H	U	N	U	U	L	L	N	U	N	Y
Leslievale	gasoline	many; 4	D	L	Y	Y(G)	U	L	L	L	N	H	Y	Y
SSA	gasoline	1100; 3	D	L	Y	Y(G)	U	L	L	H	N	H	Y	N[†]

D = diverse; G = differentiated by location; H = high; L = low; N = no; U = unknown from the judgment; Y = yes; na = not applicable

* If two numbers appear in this column, the first represents the number of firms in the industry, the second the number of firms charged with collusion

† In these cases there occurred a one-off meeting(s) specifically to deal with the problem of a price war.

> of time, character, direction and result as naturally to lead to the inference that these separate acts were the outcome of pre-concert, or some mutual contemporaneous engagement ..."[108]

The words "contract, arrangement or understanding" are not defined in the Act. It is clear, however, that the word contract takes its normal meaning of an agreement enforceable at law, while the other two terms are meant to cover informal alternatives to a legally binding agreement. But as in *Tubemakers*,[109] a number of Australian decisions have treated the terms arrangement and understanding as synonymous.[110] Judge Fisher provided a clear statement, and leading authority, of what constitutes an understanding (the term he used) in *Nicholas Enterprises*. An understanding is something in which the parties to it accept mutual rights and obligations. A necessary element is communication and an expectation being aroused therefrom by each party about future actions of the others.[111] In his words, the essential elements of an understanding are:

> "... the necessity for each of the parties to have communicated with the other, for each to have raised an expectation in the mind of the other, and for each to have accepted an obligation qua the other."[112]

Judge Fisher saw mutual obligations as the essential feature of an understanding. He thought it possible to infer an understanding from circumstantial evidence,[113] but cautioned against automatically drawing the inference, as "it is frequently possible for another explanation of the facts to be given in evidence, for example that the [conduct in question] was dictated not by commitment to an understanding but by ordinary commercial considerations".[114] This view is similar to US doctrine, as evidenced by the Supreme Court's *Matsushita* decision, where it emphasized that:

> "... conduct as consistent with permissible competition as with illegal conspiracy does not, standing alone, support an inference of antitrust conspiracy ... a plaintiff ... must present evidence that "tends to exclude the possibility" that the alleged conspirators acted independently",[115]

and also its decision in *Monsanto*, where it stated that:

> "... there must be direct or circumstantial evidence that reasonably tends to prove that [the parties] had a conscious commitment to a common scheme designed to achieve an unlawful objective."[116]

The US position is that circumstantial evidence can support a finding that the alleged conspiracy is more probable than innocent alternatives. But if the challenged behavior has a plausible alternative explanation congruent with self-interest, or if an inference of conspiracy might result in deterring otherwise pro-competitive conduct, circumstantial evidence is insufficient to infer conspiracy. US courts tend to infer conspiracy from behavior which, unless implemented jointly, would have damaged the defendants' commercial interests, such as increasing prices when demand has been falling.[117]

In *Nicholas Enterprises*, Judge Fisher found that commitment can be communicated by means other than a verbal response. But there could not be an understanding between two parties unless each aroused in the other an expectation. What was necessary was:

> "... for the adoption of the proposal to be made known in some way to the proposer, otherwise the latter will be unaware whether an understanding has been achieved. Until the proposer becomes aware, I do not see how any expectation can in the ordinary course be raised in his mind as to how the adopter will act. I exclude of course the situation in which pre-existing circumstances such as price leadership or interdependence are such that the proposer has some grounds for assuming that once he proposes, his proposal will be adopted unless he is notified to the contrary".[118]

On appeal from one of the respondents (the *Morphett Arms* decision), Chief Justice Bowen of the Federal Court qualified Judge Fisher's findings as follows:

> "... it seems to me that one could have an understanding between two or more persons restricted to the conduct which one of them will pursue without any element of mutual obligation, insofar as the other party or parties to the understanding are concerned."[119]

In deciding *Email*, Judge Lockhart endorsed the *Nicholas Enterprises* precedent as follows:

> "[f]or there to be an arrangement or understanding there must be a meeting of the minds of those said to be parties to the arrangement or understanding. In some cases this may be inferred from circumstantial evidence. There must be a consensus as to what is to be done and not just a mere hope as to what might be done or happen. Independently held beliefs are not enough."[120]

He also endorsed the finding by the Full Federal Court in *Morphett Arms*, leaning

> "... to the view that there is no necessity for an element of mutual commitment between the parties to an arrangement or understanding such that each accepts an obligation qua the other; although in practice such cases would be rare ... For my part [however] I find it difficult to envisage circumstances where there would be an understanding involving a commitment by one party as to the way he should behave without some commitment by the other party. Unless there is reciprocity of commitment I do not readily see why the parties would come to an arrangement or understanding."[121]

No case has arisen since *Morphett Arms* which has necessitated a reconsideration of the Full Bench's qualification. Thus the question of whether it takes two to tango in Australian price-fixing in effect remains unanswered.

VI. Evaluation and Issues for Reform

In terms of enforcement, it would appear that the TPC can only expect to win price-fixing cases, in the absence of admissions, where it is in possession of direct, "smoking gun" evidence, or where, when only circumstantial evidence is available, it is so "overwhelming" and inconsistent with an alternative explanation based on independent commercial considerations as to permit an inference of an understanding to be drawn. The Court has established that proof of collusion requires communication among the parties and expectations raised, but mutuality of obligation appears not to be necessary for at least one party to be found guilty of price-fixing. However, conclusions about Australian price-fixing principles must be tempered by the fact that most of the cases have involved admissions, and so a wide range of possible price-fixing scenarios has not yet been considered. In addition, there have been few cases in recent years – and there can be no doubt that the economic sophistication of judges is improving, as they grapple with complex issues relating to the misuse of market power under s. 46 of the Act.

To date, the Australian judiciary has been less than harsh towards price-fixing, despite its stated disapproval of the practice and its frequent recognition of the need to punish in accordance with the will of Parliament and to direct future business behavior. This attitude is illustrated in the comments of Judge Sheppard in the course of the *Allied Mills* trial:

> "One can imagine some very serious situations that could arise with cut-throat competition where you do really need somebody to blow the whistle ... and let everybody start off again, otherwise you might really do a great deal of harm rather than any good ... it just seems to me that to proceed upon the basis that all competition is good is not necessarily an appropriate way to look at things."[122]

While these comments occurred during trial, and did not feature in the judgment, they nevertheless illustrate the feelings of many judges towards firms caught in price wars.[123]

While one might therefore describe the success of the Act against price fixing as encouraging, but incomplete, the problem of finding a suitable methodology for proving the existence of an arrangement between firms in the presence of only circumstantial evidence remains unsolved. Because Australian courts have not had to consider many cases of this kind, they have not yet developed a structured analysis of cartel situations as is increasingly being used in the US, where firm and market characteristics are evaluated in terms of how they assist in overcoming the problems inherent in forming and maintaining a collusive arrangement. Such an approach would consider factors (which, if observed in conjunction with parallel pricing, could indicate a price-fixing arrangement), such as:

> "a. proof that the rivals had the opportunity for direct communication, or that they in fact communicated directly;
> b. evidence of anticompetitive intent behind the parallel conduct;
> c. behavior difficult to imagine as arising in the absence of detailed communication, because it appears arbitrary or unusually complex; or

d. behavior difficult to understand as rational in the absence of an agreement, including the absence of a legitimate justification for the practice." (Baker, 1993, pp.176–177).

Debate still exits in the US as to whether conscious parallelism permits an inference of conspiracy. The majority opinion appears to be that it does not, without more, in the form of extra evidence of conscious joint action by the parties. A demonstrated opportunity to conspire is insufficient, even if the evidence indicates meetings occurred where agreements could have been formed. However, if the evidence demonstrates that the meetings were held in secret, or that subsequent to a meeting all firms changed their conduct in an identical manner, or that a direct information exchange occurred such that the court could reasonably conclude that an arrangement as to future conduct had taken place, then the courts have been willing to accept that such communication involved an illegal arrangement.[124]

In Australia there is still no direct authority as to whether price leadership in the absence of agreement between rivals breaches s. 45. Hurley (1991, p. 116) submits that the decision in *Email* should not be taken to indicate that the courts will treat non-collusive price leadership as escaping this section. As she points out, in *Allied Mills*, before all the respondents withdrew their defenses, Judge Sheppard rejected price leadership reasons advanced to explain parallel price movements.[125] While this of course does not represent a final view of the Court, it does suggest that explanations of co-ordinated prices based on price leadership must be accompanied by credible evidence in order to succeed. In other words, while parallel behavior by itself may be insufficient to establish an arrangement or understanding under the Act, it may provide strong evidence of such conduct if it leads to abnormal patterns of behavior. But the evidentiary burden is high, requiring a full analysis of market competition and identification of a benchmark against which to compare the conduct at issue.

The question which is increasingly being asked in US antitrust cases, but which has not yet been addressed formally in Australia, is whether there exists a rational motive for the respondents to behave collectively, given that the market in question is characterized by behavioral interdependence.[126] In particular, it is necessary to focus on behavior which, *unless undertaken jointly*, would have damaged the individual position of each defendant. If the industry's economic environment is not suitable for joint action, then firms would be irrational to collude. Thus an agreement is unlikely to occur and it would not make economic sense to infer otherwise. If observed behavior is consistent with what firms could do by acting independently, it would be irrational for them to collude and risk antitrust prosecutions (assuming, of course, that rational action and knowledge of antitrust laws is a feature of *all* the decision makers in a firm, no matter what their position in the managerial hierarchy). If the market is conducive to concerted action, firms may establish what are called focal (self-evident) rules to fix prices without engaging in any formal arrangement. If under such circumstances no agreement is necessary for firms to achieve the observed outcome, then it would be irrational for them to agree, when the focal rule results in effective joint action without taking the risks associated with formal communication.

Australian antitrust has learned much in two decades. But, like any young adult, it has experienced growing pains. Although the learning process never stops, as antitrust policy and enforcement enters adulthood in Australia, it should be able to develop its own unique jurisprudence on price-fixing. With an increasingly sophisticated understanding of economics and with a newly enlarged arsenal of monetary penalties at its disposal, the judiciary may feel confident in the future to hit price-fixers in a manner commensurate with the damage which they do to social welfare.

Notes

* We are grateful to Rod Williams for his helpful comments on an earlier draft of this paper.
[1] As Stalley (1958, p. 259) put it, if the 1913 decision had found against the respondents, "Australia may well have entered a period of anti-monopoly enforcement not unlike that of the United States. There would have been a profound effect on business and political thinking, and the community as a whole would have been forced to face the problem of social policy towards monopoly with a much greater awareness of the issues involved."
[2] Comparatively few accounts exist, by either lawyers or economists, of Australia's antitrust history. For brief treatments of early legislation and cases, see Donald and Heydon (1978), Nieuwenhuysen (1970, 1976), Nieuwenhuysen and Norman (1976), Richardson (1967), Taperell, Vermeesch and Harland (1983) and Walker (1967).
[3] *U.S. v. Trans-Missouri Freight Association*, 166 U.S. 290 (1897).
[4] A prohibition on conspiracies in restraint of trade has not been without exception in the U.S., as exemptions periodically have been made for industries such as airlines, motor freight transportation, milk, sports leagues, and export associations.
[5] *U.S. v. United States Gypsum Company, et al.*, 438 U.S. 422 (1978).
[6] *American Society of Composers, Authors and Publishers, et al. v. Columbia Broadcasting System, et al.*, 441 U.S. 1 (1979).
[7] See Hay and Kelley (1974) for discussion of these factors.
[8] Ginsburg (1993, pp. 99–100) argues that there are two market contexts in which any opportunity for non-price competition is absent – in auction markets, and where sellers allocate customers or territories among themselves. He also points out, at p. 105, that as any agreement proceeds beyond price to cover non-price areas, the probability that it will be detected increases, as a result of either intentional or inadvertent exposure.
[9] The penalty for an infringement was five hundred pounds. In 1910 Section 4 was amended to include a prohibition on contracts or combinations which were actually in restraint of trade or commerce (and not just those done with such intent), or which actually destroyed or injured any Australian industry.
[10] Pengilley (1983, pp. 903–908 and 911–912) provides a brief evaluation of the success of this Act.
[11] Failure to register a restrictive agreement involved a maximum penalty of only $A2,000. No sanctions applied if a firm, after having voluntarily agreed after consultations on a restrictive practice with the Commissioner to behave in a certain manner, then failed to behave accordingly.
[12] For discussion of the benefits of a registration system, see Pengilley (1983, pp. 898–900).
[13] The Commissioner was able to convince those involved in hundreds of other similar agreements (albeit of varying complexity and effect) to discontinue them, without recourse to formal legal action.
[14] An account of early authorization decisions by the TPC is given by Pengilley (1978).
[15] *Quadramain Pty Limited v. Sevastapol Investments Pty Limited (Howie and Anor.)* (1976) ATPR 40–013.
[16] See Trade Practices Review Committee (1976) at para 4.3ff.
[17] What constitutes a *substantial* lessening of competition has been the subject of considerable judicial evaluation. See Hurley (1991, pp. 168–178) for commentary and related case extracts.

[18] This most fequently applies to retail buying groups but does not extend to permit them to agree on the price at which the goods are actually sold.
[19] In the US price recommendations by trade associations are illegal per se.
[20] Pengilley (1987, p. 1025) suggests the Australian position on recommended prices is an "under-kill" compared with the US, but that it has probably "not resulted in too many dramatic adverse consequences".
[21] As under the 1974 Act, no statutory definition is provided of the term public benefit. Hurley (1991, pp. 181–182) lists the public benefits which have been recognised by the TPC and the Tribunal. However, in relation to mergers that occur outside Australia, s. 50A(1B) of the Act directs the Tribunal to regard as benefits increased value of exports, import substitution, or any other matter that relates to Australian industry's international competitiveness. For more extensive discussion of the interpretation of the term public benefit in Australia, see CCH Australia Ltd, *Australian Trade Practices Reporter*, pp. 7,091–7122.
[22] The original reason for distinguishing between goods and services is not clear; the Swanson Committee certainly drew no such distinction. Donald and Heydon (1978, p. 161) suggest it might have been to accommodate small businesses, as they tend to be more involved in the provision of services. The exception has allowed the professions to persist with centralized fee-setting practices.
[23] For an earlier debate on whether price-fixing should be authorizable, see Jackson (1983) and Round (1984). Jackson, a lawyer, was concerned about the probability of penalizing an "innocent" price-fixer if authorization were not available. Round (1984, p. 94) argued that authorization would require the administrative or judicial determination of what was a "reasonable" price, and that the only defensible way to establish such a price was through "the free interplay of rivals' independent strategies".
[24] In practice, appointments to this body have been part-time ones, and the President has, since its inception, always been a senior judge of an Australian federal court.
[25] An assessment of three of the early price-fixing decisions is provided by Miller and Round (1982).
[26] It would not be true to say that all, or even many, judges are comfortable with the roles of economists in the witness box. The penchant of economists to tell judges what the answer should be has annoyed some judges. For further elaboration, see Round and Miller (1993, pp. 217–219), Brunt (1990) and the paper in this issue by Mr Justice French of the Federal Court.
[27] *The King and the Attorney-General of the Commonwealth v. The Associated Northern Collieries and Others* (1911) 14 C.L.R. 387
[28] *The Attorney-General of the Commonwealth v. The Adelaide Steamship Company Limited and Others* (1913) 18 C.L.R. 30.
[29] A list of these practices is provided in Commissioner of Trade Practices, *Seventh Annual Report Year Ended 30 June 1974*, Canberra, Australian Government Publishing Service, pp. 25–31. Among the industries involved were asbestos cement products; beer; bread; builders hardware; electric cables; cement; ceramic tiles; classified advertising; concrete pipes; concrete roofing tiles; electrical accessories; engineers cutting tools; fibreboard containers; frozen vegetables; greeting cards; gypsum plaster and plasterboard; ham and bacon; hand tools; electric hot water systems; industrial safety products; insulation materials; electric lamps; wholesale wine and liquor; metal control valves; nails; optical products and services; paint; pigments; pre-mixed concrete; pressed steel baths; rubber footwear; sand and gravel; soft drinks; sporting ammunition; stainless steel sinks; tires and tubes; vinyl tiles; vitreous china and sanitary ware; and welding electrodes.
[30] Brief summaries of each case may be found in Nieuwenhuysen and Norman (1976, pp. 28–31 and 37–40) and Commissioner of Trade Practices, *Fifth Annual Report Year Ended 30 June 1972*, Canberra, Australian Government Publishing Service, pp. 27–34, and *Sixth Annual Report Year Ended 30 June 1973*, Canberra, Australian Government Publishing Service, pp. 25–33. More detailed analysis of the frozen vegetables case is in Hatch (1972).
[31] *Re Frozen Vegetables* (1971) F.L.R. 196.
[32] This scenario is consistent with the findings of Asch and Seneca (1976), who discovered that cartels form more frequently in bad economic conditions, when the opportunity cost of a conspiracy is lower.

[33] The Australian experience apparently differed little from the US experience three-quarters of a century earlier (1897–1904), when price-fixing was illegal but anti-competitive mergers were not. See Bittlingmayer (1985).
[34] Commissioner of Trade Practices, *Seventh Annual Report Year Ended 30 June 1974*, Canberra, Australian Government Publishing Service, p. 5.
[35] *Re Fibreboard Manufacturers' Association* (1973) ATPR 8378.
[36] Commissioner of Trade Practices, *Sixth Annual Report Year Ended 30 June 1973*, Canberra, Australian Government Publishing Service, p. 2.
[37] *Supra* n. 34, p. 4.
[38] It should be noted that all dollar amounts discussed in this paper are in Australian dollars. When the 1974 Act was passed, $A1 was equal to a little less than $US1.50. Over the years since the $A has steadily declined against the $US, so that in early 1994 it is now worth only about $US 0.72.
[39] *Re Association of Consulting Engineers, Australia* (1981) ATPR 40–202.
[40] *Ibid*, p. 42,796.
[41] *Loc. cit.*
[42] The Tribunal earlier granted authorization to the Media Council of Australia's rule which established the right of all the Council's members (which included almost all mass media proprietors – radio, television, newspapers and magazine – and outdoor advertisers in Australia) to refuse to pay commissions to non-accredited advertising agencies. The Media Council had argued that its accreditation scheme could only work in the presence of such a restriction, and that it produced efficiency and cost savings, high advertising standards, the preservation of both small media proprietors and small advertising agencies, and the preservation of Australian ownership and control among advertising agencies. See *Herald & Weekly Times Ltd. & Ors.(on their behalf and on behalf of Members of the constituent and affiliated associations of the Media Council of Australia)* (1978) ATPR 40–058.
[43] *Application of G. & M. Stephens Cartage Contractors Pty. Ltd. on behalf of the Members of the Concrete Carters Association (Victoria).* (1977) ATPR 40–042.
[44] On the strength of this decision, the TPC over the next decade authorized numerous agreements for the negotiation of haulage rates, both within the ready-mixed concrete haulage market and elsewhere. In 1988, however, it denied authorization for an arrangement for jointly negotiating rates for carrying ready-mixed concrete in the Australian Capital Territory. The Tribunal (*Re Lamont on behalf of Owner-drivers in the Pre-mixed Concrete Industry.* (1990) ATPR 41–035) affirmed the Commission's determination. The proposed arrangement sought not only to reduce industrial disputes over haulage rates but also sought to ensure that drivers' incomes should rise in line with cost increases. Unlike in the 1977 matter, however, entry barriers to the ACT hauling market were high, with the established carriers having collectively threatened industrial action in response to entry unless they had approved it.
[45] A complete list of citations to these cases is available from David Round. Two cases were private actions, and in one of these the s. 45 matter was of no real consequence. The other private case is one of the major Australian decisions.
[46] In contrast, there have been many vertical price-fixing (resale price maintenance) cases, with the TPC having a winning record of over 90 per cent since 1974 (as might be expected, given that the practice has been illegal per se since 1971).
[47] *Trade Practices Commission v. Email Ltd. & Anor.* (1980) ATPR 40–172.
[48] This case, involving bread price-fixing in Canberra, was settled by the TPC during the course of the proceedings, with the defendants offering appropriate undertakings to the Court not to announce bread price increases jointly, and not to communicate with each other on proposed alterations to prices.
[49] The first prosecution for price-fixing in Australia under the 1974 Act began in 1975, involving five gas stations in Wollongong, a city south of Sydney. It was alleged that the respondents had given effect to an arrangement that they should sell gasoline at no less than the maximum price fixed from time to time by the New South Wales Prices Commissioner (the setting of maximum prices for a wide range of "essential" commodities by State governments was, until recently, a feature of Australian business). The case dragged on for years with amended statements of claim, legal disputes and attempts at settlement. The matter was finally settled in 1980–81 when by consent the Court ordered that the five firms be restrained from agreeing to sell gasoline only at the maximum

recommended price, and from agreeing to stop discounts and give-aways. Another early case was initiated by the TPC after investigations indicated that members of the NSW branch of the Australian Hotels Association had given effect to a recommended price agreement formulated and circulated from time to time by officials of the AHA. After numerous procedural matters, the Commission instituted proceedings in 1975 against 107 companies operating hotels and two individual officials of the AHA. Numerous legal and constitutional challenges followed. Meanwhile, the AHA stopped circulating recommended prices, and this role was assumed late in 1976 by a publication known as "Thomson's Liquor Guide". The Commission believed that this publication would be used by the respondents as a new vehicle for a continuance of price-fixing. Many of them indicated that they wished to settle, and settlement terms were agreed with them, whereby they would notify Thomson that they no longer wished to receive the Guide. Further legal challenges ensued from the publishers of Thomson's, arguing it could be found to be in contempt of court if it inadvertently sent copies of its Guide to these defendants (it was not a party to the proceedings). It was not until late 1982 that the matter was finally disposed of. The TPC settled the case in view of the 1977 amendments which permitted genuine price recommendations where 50 or more parties were involved, and also because the evidence was "largely non-documentary and quite stale" (Trade Practices Commission, *Annual Report 1982–83*, Canberra, Australian Government Publishing Service, at p. 64).

[50] The exception, at trial court only (*Trade Practices Commission v. Parkfield Operations Pty. Ltd. & Anor.* (1985) ATPR 40–526), was a most unsatisfactory ex tempore judgment relating to an attempt to fix retail gasoline prices in two provincial cities in New South Wales, which looked for detailed terms of the alleged arrangement, no vagueness about the alleged understanding or agreement, sufficient clarity as to what was proposed and a sufficient measure of consensus, and clear identification of the possibilities of achieving the desired result. As the editorial comment written by the ATPR editors said (at p. 46,248), there can be no justification "... for introducing the requirements of detailed terms, certainty of parties or possibility of achievement... By their very nature price fixing arrangements will generally lack the refinement and definitiveness of legitimate commercial agreements since, although when made they are frequently not adhered to, they have a logic and direction of their own which is apparent to those involved." However, on appeal (*Trade Practices Commission v. Parkfield Operations Pty. Limited & Anor.* (1985) ATPR 40–639) the decision of the trial judge was vacated, the Full Court finding that there could be no suggestion that the proposed price rise was momentary or in any sense illusory, and that it was not necessary for an attempt to fix prices to have reached an advanced stage before the action comes within reach of the Act.

[51] The economic characteristics of this case, and all those which are discussed in the following pages, are summarized in Section V.3.6, below.

[52] *Trade Practices Commission v. J.W. Bryant Pty. Ltd. & Ors.* (1978) ATPR 40–075.

[53] *Ibid*, p. 17,753.

[54] One can only but speculate as to the message that this precedential "non-nominal" set of penalties gave to other business executives contemplating the comforts of collusion.

[55] *TPC v. Culley & Anor.* (1983) ATPR 40–399.

[56] *Ibid*, p. 44,670.

[57] *Trade Practices Commission v. JJ & YK Russell Pty Limited & Ors* (1991) ATPR 41–090.

[58] *Trade Practices Commission v. JJ & YK Russell Pty Limited & Ors* (1991) ATPR 41–132. This respondent, thought by the TPC to be the ringleader of the arrangement, was found not guilty because the TPC failed in court to provide credible evidence of what he said and did at the meeting.

[59] *Supra* n. 57, p. 52,441.

[60] *Ibid*, p. 52,442.

[61] Four of the twelve cases where penalties have been awarded against price fixers involved retail markets in Adelaide, a disproportionate number. The authors, one of whom has lived in Adelaide for many years and the other who has been a frequent visitor to the city in recent years, cannot explain why "the city of churches", as it is known, has hosted so many price-fixing conspiracies. Other than the possibility that the local TPC office has been exceptionally diligent, a possible explanation may be that Adelaide, being a relatively small city, may have a well-networked community of business executives.

[62] *Trade Practices Commission v. Nicholas Enterprises Pty. Ltd. & Ors.* (1979) ATPR 40–126.

[63] Thus confirming the famous observation of Adam Smith (1937, p. 128) that "people of the same trade seldom meet together, even for merriment and diversion, but the conversation ends in a conspiracy against the public, or in some contrivance to raise prices." This case is discussed at length in Miller and Round (1982).
[64] *Trade Practices Commission v. Nicholas Enterprises Pty. Ltd. & Ors.* (1979) ATPR 40-141, p. 18,527
[65] *Trade Practices Commission v. Cook-On Gas Products Pty. Ltd. & Ors.* (1985) ATPR 40–560.
[66] The findings are found in *Trade Practices Commission v. David Jones (Australia) Pty. Ltd. & Ors.* (1985) ATPR 40–607, while the penalties were handed down in an unreported decision of the Federal Court, 8 July 1986.
[67] The distributor argued that it would have been more appropriate to have charged him with resale price maintenance, as a distributor does not compete with retailers.
[68] *Supra* n. 27.
[69] *Supra* n. 66, p. 47,412.
[70] *Supra* n. 66, unreported penalty judgment at pp. 7–8.
[71] *TPC v. Allied Mills Industries Pty. Ltd. & Ors.* (1981) ATPR 40–237.
[72] See *Trade Practices Commission v. Allied Mills Industries Pty. Ltd. & Ors.* (1981) ATPR 40–241. The judge noted that the Court had to be satisfied that the penalty was appropriate, but that it was undesirable to say much about the appropriateness of the figure because the case against the other four respondents was proceeding. However, he noted (p. 43,181–2) that

> " ... the case is by no means in the class of the worst cases one could imagine ... there is no evidence to suggest that the public was affected very much, if at all, by what was done, and the evidence tends to establish that the arrangement or understanding had a comparatively short life ... The evidence would also suggest that any arrangement or understanding ... was not, during the period of operation which it had, always observed by the ... respondent".

[73] *TPC v. Allied Mills Industries Pty. Ltd. & Ors.* (1981) ATPR 40–252.
[74] The penalty decision of the Court is *Trade Practices Commission v. Tubemakers of Australia Ltd. & Ors.* (1983) ATPR 40–390. The original decision may be found at (1983) ATPR 40–358.
[75] A penalty of $2,000 was given to the executive, who no longer was employed by the firm, due to judicial sympathy with his poor prospects of finding comparable employment.
[76] *Trade Practices Commission v. Pioneer Concrete (Vic.) Pty. Ltd. & Ors.* (1985) ATPR 40–590.
[77] *Trade Practices Commission v. Australian Autoglass Pty. Ltd. & Ors.* (1988) ATPR 40–881.
[78] *Ibid*, p. 49,555.
[79] *Trade Practices Commission v. Patterson Cheney Pty. Ltd. & Ors.* (1990) ATPR 41–059.
[80] *Ibid*, p. 51,758.
[81] This amount is very small compared with the findings of Gallo, Craycraft and Bush (1987, p. 120), who estimate the average fine per criminal *case* instituted by the US Department of Justice to be $US629,398 over the years 1980–84, and $US377,087 between 1975–1979. The Australian average penalty per case from 1974 to the present is $A72,163, roughly about, say, $US80,000.
[82] There have been no serious moves to make price-fixing a criminal offense in Australia. Given the reluctance so far of judges to hit price-fixers hard, it is unlikely that jail sentences, even if available, would be used heavily by the Australian judiciary.
[83] *Trade Practices Commission v. Leslievale Pty. Limited & Ors.* (1986) ATPR 40–687.
[84] *Trade Practices Commission v. Service Station Association Limited & Ors* (1992) ATPR 41–179.
[85] *Trade Practices Commission v. Service Station Association Limited & Ors* (1993) ATPR 41–260.
[86] *Supra* n. 84, p. 40,453. This statement has an interesting parallel in the much-criticized US Supreme Court decision in *Business Electronics Corp. v. Sharp Electronics Corp.* 485 U.S. 717 (1988), where it was held that termination of a dealer following complaints about its prices is not illegal per se if there is no evidence that the manufacturer and any non-terminated dealers agreed to set or maintain price at a *specific* level.
[87] Section 45A clearly does not extend to all arrangements which affect price, but only those which have the purpose of fixing, controlling or maintaining prices. Thus an agreement which merely had an incidental effect on price would not breach the section, as held by one of the most senior judges on the Federal Court in the *Radio 2UE* case (*Radio 2UE Sydney Pty. Ltd. v. Stereo F.M. Pty. Ltd. & Anor.* (1982) ATPR 40–318), discussed below.

[88] *Supra* n. 77.
[89] *Supra* n. 47.
[90] The decision in this case is analyzed from an economic perspective in Miller and Round (1982).
[91] *Supra* n. 47, p. 42,379.
[92] If each firm could find out its rival's price quickly through market processes, it might well be asked what was the purpose of exchanging price lists? It was suggested that the price signalling by Email, the market leader, was done to keep the ailing Warburton Franki in the market as long as it could and keep out imports or a more vigorous new competitor. In fact all this was to no avail as Warburton Franki exited the market in 1978, after six years of trading at a loss.
[93] *Supra* n. 47, p. 42,377.
[94] *Loc. cit.*
[95] It was conceded by the judge (*ibid*, p. 42,381) that "there may be cases where the exchange of current price information is likely to have significant or adverse effects on competition", but as he had found that there was no agreement to fix prices, it was not necessary to consider the effect of the practice on competition. It should be noted that this case was based on the pre-1977 version of s. 45.
[96] As defined by the US Supreme Court in *Monsanto Co. v. Spray-Rite Service Corp.* 465 U.S. 752 (1984), p. 768.
[97] *Supra* n. 47, p. 42,370.
[98] Among the cases referred to were *Theatre Enterprises Inc. v. Paramount Film Distributing Corporation* (1954) 346 U.S. 537; *Esco Corporation v. United States* (1965) 340 F.2d 1000; *U.S. v. F.M.C. Corporation* (1969) Trade Cases ¶87,405; *Bogosian v. Gulf Oil Corporation* (1975) Trade Cases ¶60,284, p. 66,104; *Pevely Dairy Co. v. U.S.* (1949) 178 F.2d 363; *U.S. v. Ward Baking Co.* (1965) 243 F.Supp. 713; and *U.S. v. National Malleable & Steel Castings Co.* (1957) Trade Cases ¶68,890, affirmed on appeal (1958) 358 U.S. 38.
[99] See Kovacic (1993, pp. 49ff).
[100] The trial court decision was referred to at *supra* n. 87. The appeal citation is *Radio 2UE Sydney Pty. Ltd. v. Stereo F.M. Pty. Ltd. & Anor.* (1983) ATPR 40–367.
[101] *Supra* n. 87, p. 43,920.
[102] *Loc. cit.*
[103] See, for example, *U.S. v. Trenton Potteries Co.* 273 US 392 (1927) and *U.S. v. Socony-Vacuum Oil Co.*, 310 US 150 (1940), especially the latter where Mr. Justice Douglas stated that "Even though the members of the price-fixing group were in no position to control the market, to the extent that they raised, lowered or stabilized prices, they would be directly interfering with the free play of market forces ... Congress has not left us the determination of whether or not particular price-fixing schemes are wise or unwise, healthy or destructive" (and this in a country where the per se rule against price-fixing is based on judicial interpretation, in contrast to the legislated per se prohibition of it in Australia).
[104] Of course, a rule of reason approach is currently possible in terms of seeking an authorization for price-fixing for services, but this is an administrative rather than a judicial task.
[105] *Supra* n. 100, p. 44,401.
[106] *Loc. cit.*
[107] The cases are listed chronologically within the two categories. With so many of the cases having involved admissions by the respondents, the courts unfortunately were not obliged to consider the economic characteristics of these industries in any great detail.
[108] *Supra* n. 27, p. 400. This passage served as precedent in *Allied Mills* and *David Jones*.
[109] *Supra* n. 74, p. 44,323 in the original decision.
[110] Corones (1990, p. 221) suggests that an arrangement is more formal than an understanding, citing the statement of Franki J. in *Trade Practices Commission v. T.N.T. Management Pty. Ltd. & Ors.* (1985) ATPR 40–512, p. 46,098 that he "... would not necessarily reject a proposition that the requirements for entering into an understanding may be somewhat different and more easily satisfied than the requirements for making an arrangement."
[111] The judge's position was derived from the views of Wilmer L.J. and Diplock L.J. in *Re British Basic Slag Ltd.'s Agreements* (1963) All E. R. 807, p. 814 and p. 819.
[112] *Supra* n. 62, p. 18,342.
[113] *Ibid*, p. 18,343.

[114] *Ibid*, p. 18,344.
[115] *Matsushita Electrical Industrial Co. v. Zenith Radio Corp.* 475 U.S. 574 (1986), p. 588.
[116] *Supra* n. 96.
[117] These cases are discussed in Kovacic (1993, pp. 39–41).
[118] *Supra* n. 62, p. 18,347.
[119] *Morphett Arms Hotel Pty. Ltd. v. Trade Practices Commission* (1980) ATPR 40–157, p. 42,234.
[120] *Supra* n. 47, p. 42,370.
[121] *Loc. cit.*
[122] The Federal Court of Australia, *Transcript of Proceedings No VG 29 of 1979. The Trade Practices Act 1974. Trade Practices Commission and Allied Mills Pty. Ltd. and Ors*, p. 2,774.
[123] The remarks of Judge Sheppard stand in strong contrast to those of Mr. Justice Douglas, reported in footnote 103 *supra*. Pengilley claims (1983, p. 924) that "emotional judicial semantics" has acted as a deterrent to potential antitrust violators in the US, and that it is important to have a judiciary with some basic business acumen. Perhaps the Australian judiciary needs to become more vocal, and possibly more colorful in its language, to convey convincingly the message that price-fixing is simply socially unacceptable, as is stated by the black letter law.
[124] See Kovacic (1993, pp. 46–48).
[125] In a preliminary hearing in the *Allied Mills* case (*Trade Practices Commission v. Allied Mills & Ors.* (1980) ATPR 40–178, pp. 42,457–8), Judge Sheppard considered the *Email* judgment and decided that:

> "In my view what his Honour has said gives the respondents little comfort ... parallel conduct may constitute circumstantial evidence from which an arrangement or understanding may be inferred. It depends on the facts of each case. Email was a prosecution which, upon its facts, failed ... *Accordingly, I do not regard the decision in Email as one which says that in no circumstances will evidence of parallel pricing provide evidence of an arrangement or understanding. There are cases in which it may do so.*" (italics added).

[126] The Court came close to this in the *Nicholas Enterprises* case, where Judge Fisher found that while each metropolitan liquor outlet would be in competition with other outlets close by, no one seller could by itself affect prices in the market, thus suggesting little interdependence between rival sellers.

References

Armentano, Dominick T. (1982) *Antitrust and Monopoly: Anatomy of a Public Failure*, New York, John Wiley & Sons.

Asch, P., and J.J. Seneca (1976) 'Is Collusion Profitable?' *Review of Economics and Statistics*, **58**, 1–12.

Baker, J.B. (1993) 'Two Sherman Act Section I Dilemmas: Parallel Pricing, the Oligopoly Problem, and Contemporary Economic Theory', *The Antitrust Bulletin*, **XXXVIII**, 143– 219.

Bittlingmayer, G. (1985) 'Did Antitrust Policy Cause the Great Merger Wave?' *Journal of Law and Economics*, **28**, 77–118.

Brunt, Maureen (1990) '"Market Definition" Issues in Australian and New Zealand Trade Practices Litigation', *Australian Business Law Review*, **18**, 86–128.

Corones, S.G. (1990) *Competition Law and Policy in Australia*, Sydney, The Law Book Company Limited.

Donald, B.G., and J.D. Heydon (1978) *Trade Practices Law*, Volume 1, Sydney, The Law Book Company Limited.

Gallo, J.C., J.L. Craycraft and S.C. Bush (1987) 'Guess Who Came to Dinner. An Empirical Study of Federal Antitrust Enforcement for the Period 1963–1984', *Review of Industrial Organization*, **2**, 106–130.

Ginsburg, D.H. (1993) 'Nonprice Competition", *The Antitrust Bulletin*, **XXXVIII**, 83–111.

Hatch, J.H., 'The Implications of the Frozen Vegetables Case for Australian Trade Practices Legislation', *Economic Record*, **48**, 374–386.

Hay, G.A., and D. Kelley (1974) 'An Empirical Survey of Price-fixing Conspiracies', *Journal of Law and Economics*, **XVII**, 13–38.

Hurley, Anne (1991) *Restrictive Trade Practices Commentary and Materials*, North Ryde, The Law Book Company Limited.
Jackson, J. (1983) 'Price-fixing Agreements and Section 45A(1) of the Trade Practices Act 1974 (Cth)', *Australian Business Law Review*, **11**, 310–326.
Karmel, P.H., and M. Brunt (1963) *The Structure of the Australian Economy*, Melbourne, F.W. Cheshire Pty. Ltd.
Kovacic, W.E. (1993) 'The Identification and Proof of Horizontal Agreements Under the Antitrust Laws', *The Antitrust Bulletin*, **XXXVIII**, 5–81.
Miller, R.A., and D.K. Round (1982) 'Price-fixing, Price Leadership or "Ordinary Commercial Considerations": Guilt under Section 45 of the Trade Practices Act', *Australian Business Law Review*, **10**, 251–269.
National Competition Policy Review (F.G. Hilmer, Chairman) (1993) *National Competition Policy*, Canberra, Australian Government Publishing Service.
Nieuwenhuysen, J.P. (ed.) (1970) *Australian Trade Practices: Readings*, Melbourne, F.W. Cheshire Publishing Pty. Ltd.
Nieuwenhuysen, J.P. (ed.) (1976) *Australian Trade Practices: Readings*, second edition, London, Croom Helm Ltd.
Nieuwenhuysen, J.P., and N.R. Norman (1976) *Australian Competition and Prices Policy*, London, Croom Helm Ltd.
Pengilley, Warren (1978) 'Public Benefit in Anticompetitive Arrangements? Australian Experience Since 1974', *The Antitrust Bulletin*, **XXIII**, 187–225.
Pengilley, Warren (1983) 'Comparative Approaches to the Enforcement of Antitrust Laws Against Price-fixing Arrangements (With Special Emphasis on the Lessons to be Learned from Antitrust Law and Enforcement in Australia)', *The Antitrust Bulletin*, **XXVIII**, 883–939.
Pengilley, Warren (1987) 'Trade Associations and Collective Boycotts in Australia and New Zealand: A Mistranslation of the Sherman Act Down Under", *The Antitrust Bulletin*, **XXXII**, 1019–1049.
Qualls, P. David (1974) 'Stability and Persistence of Economic Profit Margins in Highly Concentrated Industries', *Southern Economic Journal*, **40**, 604–612.
Ransom, A. (1981) 'Monopolization and Price-fixing – Good Cases Making Bad Law; Australian – United States Parallels and a Suggested Solution', *Federal Law Review*, **12**, 308–343.
Richardson, J.E. (1967) *Introduction to the Australian Trade Practices Act*, Sydney, Hicks Smith & Sons.
Round, David K. (1984) 'Some Thoughts on Price-fixing, Potential Competition and Constraints on Monopoly Power', *Australian Business Law Review*, **12**, 86–94.
Round, David K., and Richard A. Miller (1993) 'The Australian Merger Guidelines: A Comparison with the U.S. Merger Guidelines', *Review of Industrial Organization*, **8**, 211–229.
Smith, Adam (1776) *An Inquiry into the Nature and Causes of the Wealth of Nations*, Modern Library Edition, 1937.
Stalley, D.J. (1958) 'Federal Control of Monopoly in Australia', *University of Queensland Law Journal*, **3**, 258–289.
Taperell, G.Q., R.B. Vermeesch, and D.J. Harland (1983) *Trade Practices and Consumer Protection*, 3rd edition, Sydney, Butterworths.
Trade Practices Review Committee (1976) *Report to Minister of Business and Consumer Affairs*, Canberra, Australian Government Publishing Service.
Walker, G. de Q. (1967) *Australian Monopoly Law: Issues of Law, Fact and Policy*, Melbourne, F.W. Cheshire Pty. Ltd.

Review of Industrial Organization **9:** 607–626, 1994.

The Exercise of Market Power: Its Treatment Under the Australian and New Zealand Statutes

PHILIP L. WILLIAMS
Melbourne Business School, University of Melbourne, 200 Leicester Street, Carlton Victoria 3053, Australia

Abstract. The monopolisation sections of Australia's and New Zealand's antitrust statutes are unusual for the test by which they distinguish acceptable from unacceptable conduct: conduct is only proscribed if it is unlikely to be observed in a competitive market. This suggests that only inefficient conduct should be proscribed. However, the courts have flirted with, rather than embraced, this identification of competition with efficiency.

Key words: Monopolisation, monopoly power, vertical squeezes.

I. Introduction

Section 46(1) of the Australian *Trade Practices Act* states:

> "A corporation that has a substantial degree of power in a market shall not take advantage of that power for the purpose of:
> (a) eliminating or substantially damaging a competitor of the corporation or of a body corporate that is related to the corporation in that or any other market;
> (b) preventing the entry of a person into that or any other market; or
> (c) deterring or preventing a person from engaging in competitive conduct in that or any other market."

This section is still very much in the form it took when the legislation was enacted in 1974. The only substantive change in the economic content of the section took place in 1986 when the threshold degree of market power was reduced from one of being "in a position substantially to control a market".

The present version of s. 46 has three substantive elements: (i) the corporation must have substantial market power; (ii) the corporation must take advantage of that market power; and (iii) the taking advantage must be for one of the three nominated purposes. Those with a knowledge of antitrust in other jurisdictions will be familiar with the first and third elements: market power and purpose. They will be less familiar with the second element: taking advantage. Accordingly, this paper concentrates on the way the courts have dealt with this phrase.

The paper examines the experience of both Australia and New Zealand. The Australian New Zealand Closer Economic Relations Trade Agreement (the CER

Agreement) was executed in March 1984 but was deemed to have come into force on 1 January 1983. The CER Agreement introduced a phased reduction in barriers to trade between Australia and New Zealand, so that mutual tariffs were to be abolished by 1988. There was to be a Review in 1988 which would consider issues such as the harmonisation of company law, trade practices law and accounting standards. However, the 1984 New Zealand Labour government was not one to await lengthy reviews. As part of its vigorous program of deregulation, it introduced a bill in 1985 which became the *Commerce Act*, 1986. The New Zealand Act wrote Part IV of the Australian *Trade Practices Act* into the New Zealand statute book – with very few changes.[1] Section 36 of the New Zealand Act is very similar to s. 46 of the Australian Act, except that the New Zealand section employs the word "use" instead of the Australian phrase "take advantage of".

The meaning of taking advantage has been highly controversial in Australia – and in New Zealand – over the past five years. Perhaps the principal reason for the controversy is that for the first fifteen years of the *Trade Practices Act*, s. 46 was subject to little litigation and the meaning of the words was never clarified. But from 1974 it was clear to the most perceptive commentators that the words could well be the gateway for the introduction of economics to the courts. Two leading Australian commentators on antitrust, Baxt (a lawyer) and Brunt (an economist) wrote a detailed analysis of the first draft of the 1974 legislation. They predicted that clause 46 "... is potentially the most demanding of any that will face the Court in terms of economic analysis: there is the question of how far the Court will be prepared to go in this (or, if you like, in "adjudication of economic evidence"); there is also the matter of the quality of that analysis".[2] Baxt and Brunt proceeded to speculate on how the courts might distinguish conduct that is acceptable from conduct that is proscribed by the section. They offered three alternatives: (i) the protection of small competitors and the muzzling of large; (ii) the appraisal of conduct according to some public-interest standard; or (iii) the allowance of "fair" conduct but the proscribing of predatory conduct – when the distinguishing feature between the two is the standard of economic efficiency. They advocated this third basis of distinction:

> "But is there not a third alternative, it might be asked? Might not the Court attempt to distinguish simply between "predatory" and "fair" forms of competition? The answer is that this would be but a variant of our second alternative – and by no means simple. For unless the Court were to devise its own arbitrary rules (with consequences that could be dreadful), the distinction between predatory and fair competition that makes most sense turns upon whether the practice contributes to good economic performance. Unfair/predatory practices are then those that rest upon sheer economic power, making no contribution to producing the kind of goods consumers want in the cheapest possible way".[3]

The remainder of this paper sets out the meaning of "take advantage" as determined by the High Court of Australia in the case of *Queensland Wire*. This case suggests that economic efficiency should be an important consideration when assessing whether or not firms have taken advantage of their market power. The paper then argues that many of the cases after *Queensland Wire* have not adopted the lead of the High Court. Many of these cases have been concerned with vertical squeezes. The final section of the paper examines proposals by a recent Government inquiry (the Hilmer Committee's report) for new procedures to deal with this problem of vertical squeezes.

II. Queensland Wire and "taking Advantage"

The case of *Queensland Wire Industries Pty Ltd v. The Broken Hill Proprietary Company Limited and Anor* ("Queensland Wire")[4] was a landmark in litigation under Australia's *Trade Practices Act*. It was the first case in which substantive economic issues went all the way to the High Court – Australia's ultimate court of appeal.

The case was litigated principally on the basis of taking advantage. The Broken Hill Proprietary Company Limited ("BHP") produced some 97 per cent of Australian steel. It supplied its wholly-owned subsidiary, Australian Wire Industries Pty. Ltd. ("AWI"), with wire rod to make fencing wire and with a Y-shaped section (Y-bar) to make by far the most popular type of post used for fencing in rural Australia. Queensland Wire Industries Proprietary Company Limited ("QWI") also purchased wire rod from BHP. But, because QWI produced no fence posts, the customers for its wire had also to purchase a load of fence posts from AWI. Between them, AWI and QWI supplied nearly all the rural steel fencing in the State of Queensland, with QWI's share being about twenty-eight per cent. AWI supplied most of the rural fencing in the rest of Australia. QWI had tried to purchase Y-bar from BHP so that it could manufacture fence posts, but BHP had effectively refused, responding that its policy was to refuse supply of Y-bar, or to offer supply only at an uncompetitive price, because it wished to preserve the business of manufacturing the star picket posts to itself. The only other producer of steel in Australia did not produce Y-bar, and no significant quantities had been imported. QWI made an application against BHP and AWI claiming that they took advantage of their substantial degree of power in a market by effectively refusing to sell Y-bar to QWI.

The value to the BHP group of its monopoly in Y-bar was the advantages flowing to it in the rural fencing market from being the sole supplier of star picket posts. The advantages indicated by the evidence were the unique ability to supply a complete fencing system (an advantage emphasised in BHP's advertising) and the capacity to discourage its distributors from obtaining their other fencing requirements from other suppliers.[5]

At the trial before the Federal Court of Australia, Pincus J., judge at first instance, was satisfied of the presence of all elements of QWI's claim except taking advantage. His Honour construed taking advantage as requiring some reprehensibility of conduct. Because he considered that a refusal to supply a competitor as part of a policy of keeping the whole of a product in-house for further processing would not be regarded in commerce as deserving of criticism, the judge dismissed the proceedings. The case then went to the Full Federal Court, which dismissed the appeal on the ground that because Y-bar had never been sold outside BHP, there was no market for it; and, because there was no market, there could be no market power.

When the case eventually reached the High Court, the justices unanimously upheld the appeal by QWI. They rejected the construction of the trial judge that taking advantage required that the defendant be doing something reprehensible. A different interpretation was propounded: to take advantage of one's market power is to do something that one would not do in a competitive market. To quote the judgment of the Chief Justice and Wilson J:

> "In effectively refusing to supply Y-bar to the appellant, BHP is taking advantage of its substantial market power. It is only by virtue of its control of the market and the absence of other suppliers that BHP can afford, in a commercial sense, to withhold Y-bar from the appellant. If BHP lacked the market power – in other words, if it were operating in a competitive market – it is highly unlikely that it would stand by, without any effort to compete, and allow the appellant to secure its supply of Y-bar from a competitor".[6]

The overriding message of the High Court in *Queensland Wire* is that s. 46 is to be read as relating to economics rather than to morals. In the words of Deane J:

> "The starting point ... is the fact that the essential notions with which sec. 46 is concerned and the objective which the section is designed to achieve are economic and not moral ones. The notions are those of markets, market power, competitors in a market and competition. The objective is the protection and advancement of a competitive environment and competitive conduct by precluding advantage being taken of "a substantial degree of power in a market" for any of the proscribed purposes".[7]

To an economist, the *Queensland Wire* test for taking advantage seems to open the door for argument about economic efficiency. As was suggested by Baxt and Brunt in 1974, practices may be classified as unfair/predatory if they impair economic efficiency. BHP was found to have taken advantage of its market power because it behaved in a way that would be unlikely in a competitive market. This seems to suggest that BHP's refusal to supply was not driven by economic efficiency. In the light of the test it proposes for "taking advantage", it is surprising that the High Court decision in *Queensland Wire* contains no explicit discussion of economic efficiency. Nevertheless, as one commentator has stated "... it is patently obvious from the facts reported in the several judgments, both in the High Court and below, that in this case there were no significant efficiencies of vertical integration".[8] The facts strongly suggested that there were no efficiencies in the form of flow-on processes. The activities of BHP's steel-making were located apart from the activities of AWI.

The interpretation of the High Court in *Queensland Wire*, corresponds quite closely to the recent interpretation given by courts in the United States to s.2 of the Sherman Act. For instance, in *Berkey Photo, Inc. v. Eastman Kodak Co.* the Second Circuit Court of Appeals described a use of monopoly power as "an action that a firm would have found less effective, or even counterproductive, if it lacked market power.[9] In *Aspen Skiing Co. v. Aspen Highlands Skiing Corp.*, in its first opportunity for nearly twenty years to restate the elements of the offence of monopolization, the Supreme Court explained what it meant by "exclusionary" and "predatory": "If a firm has been attempting to exclude rivals on some basis other than efficiency, it is fair to characterize its behavior as predatory".[10]

III. Subsequent Cases

In a paper on *Queensland Wire*, Frances Hanks and the present writer predicted the course of future litigation under s. 46 – and, by inference, under the parallel section 36 of New Zealand's Commerce Act thus "... we anticipate that defendants under s. 46 will generally conduct their defence by bringing evidence about the efficiencies which would explain [their conduct]. The effect of the decision of the High Court in *QWI* is to encourage parties to argue efficiencies before the courts."[11] The prediction has yet to be vindicated. We simply have not had time to accumulate sufficient cases to assess how the courts will handle the economics of s. 46. The remainder of this paper examines four leading cases (two from Australia and two from New Zealand) to see how they have dealt with the issue of taking advantage. So far, the economic content of the test proposed by the High Court of Australia has been far more prominent in New Zealand than it has in Australia.

Only one of the four cases (*Eastern Express*) is a predatory-pricing case of the type many economists would expect under the exercise of market power. The other three cases (*Pont Data*, *Port Nelson* and *Clear*) share many characteristics in common with *Queensland Wire*. None involved any real contest as to the market power of the defendant. In each case the defendant had substantial market power in the supply of an input; but it also used the input in a downstream activity in which the plaintiff either competed or wished to compete.

Since the 1960s, it has been commonplace in the literature on Australian industrial organisation that the local markets for manufactured products are so small that they are highly concentrated.[12] The other markets that have given rise to litigation for use of monopoly are deregulated public utilities. Both Australia and New Zealand have recently deregulated and, in some cases, privatised public utilities. So, in both manufacturing and in the recently-deregulated public utilities, Australia and New Zealand have many pure public monopolies – many of which face competition in downstream markets. These competitors have complained of vertical squeezes and have produced the litigation.[13]

IV. Port Nelson

The High Court of New Zealand[14] delivered its judgment in the trial of *Union Shipping New Zealand Limited & Anor v Port Nelson Limited* in February 1990.[15] Port Nelson Limited ("PNL") operated the port at Nelson. It maintained the wharf facilities and handled cargo in the wharf. Union Shipping New Zealand Ltd ("USL") was a shipping company that was associated with Union Stevedoring Services Ltd ("USSL"). USSL provided 90 per cent of the stevedoring services at the port. Until 1987, the operation of the port had been highly regulated with clear demarcation between three groups of workers: those who maintained the wharf; those who handled the cargo on the wharf; and those who loaded and unloaded ships (stevedores). The overall waterfront system at Nelson as elsewhere was "notoriously inefficient and expensive."[16]

Demarcation caused inefficiency of two types. In the first place, there was a notional point of rest on the wharf where the stevedoring function ended and handling on the wharf began. For roll-on, roll-off vessels, watersiders would drive forklifts provided by USL and carried in the ship itself, to and fro across the ramp between the hold and the point of rest, from which point port workers would use port-owned plant to take the cargo a further distance along the wharf. This practice "...required Roro ships to waste valuable cargo space carrying large forklifts and even a truck. It also involved quite unnecessary double handling, often over short distances."[17] There were significant economies of scope to be got by combining the stevedoring with the handling of cargo on the wharf.

Demarcation caused inefficiency of a second type. The old system of regulation had caused the port to employ too many workers. In particular, cargo handling was highly seasonal; and there was no flexibility to use cargo handlers during the off-season to maintain the wharf.

> "Inflexible labour practices required [the port] to overman. As its cargo handling workers could not, or would not, do other work during slack periods, for example maintenance, frequently they were underemployed. Likewise, during slack periods watersiders were without work, although nevertheless on a guaranteed wage. Conversely, over the brief few months of the fruit export season, the port was seriously undermanned, with the necessity to bring in watersiders at considerable expense from other centres. The inefficiencies and additional expenses were passed on in charges to shippers, leading to unacceptable freight rates".[18]

The allegations made under s. 36 of New Zealand's *Commerce Act* (the exercise of market power section) related to the behaviour of PNL following deregulation. USL and USSL alleged that PNL was exercising its market power in requiring USSL to use PNL forklifts and to pay wharfage containing a component for forklift hire whether or not the forklift was used. USL and USSL argued that such terms and conditions allowed them no margin to compete with PNL in the handling of cargo on the wharf. PNL defended itself by arguing that its behavior was consistent with economic efficiency and so was not the type of behavior that could be said to constitute a use of market power according to the test proposed by the High Court of Australia in *Queensland Wire*. PNL argued (and the Court accepted) that the three functions – maintenance of the wharf, handling of cargo on the wharf, and stevedoring – were linked by significant economies of scope. Because of these economies of scope, and the transaction costs associated with achieving these economies by co-ordinating across separate enterprises,[19] Port Nelson would be forced – if it were subject to vigorous competition – to straddle all three activities.[20] Accordingly, PNL's attempt to exclude USSL from taking over part of these activities did not constitute use of market power.

The Court rejected the use of economic efficiency as a guide to what would occur under competition, finding that: "However desirable the merits of that approach as a matter of current economic theory, it carries some difficulties when the *Commerce Act* directs attention specifically to the more immediate concept of competition".[21] The Court continued:

> "We can accept that in a search for economies of scope, reaching out to insert plant and drivers into a new range of activities, PNL might (indeed, probably would) think it desirable to require stevedores to use PNL plant or make additional payments, thereby assisting PNL with such economies. However, much that is desirable is beyond achievement in a competitive world.
>
> If the situation were truly competitive, with another port nearby, PNL would not succeed in such demands. Shipping companies affiliated with stevedores with waterside orientations, such as USL and USSL, undoubtedly would respond with heavy pressure on PNL to withdraw such demands. Their strength is not inconsiderable, as this case demonstrates. In the last resort, such shipping companies and stevedores would move to the other competitor port. We are not at all persuaded that another hypothetical port alongside Port Nelson would be so obsessed by economies of scope as to shut out a USL/USSL combination willing to switch favours".[22]

As will be shown in section 6 below, this reasoning of the Court in *Port Nelson* is in striking contrast to that of the Court in the later case of *Clear*. In that case, the Court accepted that if an enterprise with substantial market power were to impose conditions of dealing that produced a form of economic efficiency, then those conditions could not be said to constitute a use of market power.

V. Pont Data

The decision of the trial judge in the Australian case of *Pont Data Australia Pty Limited v ASX Operations Pty Limited & Anor* ("Pont Data") was handed down just a few days before *Port Nelson* in February 1990. The judgments could not be more different in their approach to the issue of use of market power. In contrast to the extended discussion in the New Zealand case of *Port Nelson*, neither the trial judge nor the appeal judges in *Pont Data* offer any analysis of use of market power.

The case was a type of vertical squeeze. The supplier of the input was Australian Stock Exchange Limited ("ASX"). ASX was the parent of a group of companies including the operators of the Sydney and Melbourne exchanges. Among other products, ASX produced pricing and volume information of bids and trades. This information was used as an input by a number of data suppliers. These downstream suppliers included ASX Operations Pty Limited ("ASXO") – a subsidiary of ASX – and the plaintiff – Pont Data Australia Pty Limited ("Pont Data"). Pont Data objected to the terms and conditions which ASX insisted upon for its supply of information. In assessing the s. 46 claim, the trial judge focused on two of these: (i) the condition that Pont Data on-sell the data only to final customers; and (ii) the price at which the input was to be supplied. The trial judge and the appeal court found that each of the conditions contravened s. 46. The judgments give no hint as to why the judges considered that the behavior involved a use of market power.

In a recent paper, O'Bryan criticises the judgments for their failure to address the issue of use of market power. In considering the restriction on re-sale, the courts should have asked whether "...ASX took advantage of its market power. The question should be answered by considering whether ASX would have licensed the trading information with a restriction on wholesaling in a competitive market."[24] O'Bryan concludes that such a restriction could well be found in a competitive market. This conclusion must be correct. One could imagine a set of competitive suppliers of data each of which sells data to its own customers. Economic efficiency would be promoted if each of these suppliers of data could engage in perfect price discrimination and charge each purchaser its demand price. The restriction on re-sale may well be a necessary part of a scheme of perfect price discrimination – because the discriminator will need to estimate the extent to which the information is used. This may not have been the subjective motivation of ASX. Nevertheless, the objective behaviour is consistent with that of a firm in a competitive market.

Economists have known for many years that price discrimination can promote efficiency. However, it has been generally considered that price discrimination was inconsistent with perfect competition and so was in some way contingent upon monopoly power. This latter proposition has been questioned in the last decade for three reasons: (i) other models of competition are consistent with price discrimination – contestability is the obvious example; (ii) particular forms of price discrimination have been shown to emerge in types of monopolistic competition;[25] and (iii) casual empiricism suggests that price discrimination occurs in quite competitive markets (for example, students obtain discounts at retail book stores; airlines sell seats in aircraft with a bewildering range of prices, and so on). If models suggest that such price discrimination is caused by monopoly, then the more-insightful models are required.[26]

VI. Eastern Express

Although the economics content of *Pont Data* is close to zero, that is not true of *Eastern Express Pty Limited v General Newspapers Pty Limited & Ors* ("Eastern Express").[27] The s. 46 claim concerned predatory pricing. General Newspapers is a subsidiary of the Hannan group which publishes the 'Wentworth Courier', a local newspaper in Sydney. A substantial part of its revenue base derives from display advertisements for the sale of real estate. Until February 1990, the Wentworth Courier had substantial market power in advertising real estate within its distribution area, where it was generally thought that a local property of any significant worth had to be advertised in the paper. A competitor local newspaper – Eastern Express – was formed in 1988, and started publication in February 1990. The Wentworth Courier cut the prices of its display advertisements at about this time; that price-cutting was the behavior that was claimed to infringe s. 46.

The trial judgment contains a lengthy discussion on when price-cutting is predatory. It states: "The factor which turns mere price cutting into predatory pricing is the purpose for which it is undertaken."[28] Although this may read like the concerns of a traditional lawyer, it appears that the judge was particularly impressed by evidence about the relation of prices to costs. In particular, the judge found that, even in the alleged predatory episode, prices still allowed a margin over fully-allocated costs. The judge dismissed the claim. He found that, although "...'Wentworth Courier' is presently not unprofitable, the profit is small relative to the size of the enterprise."[29]

It is impossible to understand the precise meaning of profitable from the judgment. In particular, despite the lengthy discussion of evidence from accountants, the reader is left with no clear notion of which costs have been included in which sets of figures. Certainly, it appears that the court was given no precise analysis of the types of cost that are relevant for assessing predation.[30]

VII. Clear

The New Zealand case of *Clear Communications Limited v Telecom Corporation of New Zealand Ltd et al* ("Clear")[31] is extraordinary in two respects. Of all exercise-of-market-power cases in Australia and New Zealand since *Queensland*

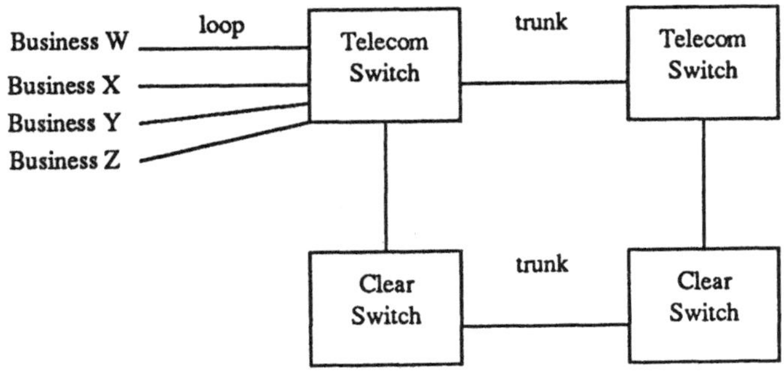

Fig. 1. Telecommunications in New Zealand.

Wire, only *Port Nelson* and *Clear* report extensive economic evidence on the issue of whether the conduct involved a use of market power. Of these two cases, only in *Clear* did the Court agree with the evidence from economists on the issue. At the time of writing, Clear has appealed; but no judgment has been delivered.

Until 1 April 1989 Telecom enjoyed statutory protection in the provision of telecommunications network services in New Zealand. Clear entered and commenced service in May 1991 by offering a toll bypass network in competition with Telecom. Clear now wishes to provide local network services, particularly to business customers, in the larger cities of New Zealand – Auckland, Wellington, and Christchurch. The dispute can be illustrated by means of Figure 1 above.

Clear's offering local network services to business customers might be represented by deleting the loops that link Business Y and Z to a Telecom switch and adding loops that link those Businesses to a Clear Switch. This will produce one local network of Business W, Business X and the Telecom switch, and another local network of Business Y, Business Z and the Clear switch. Such an arrangement is relatively straightforward providing a company wishes to call only the other company in its local network. But what contractual arrangements between Clear and Telecom should govern a call from Business Z to Business W? This was the real issue before the Court.

For most of the negotiations Telecom had insisted that it would charge Clear as it would charge a final consumer in the form of a PABX customer. Clear insisted it was not a normal PABX customer; it intended to operate a competitive local network. Just as calls would go from Business Z to Business W, they would also go from Business W to Business Z. So, Clear argued, any arrangements must acknowledge that each network would need the other and was providing a service for the other.

This notion of reciprocity was accepted by the Court at a number of points in the judgment. For example:

"Telecom was faced with responding to the demands on its merits. Instinctively its response was that it was entitled to be paid for access to and use of its ubiquitous network, and its views were that it had no need of access to the Clear system because it could provide all network loops itself. This failed to grapple with the concept of a fully fledged up-and-running competitor offering toll service and a network of customer loops that Telecom would need access to for its own network to have ubiquity of reach".[32]

"Telecom accepts the necessary periodic adjustments. It accepts that when Clear's local network is 'big enough' there will be reciprocity in the access levy to each competitor's network".[33]

"The economists called by Telecom, and Professor Baumol in particular, stressed that the model must eventually be applied reciprocally".[34]

"Perhaps it is easy to say so now, but it is hard to accept that Telecom did not realise early in the piece that a competitive environment must involve Telecom accepting certain of its sunk costs (e.g. for some existing loops) becoming irrecoverable and the competitor entitled to be paid for the services it provided Telecom just as Telecom would be entitled to be paid for services it provided to the competitor".[35]

The possession of market power was not an issue in the proceedings. The two issues were (i) whether Telecom's demands constituted a use of market power; and (ii) whether they were for one of the proscribed purposes.

Clear argued that there should be no financial flows, either from Clear to Telecom or from Telecom to Clear. They argued that calls from their network to Telecom's network would roughly balance calls in the other direction. If calls failed to balance, there may be a need for some compensation. In contrast, Telecom argued for a charging regime based on the opportunity cost of losing a customer to Clear. Consider a one-minute call from Business Y to Business X. The current price for such a call is 3.55 cents during the peak. As the call is depicted in Figure 1, the call is conducted wholly within Telecom's network, and Telecom keeps the 3.55 cents. Now suppose that Business Y is linked to the Clear switch and calls Business X. Telecom loses the 3.55 cents but it also saves something (say 0.5 cents) as a result of having part of the call provided by Clear. The net loss to Telecom is the difference between the two amounts, 3.05 cents. This is the amount that Telecom argued it should be able to charge.

Figure 2 is reproduced from p. 71 of the judgment. It shows that Telecom's price consists of three components: average incremental cost, contribution to common costs and contribution to monopoly profits (if any). Telecom argued (and the Court accepted) that it should be able to charge the opportunity cost of the customer switching from Telecom to Clear. The argument is similar to the argument of Port Nelson that it should be able to charge a fee for the use of its fork lifts even when USSL chose to use its own forklifts.

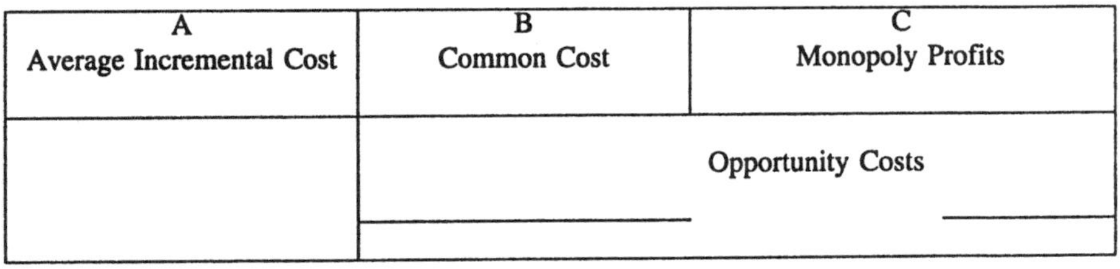

Fig. 2. Components of price.

Telecom argued that the result was consistent with a type of economic efficiency and was, therefore, consistent with a competitive result. Telecom argued, and the Court accepted, that this make-or-buy charging would promote production efficiency – because Clear would only provide the loop to Business Y if that provision generated a net saving to society. The argument was that Clear would only get the business of the call from Y to X if it could charge 3.55 cents or less. It would only be able to do this if its average incremental costs were less than 0.5 cents – because it would have also to recover the 3.05 cents it would have to pay to Telecom.[36] It was clear to the Court that this pricing regime would preserve the monopoly profits (if any) of Telecom. "The first link in this chain of argument is the assertion that the Rule would enable the recovery of monopoly profits and recoupment of uneconomic costs. It is plain that, logically, this must be so".[37]

There was no claim by Telecom that the make-or-buy pricing arrangement was consistent with allocative efficiency. Baumol, who gave evidence for Telecom, argued that the make-or-buy pricing rule achieved only one type of economic efficiency – an allocation of business between Clear and Telecom that would minimise the cost of production:

> "Now the input pricing rule is there for one purpose and it does not serve other purposes, it does not cure AIDS or baldness, it does not get rid of business cycles and it is not in my view the proper instrument to get rid of monopoly profits....just because if it is used for that purpose, it will have serious side effects, in effect providing terms which make the competitive position of the two firms unequal, it makes the playing field unlevel".[38]

The judgment in Clear seems to set out principles for the implementation of this pricing rule. The particularly odd feature of these principles is that the pricing rule is not applied symmetrically to calls from Clear to Telecom as to calls from Telecom to Clear – despite the evidence from Baumol that the rule should be applied symmetrically.

The judgment offers as 'Conclusions from the Baumol-Willig Economic Model':

1. In respect of calls from a Telecom customer into the Clear network, Clear can charge Telecom, Telecom's AIC saved by Clear carrying part of the call.
2. In respect of calls from a Clear customer to the Telecom network, Telecom can charge Clear its call rate less Telecom's AIC saved by Clear carrying part of the call.
3. In respect of access to the PSTN Telecom can charge Clear the equivalent of its line rental less Telecom's AIC saved by Clear providing part of the loop.
4. Actual expenses incurred by Telecom in connecting Clear to the PSTN are payable by Clear as agreed".[39]

If the pricing rule were applied symmetrically, and Clear and Telecom had similar prices and cost structures, the flow of funds from Clear to Telecom would equal the flow of funds from Telecom to Clear – providing calls were to balance. This invites the question as to why the Court so prefers the Telecom pricing proposal to that of Clear. This question is not directly addressed by the judgment.

Finally, one must question (as Clear did at the trial) whether the pricing rule will produce even the one type of efficiency claimed for it – if it is applied in a world of positive transactions costs. The judgment acknowledges that the translation of pricing principle to actual numbers will be the subject of regular negotiation. It proposes an administrative mechanism to deal with the problem – although the Court provides little by way of detail:

> "If the Baumol-Willig Rule is implemented there would be a need for careful design of the administrative mechanism. Regular reviews would be necessary to adjust for shifting prices and costs. It would be important to design an arms length mechanism that would minimise the possibility of collusion. This is another point in which some regulatory presence may be needed. It would be important for the reviews not to take place at too frequent intervals, for that would reveal sensitive market information; the adjustments should be back-dated, with interest covering the time-value of money".[40]

The irony of this proposal must have been apparent to the Court when writing its judgment. The New Zealand Parliament had legislated to privatise Telecom and to leave telecommunications with no regulatory authority. As was noted in section one above, such privatisation and deregulation demands a great deal of the statutory provision governing the use of market power (s. 46 in Australia and s.36 in New Zealand). Nevertheless, in *Clear* the High Court of New Zealand, by its proposal of a regulator, has acknowledged that the Courts are scarcely well-suited to the regular reviews of shifting prices and costs that are needed for the remedy they propose.

VIII. The Vexed Issue of Remedies

The Australasian provisions governing the use of market power are unusual in the test they employ for distinguishing acceptable conduct by a monopolist from unacceptable conduct. Unacceptable conduct is conduct that one would be unlikely to observe in a competitive market. Although this test of the use of market power is peculiar to Australia and New Zealand, the other elements in the section would be familiar to non-Australasian students of antitrust. One of these familiar problems is that of remedy in monopolisation cases.

In the 1912 edition of *The Control of Trusts*, J.B. Clark and J.M. Clark argued that it was inappropriate to rely only on proscriptions of anticompetitive conduct: structural remedies may be needed.[41] This view has been reiterated many times by writers on antitrust.[42] The issue arose in Australia as soon as the High Court found that BHP's refusal to supply Y-bar to Queensland Wire was a use of its market power for one of the purposes proscribed by s. 46 of the *Trade Practices Act*.[43] The issue of remedy was sent back to the trial judge to resolve. The parties relieved the judge of this difficult responsibility by agreeing on terms of supply.

The issue arose again in *Pont Data*. The trial judge fixed a remedy for the offence of charging too high a price for the information feed. The remedy was for the ASX to charge a price that reflected cost:

> "Once it is accepted that ASXO is not entitled to misuse its monopoly position, it ought not to be regarded as unfair to compel ASXO to supply Signal "C" at a price which reflects the cost of supplying that signal together with a margin of profit similar to that charged by competitive suppliers in the data industry. I accept that such a price is likely to be low, compared with the fees charged in the subject contracts. But that is because the cost of supply is low. In a competitive situation that low cost would be reflected in a low price".[44]

The trial judge gave ASXO further time "... to demonstrate, if they are able, that there is some cost attached to the supply of Signal 'C' which they would not otherwise incur; and, if so, its extent".[45] It appears that the trial judge was suggesting that an appropriate supply price would be long-run incremental cost – which would make no contribution to common costs. This suggestion was rejected by the Full Federal Court on appeal. The Appeal Court did not canvas arguments about the commercial sense of the order by the trial judge. Rather, it found that the Court "... must be slow to impose upon the parties a regime which could not represent a bargain they would have struck between them".[46] It ordered a price equal to that which was agreed prior to the offensive contract that ASX tried to impose on Pont Data.

The remedies suggested by the *Clear* case are perhaps most interesting because, if the case is upheld on appeal, they suggest a general rule that could be applied in the vertical squeeze cases that are so common in Australia and New Zealand. If the monopolist is found to have infringed by using its market power, courts could well follow the lead of *Clear* and order a price that represents the opportunity cost to the monopolist of supplying its downstream competitor. It is far too early to speculate on the likelihood of this development.

IX. Vertical Squeezes and the Hilmer Committee

In August 1993, the Australian Government received the Report of a major inquiry into National Competition Policy known (after its Chairman) as the Hilmer Committee.[47] Chapters 10 and 11 of the Report are concerned principally with the problem of the vertical squeeze – imposed by an upstream monopolist on its downstream competitor. The Report canvasses two solutions; one is for the courts or regulators to demand that the input be supplied on terms that would allow an efficient competitor to be viable, while another solution would be to prevent the monopolist from undertaking the downstream activity. In this case, there would be less need for the State to be worried that the terms and conditions of supply may be discriminatory. The Report favours the solution of structural separation, but it realises that structural separation may not always be adopted, and so a regime is proposed by which prices may be regulated to secure access.

The Report's advocacy of structural separation does not extend to advocacy for insertion of divestiture provisions in the Trade Practices Act.[48] Nevertheless, the Report recommends (10.2) that privatisation and deregulation should be used as opportunities to introduce structural separation in public utilities, i.e., the units which are potentially subject to competition should, where possible, be under separate ownership or control from the units that are monopoly suppliers of inputs or purchasers of outputs.

Experience of use-of-market-power cases in Australia and New Zealand indicates that the presumption in favour of vertical separation is appropriate. However, the presumption is only appropriate where an entrenched monopoly is the supplier or purchaser of a process that is potentially competitive. If a monopoly is supplying a monopoly, economic theory suggests that the presumption should be the opposite – in favour of vertical integration.[49]

The Report proposes an access regime that is intended for: (i) public utilities that were not vertically separated at the time of privatisation/deregulation; and (ii) private monopolies that face no real threat of competition. The Committee's opinion is that "almost all" "essential facilities" are in the public sector.[50] But the Report envisages that the access regime should also apply to privately-owned entrenched monopolies.[51] It is recommended that a Federal Minister shall have power to declare access under legislation.[52] That declaration should only be made if

(i) Access to the facility in question is essential to permit effective competition in a downstream or upstream activity;
(ii) The making of the declaration is in the public interest, having regard to:
(a) the significance of the industry to the national economy; and

(b) the expected impact of effective competition in that industry on national competitiveness;

(iii) The legitimate interests of the owner of the facility must be protected through the imposition of an access fee and other terms and conditions that are fair and reasonable, including recognition of the owner's current and potential future requirements for the capacity of the facility; and

(iv) The creation of such a right must have been recommended by an independent and expert body.

The Report does not address the relationship between the proposed access regime and the courts' dealing with access cases under s. 46. There are two points of conflict. The first point of conflict is over the circumstances in which the system would intervene to provide access. The courts will only intervene under s. 46 if the refusal to provide access constitutes a taking advantage of the firm's market power. The High Court in *Queensland Wire* construed taking advantage as behaving in a way that is inconsistent with behavior in a competitive market. In discussing s. 46 the Report[54] assumes that any refusal to supply by an essential facility constitutes taking advantage. This view is a clear misinterpretation of the High Court in *Queensland Wire* – as that interpretation has been applied in subsequent cases. The criterion for intervention under the proposed new access regime is that the facility is "... essential to permit effective competition in a downstream or upstream activity". It is not at all clear whether the Committee is proposing a precise test of the form the courts have developed under s. 46 or whether a much-wider test for intervention is proposed. It would be regrettable if the principles that have been developed by the courts in recent years were to be by-passed by the introduction of a new access regime.

The second point of conflict between access under s. 46 and the proposed new regime involves the principles governing the terms of access. Under the new proposals, the appropriate Federal Minister would determine the appropriate principles for access pricing after considering the advice of the newly-constituted National Competition Council.[55] The Report does not lay down definite criteria for these principles except to say that the prices should be "fair and reasonable".[56] It is odd that these criteria differ so markedly from the Report's emphasis on economic efficiency in its Introduction. To be consistent with the bulk of the Report, the criterion for access prices should be the promotion of economic efficiency. One of the real benefits of the approach of the courts is that, even if the application is somewhat patchy, their interpretation of take advantage places efficiency considerations at the forefront of monopolisation cases.

X. Conclusions

Following the judgment in *Queensland Wire*, it appeared that arguments over economic efficiency would be central to cases involving the exercise of market power in Australia and New Zealand. In the subsequent few years this has not been true of any case in Australia. It has, however, been true of two cases in New Zealand. In *Port Nelson* the Court accepted that the monopolist was acting consistent with economic efficiency but rejected the proposition that this established that the action was consistent with a competitive outcome. In *Clear*, the Court accepted the monopolist's prices were consistent with one type of economic efficiency and, because of this, accepted that the prices did not constitute a use of market power. Remedies represent an intractable problem in Australia and New Zealand – as in other jurisdictions. The Hilmer Committee does little to solve the problem.

Notes

* An earlier version of this paper was presented at the Trade Practices Workshop of The Business Law Section of the Law Council of Australia, Canberra, 16–18 July 1993. I am grateful to the discussant of the paper at the Workshop, Ian McEwin, and to the participants for their helpful comments. The Special Editor for this issue has also been most helpful. He suggested that I should disclose my interest in the cases I discuss. I gave expert economic evidence: (i) for Queensland Wire at the trial of *QWI and BHP*; (ii) for Port Nelson Limited at the trial of *USNZL and PNL*; and (iii) for Clear at the trial of *Clear and Telecom NZ*.

[1] For background on the CER and the Commerce Act, see Bollard and McCormack (1985, p.48) and Farmer (1989, p.171).
[2] See Baxt and Brunt (1974, p. 19).
[3] *Ibid*, p. 25.
[4] *Queensland Wire Industries Pty. Ltd. v The Broken Hill Proprietary Company Limited & Anor.* Trial Judgment: (1987) Australian Trade Practices Reporter (ATPR) 40–810. The Full Court of the Federal Court (1988) ATPR 40–841. The High Court of Australia (1989) ATPR 40–925.
[5] Judgment of the Federal Court, p. 48,813.
[6] Judgment of the High Court, p. 50,011.
[7] Judgment of the High Court, p. 50,0111–12.
[8] Brunt (1993, p.172).
[9] *Berkey Photo, Inc. v. Eastman Kodak Co.*, 603 F. 2d 263 (2nd Cir. 1979), p. 291.
[10] *Aspen Skiing Co. v. Aspen Highlands Skiing Corp.*, 472 U.S. 585 (1985) p. 605.
[11] See Hanks and Williams (1990, p. 446).
[12] For studies on concentration in Australian manufacturing markets, see Karmel and Brunt (1962, pp. 77–92); Round (1975); and Caves (1984).
[13] See Brunt (1993, pp. 178ff).
[14] Unlike Australia, the High Court of New Zealand is a court of first instance.
[15] *Union Shipping New Zealand Limited and Anor v Port Nelson Limited* (1990) *New Zealand Business Law Cases*, 3, pp. 101,618–54.
[16] *Ibid*, p. 101,624.
[17] *Ibid*, pp. 101,624–5.
[18] *Ibid*, p. 101,625.
[19] See Teece (1980).
[20] See Panzar and Willig (1981).
[21] *Supra* n. 15 at p. 101,642.
[22] *Ibid*, p. 101,646.
[23] *Pont Data Australia Pty. Limited v ASX Operations Pty. Limited & Anor* (1990) ATPR 41–007 (Trial Judgment). Full Court of the Federal Court is at (1990) ATPR 41–069 and 41–109.
[24] O'Bryan (1993, p. 10).
[25] See Borenstein (1985) and Katz (1984).
[26] See Varian (1989) and Klein (1990).
[27] *Eastern Express Pty. Limited v General Newspapers Pty. Limited & Ors* (1991) ATPR 41–128.

[28] *Ibid*, p. 52,895.
[29] *Ibid*, p. 52,897. The case went on appeal to the Full Court of the Federal Court. See (1992) ATPR 41–167. The Full Court found that the Wentworth Courier did not enjoy sufficient market power to infringe the section.
[30] See Ordover and Willig (1981).
[31] *Clear Communications Limited v Telecom Corporation of New Zealand et al* (1993), unreported High Court of New Zealand, Wellington Registry, No. CP 590/91.
[32] *Ibid*, p. 38.
[33] *Ibid*, p. 49.
[34] *Ibid*, p. 74.
[35] *Ibid*, p. 97
[36] *Ibid*, p. 26.
[37] *Ibid*, p. 85.
[38] *Ibid*, pp. 89–90.
[39] *Ibid*, p. 74.
[40] *Ibid*, p. 93.
[41] Clark (1912, pp. 130–1 and 145).
[42] For examples, see Kaysen and Turner (1959, pp. 93ff), and Comanor (1990, p. 55).
[43] See Pengilley (1991).
[44] *Supra* n. 23, trial judgment at p. 51,132.
[45] *Loc. cit.*
[46] *Ibid*, Full Court judgment 41–109 at p. 52,666.
[47] See Australia, National Competition Policy Review (1993).
[48] *Ibid*, pp. 233–4.
[49] See Blair and Kaserman (1985, pp. 295–302).
[50] *Supra* n. 47 at p. 239.
[51] *Ibid*, p. 256.
[52] *Ibid*, p. 250.
[53] *Ibid*, pp. 251–2.
[54] *Ibid*, p. 243.
[55] *Ibid*, p. 255.
[56] *Ibid*, p. 253.

References

Australia, National Competition Policy Review (1993), *National Competition Policy, Report by the Independent Committee of Inquiry*. Canberra: Australian Government Publishing Service.

Baxt, Robert, and Brunt, Maureen (1974) 'The Murphy Trade Practices Bill: Admirable Objectives, Inadequate Means', *Australian Business Law Review*, **2**(1), 1–79.

Blair, Roger D., and Kaserman, David L. (1985) *Antitrust Economics*, Homewood, Illinois: Irwin.

Bollard, Alan, and McCormack, Darcy (1985) *Closer Economic Relations: A View from Both Sides of the Tasman*. Wellington: NZIER.

Borenstein, S. (1985) 'Price Discrimination in Free-entry Markets', *Rand Journal of Economics*, **16**, 380–97.

Brunt, Maureen (1993) 'Australian and New Zealand Competition Law and Policy', in Barry Hawk, ed, *Annual Proceedings of the Fordham Corporate Law Institute, International Antitrust Law and Policy*. New York: Transnational Juris Publications.

Caves, R.E. (1984) 'Scale, Openness and Productivity in Manufacturing Industries', in R.E. Caves and L.B. Krause, eds, *The Australian Economy: A View from the North*. Sydney: Allen and Unwin.

Clark, J.B., and Clark, J.M. (1912) *The Control of Trusts*, Revised Edition. New York: Macmillan.

Comanor, William S. (1990) 'U.S. Antitrust Policy', in W.S. Comanor *et al.*, *Competition Policy in Europe and North America: Economic Issues and Institutions*. Switzerland: Harvard Academic Publishers.

Farmer, James (1989) 'CER and Competition Law: A Lawyer's Perspective', in Michael James, ed, *Regulating for Competition? Trade Practices Policy in a Changing Economy*. Sydney: Centre for Independent Studies.

Hanks, Frances, and Williams, Philip L. (1990) 'Implications of the Decision of the High Court in *Queensland Wire*', *Mebourne University Law Review*, **17**(3), 437–61.

Karmel, P.H., and Brunt, Maureen (1962) *The Structure of the Australian Economy*. Sydney: F.W. Cheshire.

Katz, M.L. (1984) 'Price Discrimination and Monopolistic Competition', *Econometrica*, **59**, 1453–71.

Kaysen, Carl, and Turner, Donald F. (1959) *Antitrust Policy, An Economic and Legal Analysis*. Cambridge: Harvard University Press.

Klein, Benjamin (1990) 'The Use of Economics in Anti-trust Litigation: Realistic Models of the Competitive Process', in Frank Mathewson, Michael Trebilcock, and Michael Walker, eds, *The Law and Economics of Competition Policy*. Vancouver: The Fraser Institute.

O'Bryan, Michael (1993) 'Section 46: Law or Economics', Paper presented at the Trade Practices Workshop of The Business Law Section of the Law Council of Australia, Canberra, 16–18 July.

Ordover, J.A., and Willig, R.D. (1981) 'An Economic Definition of Predation: Pricing and Product Innovation', *Yale Law Journal*, **91**, 8–53.

Panzar, J.C., and Willig, R.D. (1981) 'Economies of Scope', *American Economic Review*, **71**, 268–72.

Pengilley, Warren (1991) 'The High Court Decision in Queensland Wire: Who now has to supply what and on what terms?', *The Antitrust Bulletin*, **36**, 201–16.

Round, D.K. (1975) 'Industry Structure, Market Rivalry and Public Policy: Some Australian Evidence', *Journal of Law and Economics*, **18**, 273–81.

Teece, David J. (1980) 'Economies of Scope and the Scope of the Enterprise', *Journal of Economic Behaviour and Organization*, **1**, 223–47.

Varian, Hal R. (1989) 'Price Discrimination', in Richard Schmalensee, and Robert Willig, eds, *Handbook of Industrial Organizations*, vol. I. Amsterdam: North-Holland, 597–654.

Postscript

Shortly before the final deadline for this issue, the New Zealand Court of Appeal handed down its decision in *Clear*. Clear had appealed against the finding of the High Court that the Baumol/Willig rule, if implemented, cannot be a breach of s. 36 of the Commerce Act. The three judges on the Court of Appeal unanimously upheld the appeal.

The lead judgment by Gault J. begins by explaining the background to the privatization and deregulation of telecommunications in New Zealand. From 1987, the stated policy of the government was to permit competition. Indeed, the Government stated that it placed primary reliance on the operation of the Commerce Act to maintain conditions of effective competition.[1]

The Court of Appeal criticized the proposition that the question of Telecom's use of dominance could be resolved by a debate about economic efficiency thus: "In a fully competitive market the firm might still be in a dominant position because of superiority in efficiency over its existing and potential rivals. But any assumption of efficiency may be question-begging if in the particular case competitive efficiency is an issue. It is important therefore to keep firmly in mind the commercial context and the purpose of the enquiry when considering whether particular behaviour could occur in a fully competitive situation".[2]

The Court decided that Telecom's attempt to implement the Baumol-Willing pricing rule did constitute a use of dominance, because the rule would enable Telecom to continue to earn a monopoly margin even if it lost business to Clear. As Gault J. states, "[t]he reason I have rejected the opportunity cost method of pricing in the circumstances of this case is that it does not exclude monopoly profits".[3] He acknowledged that there was also force in Clear's argument that the transactions costs generated by complex reviews of the application of the Baumol-Willig rule would themselves "increase the height of the entry barrier".[4] And this point was chosen for elaboration in the judgment of Cooke J., President of the court ". . . constant price reviews would be required to ascertain lost opportunity compensation . . . I cannot avoid the conclusion that such a system would mean a vista of continual disputes or arbitrations, so daunting in itself as to transgress the Commerce Act. Such a system would never be agreed to by an entrant not faced with the hurdle of market dominance by the monopolist."[5]

The Court declined to give a precise order as to the rule that should determine the prices of interconnection. In effect, the parties were ordered to resume negotiations in the light of the decision of the Court. If the parties cannot agree they may need to face arbitration or direct Government regulation. As Cooke J. noted in his judgment, "... the long drawn-out proceedings have benefited no-one apart from Telecom, for the entry of Clear into the market has been delayed."[6]

The saga of the *Clear* litigation raises a number of critical issues. Not the least is whether the Courts are the most suitable institutions for deciding issues of access to public utilities. For the purpose of this paper, the Court of Appeal's rejection of the Baumol-Willig argument means that, to date in Australia and New Zealand, no economist has successfully defended a monopolist from a charge of monopolization by arguing that its conduct does not constitute a use of monopoly power because the conduct is efficient. The High Court of Australia in *Queensland Wire* seemed to invite such defenses if they were available. To date we have observed either that such defenses have not been available; that the defendants have failed to argue them persuasively; or that the Courts have refused to follow the avowedly economic approach suggested by the High Court of Australia in *Queensland Wire*.

Notes

1 *Clear Communications Limited v Telecom Corporation of New Zealand Limited et al.* (1993), unreported Court of Appeal of New Zealand, No. C.A. 25/93, judgment of Gault J., at p. 4.
2 *Ibid*, judgment of Gault J., at pp. 24–25.
3 *Ibid*, judgment of Gault J., at p. 42.
4 *Ibid*, judgment of Gault J., at p. 35.
5 *Ibid*, judgment of Cooke J., at p. 6.
6 *Ibid*, judgment of Cooke J., at p. 7.

Review of Industrial Organization **9:** 627–647, 1994.

Vertical Restraints in the Australian Trade Practices Act

R. IAN MCEWIN*
Department of Economics and Management, University of New South Wales, ADFA, Campbell ACT 2600, Australia (Consultant, Sly and Weigall)

Abstract. Vertical restraints are singled out for detailed legislative treatment in the Australian *Trade Practices Act*. Resale price maintenance and third-line forcing (tying another firm's products) are illegal per se while price discrimination and non-price vertical restraints (apart from third-line forcing) are subject to a competition test. Most vertical restraints may be either authorised by the Trade Practices Commission or given statutory exemption from the Act under a notification procedure unique to vertical restraints. The ability to seek an authorisation or to notify the Commission about a vertical practice has meant that the economic issues in this area have been dealt with mainly in administrative processes outside the courts. While issues of economic efficiency have been important, the main objective of the Commission has been to benefit consumers by promoting competition as a process. This paper briefly overviews what is probably the most complex area of antitrust in Australia yet, which has received negligible academic comment.

Key words: Vertical restraints, antitrust, economic efficiency, public benefits

I. Introduction

Restrictive terms imposed by either buyers or sellers in a vertical relationship have been one of the most troublesome areas for competition policy in the last twenty years. Mathewson and Winter (1990) argue that there are two main reasons for antagonism to vertical restraints. The first is based on the notion that buyers should be able to do what they like with the goods they buy. Once sold, the seller has no further interest. The response is that sellers have an interest in ensuring that their goods are produced and distributed in such a way as to maximise their own advantage. The second main reason is a belief that restraints reduce competition in either the sellers' or buyers' markets. Resale price maintenance and setting exclusive territories may reduce competition in the buyer's market by limiting intrabrand competition. Exclusive supply arrangements can reduce competition in the seller's market by either foreclosing markets at the buyer's level to other sellers or facilitating seller collaboration by making breaches of any agreement more visible (sellers cannot offer dealers secret deals to promote their own products at the expense of the other members if outlets deal in only one product).

While Australian competition policy towards vertical restraints has been largely influenced by the developments in economic theory and antitrust doctrine in the United States, particularly in the 1970s, there are significant differences. In particular, special attention is given to non-price vertical arrangements which are singled out for detailed legislative treatment in s. 47 of the *Trade Practices Act* (the 'Act' hereafter). Some vertical practices are illegal per se while others are made subject to a competition test. In addition, notification and authorisation procedures are available for non-price vertical restraints. Under these processes firms may seek exemption for otherwise illegal behavior under the Act by applying to the Trade Practices Commission ('The Commission' – the administrative body responsible for the Act).[1] Decisions by the Commission on authorisations and notifications can be appealed to the Trade Practices Tribunal (while headed by a judge, the Tribunal has an administrative role, serving to review Commission decisions). However, neither resale price maintenance (RPM) nor price discrimination can be authorised.

II. The Basic Prohibitions

The Act prohibits vertical restraints in several sections. Section 45 prohibits the inclusion of a term in a contract, arrangement or understanding which has an anti-competitive effect (but which excludes certain vertical arrangements such as resale price maintenance and (legislatively defined) exclusive dealing which are covered in separate sections). Section 46 deals with a corporation taking advantage of substantial market power for the purpose of damaging a competitor or preventing entry (which includes refusal to supply). Section 47 is the main section dealing with non-price vertical restrictions while s. 48 prohibits RPM and s. 49 prohibits price discrimination. While ss. 45 and 46 are important to controlling vertical restraints they are not discussed here.[2] Nor are buyer-imposed restraints discussed. Instead, this paper focuses solely on the way the courts, the Commission and the Tribunal have dealt with price and non-price restraints imposed by sellers on the supply of goods and services.[3]

While RPM is illegal per se, price discrimination and all s. 47 non-price exclusive dealing (except for third-line forcing which is illegal per se) are subject to a rule of reason 'competition test'. That is, the conduct is prohibited if it has the purpose or has, or is likely to have, the effect of substantially lessening competition. All vertical prohibitions can be *authorised* except for RPM and price discrimination. Non-price restraints can be *notified*, with the exception of third-line forcing.

Exclusive dealing is defined widely in s. 47 of the Act to include:

- exclusive dealing as commonly understood in the United States (buyers agree to buy all or some stipulated quantity of their goods or services from the seller, at the expense of rival sellers;
- product forcing (either one's own product [tying] or another's [third-line forcing]);
- territorial and customer (re-supply) restrictions.

Prior to 1977, s. 47 did not apply to restrictions imposed by buyers on suppliers (this practice was caught, if at all, by s. 45). Following a review by the Swanson

Committee (1976) s. 47 was amended to include buyer-imposed restrictions because it was considered undesirable to treat differently similar restraints operating in the opposite direction.

Section 47 has not generated much litigation. In particular, the Commission has brought few cases dealing with non-price vertical restraints, with the exception of third-line forcing (s. 47(6)).[4] Instead, enforcement activity has been concentrated outside the courtroom in authorisation and notification applications before the Commission and Tribunal. Both the Commission and the Tribunal have tended to focus on the extent of seller market power and so have ruled against exclusive dealing in situations where the relevant market is highly concentrated and has high barriers to entry.[5] Issues of economic efficiency have been largely ignored. In one of the very few articles dealing with the economics of vertical restraints in Australia, Hanks and Williams (1987) criticised the tendency by the courts, the Commission and the Tribunal to dismiss potential economic efficiencies.

III. Notification and Authorisation

Non-price exclusive dealing is singled out for special treatment in the Act through a unique *notification* procedure, introduced in 1977, which allows a restraint, if notified to the Commission, to gain a statutory interim exemption from the Act until the Commission demonstrates and gives notice that the restraint is anti-competitive and does not yield a net public benefit (s. 93). Thus the restraint is protected from third party or government litigation until the Commission issues a notice.[6] This special procedure does not apply to third-line forcing (the only non-price conduct illegal per se). The Act does not define 'public benefit' but the Commission has listed the following factors as relevant in determining public benefit: economic development; business efficiency; more efficient allocation of resources; expansion of employment (including in certain regions) as well as the prevention of unemployment in efficient industries; industrial harmony; improvement in product quality; and better consumer information.[7]

If a firm applies for an *authorisation*, the Commission may authorise non-price vertical restraints if the benefit to the public outweighs any anti-competitive effect. Even though third-line forcing is illegal *per se* it may be authorised. However, the test for third-line forcing is slightly different. The extent of anti-competitive detriment is not examined (being illegal per se). Instead, the conduct must, in all the circumstances, result in a benefit to the public such that it should be allowed. Reflecting a general aversion to price restraints of any form in the Act, RPM cannot be authorised. The attitude towards RPM is summed up by Smithers J. as follows:

> "So far as resale price maintenance is concerned the object of the Act is to create conditions in which the public will benefit from traders competing with each other in respect of prices unfettered by price restraints imposed by suppliers of goods upon retailers."[8]

For notifications the burden of proving that the conduct has a significant adverse effect on competition without an offsetting public benefit lies with the Commission. On the other hand, the burden for an authorisation rests with the applicant. This view reflects the prevailing orthodoxy at the time the legislation was enacted, namely that vertical relationships were, in general, efficiency enhancing. Because the notification procedure is more beneficial to an applicant (automatic exemption with the burden of proof on the Commission) than authorisation, the latter is only likely to be sought for third-line forcing.

The open-ended nature of 'public benefit' means that goals other than (say, distributive) efficiency may be pursued. Thus the Australian approach to vertical restraints may have more in common with the multi-goal approach of the European Community than the tendency in the United States to focus on allocative efficiency.[9]

IV. The Competition Test

Price discrimination and all non-price prohibitions (apart from third-line forcing) are subject to a competition test. In practice this is the most difficult issue in s. 47. As with the other sections in the Act, the competition test revolves around whether the conduct has the purpose or has, or is likely to have, the effect of substantially lessening competition, where substantial means non-trivial, judged in the context of the actual situation in the relevant market.[10] For example, Keeley J. has noted that "It must be capable of being fairly described as a lessening of competition that is real or of substance as distinct from a lessening that is insubstantial, insignificant or minimal."[11] A relevant market includes markets in which the exclusive dealer or a related body corporate operates or a market in which a person affected by the restriction operates and so includes markets in which either buyers or sellers operate. The inclusion of 'likely' means that the impact on future competition (including potential competition) can be taken into account. Thus the s. 47 test appears to be stricter than s. 3 of the *Clayton Act* which requires a substantial foreclosure effect.[12]

In general, where supply has been refused because a dealer stocks the product of another supplier (exclusive dealing in the US sense) it has been difficult to show that the conduct has had the required effect on competition in a market For example, in *Dandy Power Equipment Pty. Ltd. & Anor. v. Mercury Marine Pty. Ltd.*[13] a manufacturer of outboard marine engines was found not to have engaged in exclusive dealing by cancelling a retail franchise because the dealer had obtained outboard motors from another manufacturer. There was no substantial lessening of competition in the retail market for outboard motors because consumers could buy the withheld product at another showroom a few kilometres away.

Similarly in *Outboard Marine Australia Pty. Ltd. v. Hecar Investments (No 6) Pty. Ltd.*[14] it was held that a manufacturer of marine engines did not breach s. 47 by terminating Hecar's dealer franchise. Hecar could continue to obtain the engines from another dealer but at a higher price. It was held that even though this put Hecar at a competitive disadvantage it was not sufficient to substantially lessen competition. The trial judge had found that the termination would deprive consumers of the opportunity of viewing the competing engines side by side. This approach was rejected on appeal on the basis that the convenience of consumers is not important in determining the state of competition. Thus the definition of the geographic market precluded the conduct having the necessary anti-competitive effect.

Courts balance the pro- and anti-competitive impact of restraints on competition. However, because the analysis is concerned with assessing any diminution of competition, courts tend to focus on the effects of constraints on the competitive *process*. In *Outboard Marine* Bowen C.J. and Fisher J. said:

> "It would seem that 'competition' for the purposes of sec. 47(10) must be read as referring to a process or state of affairs in the market. In considering the state of competition a detailed evaluation of the market structure seems to be required."[15]

This approach is in line with the general goal of antitrust policy in Australia which has been seen by the Commission, the courts and academic commentators as the promotion of 'workable competition' and the welfare of consumers.[16] For example, in a recent submission to a Parliamentary Inquiry, the Commission (1988) said that the Act was intended to provide consumers with the lowest possible prices, to protect small firms from powerful firms and to allow firms to respond to market opportunities. In examining vertical restraints, courts and the Commission have a tendency to balance any efficiencies in distribution with other goals such as the preservation of small business. However, as noted above, efficiency is not seen as the most important goal of competition policy in dealing with vertical restraints. Thus, a dominant firm which increased its competitive strength at the expense of rivals would be seen to have reduced market competition.[17]

V. Supplier Restrictions that Limit Competition in the Buyer's Market

Supplier-imposed customer and territorial restrictions which prevent dealer competition on the basis of service, advertising etc. are permitted as long as the restrictions do not have the purpose, or have or are likely to have the effect of substantially lessening competition. However, vertical price fixing via resale price maintenance is prohibited outright in s. 48. Thus suppliers may restrict dealer competition in any dimension apart from price, subject to the competition test.

V.1. Resale Price Maintenance

Resale price maintenance was prohibited for the first time by the *Restrictive Trade Practices Act 1971*. In 1971 the Australian Council of Trade Unions (ACTU) operated a retail store in Melbourne. About 30 manufacturers who practised RPM refused to supply the ACTU store for selling below the stipulated price. The

ACTU instigated a trade union ban on goods entering or leaving the premises of one of the major manufacturers, Dunlop. As a result Dunlop's stock price dropped considerably. Dunlop then agreed to supply without restriction. The following month the Federal Government announced that RPM would be banned.[18]

Section 48 prohibits the 'practice of RPM' which occurs where a corporation (manufacturer or wholesaler) attempts to specify a minimum price below which goods (not services – although the Hilmer Committee (1993) has recommended that services be included) cannot be resold. RPM is defined in s. 4(1) which, in turn, refers to s. 96(3) which lists six types of conduct by a supplier which constitutes RPM. These are:

- making it known that there will be no supply unless a specified resale price is maintained (s. 96(3)(a)).
- inducing (or attempting to induce) the sale of goods supplied directly or indirectly at or above a specified price (s. 96(3)(b)).
- entering into an agreement (or offering to do so) for supply which includes a provision for resale at or above a price specified by the supplier (s. 96(3)(c)).
- withholding the supply of goods unless the buyer agrees not to sell below a price specified by the seller (s. 96(3)(d)).
- a supplier withholding the supply of goods to a second person because a third person who obtains goods from the second person sells or will not agree not to sell below the price set by the supplier (s. 96(3)(e)).
- the use of a price statement likely to be understood as the price below which goods may not be sold (s. 96(3)(f)). However, recommended prices are not included (s. 97).[19]

The Australian position on RPM is much tougher than the position in the US, where RPM is perceived to be little different in its impact from non-price restraints and so a rule of reason approach is considered more appropriate.[20] In Australia, "...unilateral acts may constitute resale price maintenance ... whereas, in the United States, the *Sherman Act* 1890 (US) only prohibits agreements on resale price."[21] The prohibition on RPM is not confined to the retail level but covers RPM at all stages of distribution.

The Commission has actively prosecuted s. 48. Hurley (1991, p. 419) points out that:

> "In many of the cases brought, the supplier has admitted the contravention or withdrawn its defence to the allegations after proceedings have commenced, leaving the court to determine the appropriate penalty under s. 76. The highest penalties imposed under the Act have been in relation to breaches of s. 48."

Between 1971 and June 1990, 39 RPM cases were litigated. Of these the Commission started 33. Of the remaining six cases, two were started by private litigants to obtain damages on the basis of decisions in cases won by the Commission. The Commission's preoccupation with RPM may be explainable, at least in part, by the lower evidentiary requirements of a per se test. Of the 39 cases, only two were lost by those instituting the litigation. The situation in Australia contrasts starkly with that in the United States where more than 60 per cent of RPM cases are started by private litigants.[22] However, the relatively low level of private litigation can be largely explained by the absence of triple damages and contingency fees, in general, in Australia.

The per se nature of the test and the inability to obtain an authorisation has meant that enforcement has been solely concerned with whether the statutory test for RPM has been satisfied. The courts see RPM as preventing price competition. In *BP Australia Limited. v Trade Practices Commission*,[23] a wholesaler of petroleum products discounted its motor spirit (gasoline) wholesale price to dealers in order to compete with prices charged by competitors. BP gave support to a dealer whereby the dealer's wholesale "buying price [will] be 40.9 [cents per litre] to retail at 43.4" (at p. 47,653). The dealer sold at 41.8 c.p.l. and was told by BP that the price support would be withdrawn unless the price was increased. This was found to be RPM by the Full Federal Court. RPM, it said, is "designed to promote competitive pricing at the point of resale." (at p. 47,655).

The economic debate about the merits of RPM in the United States has had little impact in Australia. Hanks and Williams (1987, p. 156) point out that:

> "The published records of Court and Commission decisions on vertical restraints on distribution (geographic and customer restraints and RPM) contain no direct references to the possibility that the restraint may be justified as a means of preventing one dealer from free-riding on the services of another."

This conclusion is not surprising given that there is little opportunity to advance efficiency arguments in court. In the only empirical study of court cases involving RPM in Australia, Wang and Davison (1992) found that between 1971 and mid 1990, most RPM cases involved individual suppliers and about half involved complex products, both factors suggesting possible efficiency explanations for RPM (the promotion of dealer services). However, they concluded that "RPM in most cases lessens competition with little redeeming social benefit and the arguments from the Chicago School of Economics that it is pro-competitive are largely inapplicable in Australia for a number of reasons."[24] However, this conclusion is not warranted given that their study focussed on cases in which neither the impact of RPM on competition nor economic efficiency was argued.

The onus of proof in RPM cases is reversed where it can be shown that a supplier has withheld supply, having become aware within the previous six months that the buyer was discounting the product (s. 100). The supplier must prove that the withholding was not the result of an attempt to impose RPM.

While RPM cannot be authorised at the moment, the former 1971 Act allowed for an exemption if the Tribunal was satisfied that there was a detriment to consumers if an exemption was not granted. Only one application was lodged but was disallowed. In that case an Australian publisher applied for an application with respect to books claiming, inter alia, that without RPM, consumers would suffer because the range and quality of books would be reduced, the number of retail outlets would be reduced and, ultimately, prices would increase. The Tribunal rejected these arguments and concluded that the abolition of RPM would have little impact on the book trade.[25] The 1974 Act does not provide for exemptions but there is one RPM exception. Goods may be withheld from a reseller who engages in 'loss-leadering', ie selling below cost where cost is the cost of the goods to the reseller (ie net acquisition cost which includes the price less any rebates plus freight and insurance costs to deliver). The exception does not extend to genuine seasonal or clearance sales. Note that the Act does not prohibit loss-leadering, but only allows sellers to prevent it.

Despite RPM's per se illegality, benefits from the provision of dealer services have been argued in a number of cases. For example, in *Trade Practices Commission v. ICI Australia Petrochemicals Ltd. & Anor.*,[26] ICI introduced a new distribution system following the unsuccessful launch of a chemical for cleaning swimming pools. Many consumer complaints had been received because retailers did not provide advice on the proper use of the chemicals. The new arrangements did not require retailers to maintain a certain retail price, but ICI encouraged retailers not to engage in price cutting so that they could make sufficient profits to provide effective service and technical support. Nevertheless ICI was fined – although the judge thought that the distribution system could have been introduced in a way which did not breach the Act.[27]

In one of the few RPM cases lost by the Commission, the Full Federal Court in *Trade Practices Commission v. Penfolds Wines Pty. Limited. & Anors.*[28] held that Penfolds did not engage in RPM by 'inducing' a major liquor wholesaler to 'come into line' with Penfolds' prices. The Court said that RPM related to the specification of a minimum price. In this case the liquor wholesaler could still set prices greater or less than Penfolds' specified price.

The Commission often uses the threat of litigation to force companies to introduce compliance programs. For example, following an admission by Toshiba (Australia) Pty. Ltd. that it had engaged in RPM, Toshiba entered into an agreement with the Commission which required the company to set up a staff training program and report on its success to the Commission. Every Toshiba dealer in Australia received a letter from Toshiba telling it that it was free to advertise and set its own prices for Toshiba products.

Unlike the United States, there has been little pressure for a relaxation of the absolute prohibition on RPM.[29] The Blunt Committee (1979) recommended the continuation of the absolute prohibition and said that: "... the prohibition of resale price maintenance is fundamental to the fostering of price competition and in line with the competitive thrust of Pt IV of the Act."[30] Many economists doubt the wisdom of banning RPM outright. RPM does not prevent non-price intrabrand competition, whereas territorial or customer restrictions eliminate all intrabrand competition. RPM maintains an incentive to provide services while territorial restrictions do not. Posner (1975, p. 292) considers RPM and territorial restrictions are in the same category, while customer restrictions are less dangerous.[31] Despite these arguments RPM cannot be authorised. However, pressure for change is developing. The Hilmer Committee (1993) recommended that the per se prohibition on RPM continue but that "... authorisation should be available to permit firms to argue their case if they believe that their proposed RPM would enhance economic efficiency".[32] The Committee recommended this course of action because:

> "The Committee has not been presented with convincing evidence that efficiency-enhancing RPM occurs with such frequency that the per se prohibition should be relaxed. ... The economic theory associated with RPM does, however, present convincing argument that RPM can, in certain circumstances, enhance economic efficiency."[33]

V.2. Customer and Territorial Restrictions

Section 47(2)(f) provides that exclusive dealing occurs where a supplier places customer and geographic restrictions on the buyer. Section 47(3)(f) covers refusals to supply because the restrictions will not be agreed to. Similar to the situation in the United States,[34] customer and territorial restrictions are subject to a rule of reason and are only prohibited if they substantially lessen competition. The Act also covers restrictions in the opposite direction, i.e. where the distributor or dealer demands the restriction. Section 47(4) designates exclusive dealing as occurring where a dealer acquires goods or services subject to the supplier agreeing to a restrictive condition (eg that the manufacturer will not supply goods of a particular kind to certain customers or to certain places – and so covers franchise agreements).[35]

Under the notification procedure the benefits of the restrictions on interbrand competition can be weighed against possible detriment to intrabrand competition. However, as Heydon points out:

> "Section 47(13)(b) states that a reference to competition shall be read as a reference to competition in any market in which the party practising exclusive dealing competes, or any market in which the person whose business dealings are restricted competes. It does not say that one can be offset against another. If at one level, the brand constitutes a market and competition is substantially affected in that market, does that not end the inquiry, no matter how beneficial the conduct may be in other markets at other levels which may extend beyond the brand?"[36]

Firms have an incentive to seek notification/authorisation and so argue that the benefits of interbrand competition outweigh any losses from reduced intrabrand competition. The alternative is to run the risk of legal action by the Commission, where a court may find the relevant market to be restricted to a market for the firm's brand.

There have been very few court cases dealing with customer and territorial restrictions in Australia – most have not progressed beyond the Commission. Refusing to supply a discounter was found by the Federal Court to substantially lessen competition in a market for ski boots.[37] The Commission has approved a restriction intended to ensure that dealers had sufficient training to meet customer and safety needs.[38]

In general, the Commission has not found geographic constraints at the wholesale level to be anti-competitive, provided the wholesaler was faced with competition from other brands or there were large buyers willing to buy in another geographic area. Customer or geographic restrictions are less likely to be approved by the Commission if the restriction is accompanied by another restriction (e.g. a requirements contract or an exclusive franchise).

On the other hand, in the few cases dealing with geographic areas at the retail level, the Commission has been unwilling to grant authorisations. A major exception has been newspaper and magazine distribution. While the arrangements differ from state to state, the distribution of newspapers and magazines are generally organised as follows. Publishers collectively (through a Newsagency Council) give a newsagent a territorial monopoly to sell and home deliver newspapers and magazines. In return, the newsagent must agree not to sell or home-deliver outside the allotted area. The publisher sets a maximum fee for home delivery of newspapers and any loss on home delivery of newspapers is covered by profits on magazine sales. The system is designed to maximise newspaper circulation. In addition a sale or return system operates so that the publisher bears the risk of unsold stock. As a result newsagencies are able to carry a wider range of stock. Publishers effectively control entry and exit at the retail level because newsagents must agree to dispose of the newsagency through a publisher transfer system. In *John Fairfax and Sons Ltd.* the Commission granted authorisation to the system in New South Wales and the Australian Capital Territory on public benefit grounds.[39] Benefits included greater availability of newspapers and magazines and an efficient home delivery service. However, an interim authorisation in South Australia was later withdrawn by the Commission because the Commission was dubious about the benefits of distribution. The fact that there was greater concentration in the printing and distribution of newspapers and magazines in South Australia than in New South Wales seemed to be of importance. The Commission has recently authorised a Victorian newsagency distribution system on the basis that the scheme provided public benefits (low cost, efficient home delivery service and the widespread availability of a broad range of publications). Of major importance to the Commission's findings was the inclusion of rules that allowed for the development of cross-territory home delivery which might lead to the development of delivery-only newsagents.[40]

In examining exclusive franchises, the Commission considers both the product and geographic markets. Australia-wide franchises are approved, providing the products only involve a small proportion of total sales. However, exclusive franchises in a small geographic area may be prohibited if competition from other suppliers is inadequate.[41] Agreements will be illegal if a supplier enters into similar agreements with a large number of dealers which foreclose the market. The length of time involved in the restriction is also important. For example, the Queensland Rugby Football League gave a radio station a five year exclusive right to broadcast rugby league (football) games, but this was held to be too long because it prevented other commercial radio stations from competing in the broadcasting of rugby league matches and so reduced their ability to obtain advertising.[42]

VI. Supplier Restrictions that Limit Competition in the Supplier's Market

Supplier restrictions can be anti-competitive if these restrictions attempt to foreclose part of the downstream market to competitors of the supplier. Suppliers can do this in two ways. First, by placing restrictions on a dealer's ability to buy from a competitor of the supplier. Second, if a supplier has market power in one product, to use that power by making its supply conditional on the dealer agreeing to take another of the supplier's products or (in collaboration with another supplier) that other supplier's products. In assessing the impact of an exclusive dealing arrangement regard will be had to whether the arrangement furthers a seller cartel or impacts in other ways such as raising barriers to entry in the seller's market.

Section 47(2)(d) regulates the situation where a supplier restricts the ability of a buyer to buy from a competitor of the supplier (which is the meaning of exclusive dealing in s. 3 of the *Clayton Act*). Thus s. 47(2)(d) covers solus agreements, requirements contracts and tying arrangements. Section 47(3) covers refusing to deal because the buyer will not agree to a condition. To infringe s. 47(2)(d) a supplier must either supply or offer to supply goods or services or supplies or offers to supply goods or services at a particular price or gives a rebate, discount etc. (or refuses to supply) on condition that the buyer:

(a) agrees not to buy goods and services from another supplier (solus agreements);

(b) agrees to buy all or part of its requirements of goods and services from the supplier (a requirements contract);

(c) agrees to take a second (tied) product from the (same) supplier (tying).

The phrase 'on condition' is defined very broadly in s. 47(13)(a). There is no need for direct proof and so the

> "... condition may be inferred from the behaviour of parties; it must be possible to state that they are only behaving as they are because of the condition .... the dealer need not agree not to do certain things; it is enough that it accepts goods or services unwillingly on certain conditions which have the same effect as if it had agreed not to do certain things."[43]

VI.1. Solus Agreements and Requirements Contracts

The main issue here is whether solus agreements (full requirements) or requirements contracts substantially lessen competition, i.e. the extent to which the agreement affects interbrand competition (or forecloses markets to competitors of the supplier). There seems little doubt that s. 47(2) covers the situation where a distributor agrees to supply the 'requirements' of the retailer (there is an implied condition

– you take none from elsewhere) or even where the distributor agrees to supply a certain percentage.[44] But it is not clear where the boundary should be drawn – does the sale of a durable product mean that the customer has agreed not to buy the good or service from a competitor? A single purchase is unlikely to substantially lessen competition or even to be supplied 'on condition' that the buyer not buy from someone else. As usual the limits are determined by the practical consequences of exclusive dealing on competition.

In *Streets Ice Cream Pty. Ltd.* the Commission found that the practise of ice-cream manufacturers hiring refrigeration equipment to retailers on the condition that the retailers only stocked that manufacturer's products in it breached s. 47(2) because smaller retailers did not have space for more than one refrigerator.[45] In *Val Morgan & Co (Aust.) Pty. Ltd.*[46] agreement to take a certain quantity of advertising slides and films, which were above the amount a cinema could reasonably show, was found to exclude rivals.

Like courts in the United States,[47] the Commission considers, in relation to the competition test, the percentage of the market affected by the restriction and the length of time of any solus agreement or requirements contract. In *Shell Co of Australia Ltd.*[48] the Commission refused to give a clearance to exclusive dealing agreements between petrol (gasoline) suppliers and retailers because the agreements restricted competition between suppliers and between retailers.[49] At a later authorisation proceeding the Commission placed considerable emphasis on barriers to entry at the wholesale level.[50] These barriers included:

- no independent refiners (wholesalers would have to refine or get supplies from integrated major companies who both refined and wholesaled);
- major companies (other than Caltex and Shell) refined to satisfy their own market requirements only;
- imported refined petrol was at a high price;
- new entrants would have difficulty because the Transport Workers Union would not deliver petrol to pumps not branded with a major company's brand, i.e. the union would only allow delivery of petroleum products from refineries in company-branded tankers into the branded tanks of the same company.

The Commission made no mention of barriers to entry at the retail end but was concerned with the fact that these contracts were the norm in the industry. Thus its decision was made essentially on the basis of the limited number of wholesalers coupled with the extensive use of exclusive requirements contracts. The Commission did not balance increased interbrand competition against reduced intrabrand competition. Instead, retailer competition was seen as an extension of wholesaler competition. It said:

> "Competition in the retail market is competition for motorist consumers, and exclusive dealing makes it significantly competition between the companies, with the tied dealers acting as 'conduits' of the branded products. Shell gets much of the control over supply of its products that it would get by selling itself to the consumer... without the disadvantages of employer-employee

relationships. In general the companies do not encourage price competition, although they do react to it when it occurs in particular localities."[51]

The Commission found no public benefits from the arrangements. Shell had argued that exclusive dealing reduced costs through a better distribution system, more certainty and hence greater investment. It was argued that consumers would get lower prices and better service via the training of retailers. But the Commission said, citing United States experience,[52] that multi-brand trading would only occur on very high gallonage sites if the exclusive dealing arrangements were abolished. The Commission accepted that solus trading created economic efficiencies but did not accept that solus trading would cease if the practice was not authorised, i.e. the benefits would continue without authorisation.

In the matter *In re Tooth & Co. Ltd.; In re Tooheys Ltd.*,[53] brewers had sole supply agreements with hotels (which lasted for 70 to 100 years for non brewery-owned hotels). The brewers argued that if exclusive dealing were not permitted, hotels would serve competing draught beers which would lead to reduced quality control, increased delivery costs and the replacement of independent lessees or hotel owners with brewery employees in brewery owned hotels. The Commission found the arrangements anti-competitive for a number of reasons, which were confirmed when the case was appealed to the Trade Practices Tribunal. The Tribunal found that the arrangements denied brewers access to each other's tied hotels; impeded market penetration of interstate brewers; enhanced barriers to entry by new brewers; contributed to barriers to entry for new hoteliers; and operated in much the same way as a market sharing agreement.

A requirements contract was considered by the Full Federal Court in *O'Brien Glass Industries Ltd. v. Cool and Sons Pty. Ltd.*[54] O'Brien Glass was a wholesaler and fitter of windscreens in a country town. Cools and Sons fitted windscreens. O'Brien offered discounts of up to 50 per cent if retailers purchased all or most of their windscreens from it. Cool purchased windscreens from another supplier and O'Brien reduced its discount. While there was another major wholesaler in the area and several smaller ones, O'Brien was the only one that operated 24 hours per day, seven days per week. Cool complained that it would lose sales because it could not compete. The Full Federal Court accepted that the behavior was exclusive dealing which substantially lessened competition in the wholesale market – in a geographic area of 100 miles in radius from the town. The majority judges accepted evidence from the other major wholesaler that O'Brien was trying to exclude it from selling to retailers. As Fox J. put it:

> "There can be no doubt that there was a purpose in this requirement. It was to coerce retailers into dealing with it and not, to a limited extent, its competitors. The tendency was to lower the forces of competition in the market, by reducing the capacity of retailers to choose between sources of supply, to weaken the trading position of competitors, and to inhibit the entry of other competitors." (at p. 44,456)

The dissenting judge found no substantial lessening of competition because, in practical terms, the market after Cool's loss of discount was just as competitive as before and that most windscreens could be obtained at the same price from both major wholesalers during business hours.

VI.2. Tying (or Full Line Forcing)

There is a close relationship between requirements contracts and tying. With ties, the dealing in one product (the 'tying' product) is conditional on dealing in a second product (the 'tied' product). In a requirements contract the dealing in one product is conditional on dealing in more of the same product. To succeed, the supplier must have some market power over the tying product. But the question remains why would a rational firm with monopoly power in one market tie a second product when the gains from market power can be exploited in the first market? The answer lies in whether additional profits can be made in the tied product's market. If the tied product market is competitive, then the monopolist will gain nothing by tying unless tying leads to the firm gaining monopoly power (for example, where the tying and tied products are complements). If successful, tying may raise the barriers to entry into the tied product market because new entrants may have to make the tying product as well.

Tying is prohibited in Australia if it substantially lessens competition. To date there have been no judicial decisions on tying. Tying falls within s. 47(2) even though the buyer is able to determine whether to take the tying product or not. For example, the supply of photocopiers on the condition that the electrostatic paper be obtained from the same supplier was found to fall within s 47.(2).[55] Nashua had the second largest share of copiers in a highly concentrated market. The Commission found that independent paper suppliers were foreclosed from competing with Nashua. In its determination the Commission made special note of the fact that Nashua had attacked similar behaviour by SCM in the United States and had argued that the action of SCM in tying service contracts to sales was done solely for anti-competitive purposes.

While the 'single product defence' in which the tying and tied products are determined to be one product has been accepted in the United States,[56] the issue has not arisen, at least in the context of tying, in Australia except for a third-line forcing case, to be discussed below. While tying is illegal, per se, in the United States, to prove it requires showing that the firm has "appreciable economic power" in the tying market and that there is a "not insubstantial foreclosure" of trade in the tied product market.[57] There are some similarities in Australia with the approach in the United States. In examining tying arrangements, the Commission puts considerable emphasis on the size of the tying firm, the proportion of the market protected and the length of the arrangement. However, there is no direct concern with whether there is sufficient market power in the tying market to affect the outcome in the market for the tied good. This may change in the future. Hurley (1991, p. 378) suggests that:

> "It may be that some of the factors which the American Courts and writers have identified as being significant in the characterisation of the transaction will also have relevance as matters going to public benefit of tying one product to another."

VI.3. Third-Line Forcing

The Commission has been active in pursuing breaches of ss. 47 (6) and (7) which cover what is termed third-line forcing in Australia. This is the situation in which a supplier will only supply goods and services on condition that the acquirer takes goods or services from another supplier. While third-line forcing is illegal outright it is still subject to authorisation (s. 88(8)) if it can be justified on public benefit grounds.

The per se illegality of third-line forcing is curious. While tying is subject to a competition test, third line forcing is illegal. Thus instead of tying one's own product (which is prohibited under s. 47(2) (a))

> "... manufacturers might instead stipulate that the second product, instead of being taken from it, could be taken from a specified range of competent manufacturers. This is regarded as a lawful alternative to tying in America. But these less restrictive alternatives seem to be caught by s. 47(6), no matter how slight their effect on competition. Thus a less restrictive alternative is treated more harshly than the more restrictive one."[58]

The High Court has taken a literal approach to the interpretation of s. 47(6). For example, in *Castlemaine Tooheys Ltd. v. Williams and Hodgson Transport Pty. Ltd.*,[59] Castlemaine sold 'Fourex' beer either through one of four regional outlets in Queensland or from Brisbane. License fees were paid either on the Brisbane price or if bought from a regional outlet, on the cost to the retailer, including freight. As North Queensland retailers faced high transport costs, their license fees could be reduced considerably by buying from Brisbane. However, if bought from Brisbane delivery could only be effected through Castlemaine's approved carrier. The High Court held that the supply of beer on condition that it be delivered by a designated carrier was a supply of delivered beer and not two separate supplies of beer and transport. The conduct did not fall within s. 47(6) essentially because retailers were not 'forced' to buy from Brisbane – they could buy from a regional centre and pay higher license fees. The 'condition' was that the brewer arrange delivery, not that the acquirer buy transport services.

Hurley (1987) has criticised the *Castlemaine Tooheys* case because, interpreted literally, s. 47(6) is meaningless. It seems that the High Court was reluctant to find that a normal commercial practice was illegal because of the possible consequences. The Court did not lay down any principles for distinguishing a 'package' or single good from the supply of separate goods and services. She suggests that, in future, courts should look more to the anti-competitive effects of the section rather than concentrating on "the strict characterisation of the conduct."

In *Re Ku-ring-gai Co-operative Building Society (No. 12) Limited.*,[60] third-line forcing was found where a building society imposed a requirement that insurance on the mortgaged property be taken out with a designated insurance company. In the High Court, Deane J. said that third-line forcing would not be found if the borrower was only required to insure the interest of the building society as mortgagee. In this case the building society would be buying insurance through the borrower as agent. In *Castlemaine Tooheys*, Gibbs C.J. used this argument from *Ku-ring-gai* to argue that the carrier's services were bought by Castlemaine Tooheys. But in *Ku-ring-gai* the benefit accrued to the building society, while in *Castlemaine Tooheys* the brewer was not using the buyer as agent in buying transport on behalf of the brewer and so did not receive a direct benefit. Both cases illustrate the literal approach to interpreting the section – the purpose of the section being lost.

The issue whether third-line forcing be prohibited at all has not been the subject of much debate in Australia. The Hilmer Committee (1993) recommended that third-line forcing be subject to the competition test and be subject to notification. The Committee recommended these changes because:

> "In some cases third line forcing will be less restrictive than full-line forcing conduct ... there appears to be no significant policy rationale for distinguishing between third-line forcing and other vertical agreements."[61]

In a recent paper, McEwin (1994) argues that third-line forcing would be better approached by introducing a separate test (perhaps in s. 46 which deals with misuse of market power) which concentrates on the two perceived evils of third-line forcing – the extent to which monopoly was extended to the tied market and whether a commission was paid by the tying firm to the tied firm.

VII. Price Discrimination

The price discrimination section of the Act (s. 49) is based on the *Robinson-Patman Act* in the United States. It covers situations where a supplier discriminates (for example via discounts) between different buyers of similar quality where the effect is to substantially lessen competition. Price discrimination does not occur where the price differential reflects cost differences or has a pro-competitive effect on the market. Buyers are also prohibited form inducing a supplier to discriminate if they are aware that the effect will be to substantially lessen competition.

The Commission has never litigated s. 49. Both the Swanson Committee (1976) and the Blunt Committee (1979) recommended that s. 49 be repealed. In addition:

> "The Industry Commission Report on Raw Materials Processing expressed concern that the existence of the section may be hindering some raw materials processors from price discriminating as between export and domestic sales. Concerns have also been expressed that s. 49 may hinder firms in oligopolistic markets from offering discounts."[62]

The Commission (1993) in its submission to the Hilmer Committee also recommended its repeal, mainly because undesirable behavior could be dealt with under the headings of misuse of market power and unconscionable conduct in other sections of the Act. The Hilmer Committee agreed and concluded that:

> "The Committee considers that price discrimination generally enhances economic efficiency, except in cases which may be dealt with by s. 45 (anti-competitive agreements) or s. 46 (misuse of market power). To the extent that s. 49 has any effect it seems to have been to diminish price competition. The Committee does not consider that competition policy should be distorted to provide special protection to any interest group, including small business, particularly where this is potentially to the detriment of the welfare of the community as a whole."[63]

VIII. Some Concluding Comments

Public policy towards vertical restraints is complex. This paper has only attempted to provide a broad overview of some of the more important cases and issues in this area in Australia. The *Trade Practices Act* spells out prohibitions on vertical restraints in considerable detail. Because most vertical restraints are subject to an examination of public net benefit, economics has had more impact in administrative rather than judicial processes. Apart from the per se prohibitions, most of the action has taken place outside the courts in notification and authorisation proceedings. When issues have reached the courts the outcome has tended to reflect more the complexities of statutory interpretation and less the economics – but litigation has been few and far between, no doubt because of the avenues open to applicants through the notification and authorisation processes. Whereas courts can only consider anti-competitive detriment, the Commission and Tribunal can consider not only anti-competitive detriment but also public benefit.

The Commission believes that the substantial lessening of competition tests in ss. 47 and 49 will not be met unless the corporation has substantial market power (the Commission may have been influenced by the US Justice Department's Vertical Restraints Guidelines (1985) which require evidence of market power). The Commission (1988), in its submission to the Griffith Committee (1989) recommended that with the exception of s. 48 (RPM) all vertical conduct (i.e. s. 47 (exclusive dealing) and s. 49 (price discrimination)) should be included in a new 'misuse of market power' s. 46 which "prohibits a corporation with a substantial market power from engaging in conduct which has the purpose or has or is likely to have the effect of lessening competition in any market." (p. 2). The Commission's proposal would extend, considerably, the reach of the Act by omitting 'substantially' from the competition test.

Competition policy towards vertical restraints in Australia reflects a belief that vertical price restraints are not desirable, but that non-price restraints are worthy of investigation to assess public benefit. Apart from third-line forcing, non-price restraints are not only subject to a competition test, but may be sanctioned, even if anti-competitive, if the benefits exceed the anti-competitive detriment, through the notification (where the burden of proof lies with the Commission) and authorisation (where the burden lies with the applicant) proceedings. Even third-line forcing, which is illegal per se, can be authorised if the benefits are sufficient. Following the Hilmer Committee recommendation it seems likely that, in the future, third-line forcing will be brought under the competition test and made eligible for notification, thus making all non-price vertical restraints subject to the same test.

In the absence of any empirical studies it is difficult to decide whether, on balance, the detailed approach to vertical restraints in Australia has provided a net public benefit. Certainly, the approach to non-price restraints is more likely to have provided a positive net public benefit partly because of the ability offered by the Act to demonstrate public benefit, and partly because these issues have been determined outside the courtroom. Vertical price restrictions have not fared as well, and some would argue that there is a case for extending the non-price rule of reason and its associated administrative processes to the per se price prohibitions.

Economic efficiency has not been as important in the enforcement of non-price vertical restraints as many economists would like. The authorisation/notification processes have given the Commission the opportunity to consider and promote many objectives, although it has not fully taken up the opportunity to consider whether economic efficiency rationales lie behind vertical non-price restraints in Australia. An important reason for this may be the limited resources available to the Commission.

Notes

* I would like to thank David Round for suggestions and comments on an earlier draft.

[1] Third-line forcing (the tying of another firm's product) cannot be notified but may be authorised. A recent Federal Government Committee has recommended that third-line forcing be notifiable – see Hilmer (1993).

[2] For a discussion of the overlap see Callaway (1980) and McEwin (1992). See the paper by Williams in this issue for a discussion of the application of s. 46 to vertical issues.

[3] Section 47 also cover leases and licenses but these are not discussed here.

[4] The Commission has brought a high proportion of s. 47 cases against financiers which have insisted that borrowers insure with a designated insurance company – see McEwin (1994).

[5] See Hurley (1991, p. 327).

[6] This flowed from a recommendation in the Swanson Committee Report: "We recommend that there should be a procedure which would enable registration of such conduct with the Trade Practices Commission. Thereafter, the conduct would be lawful unless there was or was likely to be a substantial adverse effect on competition in a market for goods or services, and that the agreement or practice did not result, or was not likely to result, in a net benefit to the public. By requiring the Commission to determine these matters positively, we believe that much of the present criticism relating to the problem of proof (sometimes put to us as 'guilty until innocence can be proved') is alleviated." (1976, para 4.121) The Committee intended that the notification procedure would replace the authorisation procedure for exclusive dealing by changing the burden of proof.

[7] See *Re ACI Operations Pty. Ltd.* (1991) ATPR 50–108. While economic considerations are important, it is still possible that there be no economic benefits at all – see *Re Westralian Farmers' Co-operative Ltd* (1979) 37 FLR 244.

[8] *Trade Practices Commission v. Stihl Chain Saws (Aust.) Pty. Ltd.* (1978) ATPR 40–091, at p. 17,896.
[9] This was originally pointed out by Brunt (1975, p. 11).
[10] If there is more than one purpose, it is enough that one of the purposes will substantially lessen competition.
[11] *Cool & Sons Pty. Ltd. v. O'Brien Glass Industries Ltd.* (1981) ATPR 40–220 at p. 43,003.
[12] See *Standard Oil Co of California v. US 337* US 293 (1949).
[13] (1982) ATPR 40–315.
[14] (1982) ATPR 40–327.
[15] *Ibid*, p. 43,983.
[16] See the discussion in Chapter 1 of Corones (1990).
[17] See *Re Ford Motor Co. of Australia Ltd.* (1977) ATPR 40–043.
[18] Bob Hawke, a future Prime Minister of Australia, was an active participant on the ACTU side.
[19] For example, putting the words "recommended price" on goods does not breach the Act. However, courts may treat recommendations as being mandatory and so breach the Act. Each situation depends on its facts – see *Trade Practices Commission v. Bata Shoe Company of Australia Pty. Ltd.* (1980) ATPR 40–161.
[20] See *Monsanto Co. v. Spray-Rite Corporation* 104 Sup. Ct. 1464 (1984).
[21] Wang and Davison (1992, p. 35).
[22] Ippolito (1988) *Resale Price Maintenance: Economic Evidence From Litigation* (FTC, Bureau of Economics Staff Report. p. 40), reported in Wang and Davison (1992, p. 62).
[23] (1986) ATPR 40–701.
[24] Wang and Davison (1992, p. 96).
[25] *Re Application By A.H. and A.W. Reed Pty. Ltd.* (1972) ATPR 36–005. A subsequent study showed that the Tribunal was largely right – see Table H of Chapter 6 of Nieuwenhuysen and Oakley (1975).
[26] (1983) ATPR 40–364.
[27] *Ibid*, at pp. 44,369–44,370.
[28] (1991) ATPR 41–071.
[29] Hanks and Williams (1987, p. 150).
[30] Blunt (1979, p. 60).
[31] RPM, Posner considers, controls the amount of service given, ie. the higher the price the more service. Also, if territorial restrictions are needed to get dealers to take a new product then same argument applies to RPM. There has been little public debate in Australia on this issue.
[32] Hilmer (1993, p. 58).
[33] Hilmer (1993, p. 57).
[34] See *Continental T.V. v. GTE Sylvania, Inc.* 433 U.S. 36 (1977).
[35] It should be noted that an agreement between dealers or suppliers to seek customer or territorial restrictions is covered by s. 45. As well, the prohibition on sellers placing customer and territorial re-supply restrictions on buyers only applies to the re-supply of goods and so does not apply where a franchisor simply licenses a trademark.
[36] Heydon (looseleaf service, para 6.1180).
[37] *Mark Lyons Pty Limited. v. Bursill Sportsgear Pty. Limited* (1987) ATPR 40–809.
[38] *Hoover (Australia) Pty. Ltd.* (1976–77) ATPR 15,901.
[39] (1980) ATPR (Com) 35–200.
[40] *Newsagency Council of Victoria Limited and Others* (1993) ATPR (Com.) 50–134.
[41] See *Pioneer Concrete (Vic) Pty. Ltd.* (1975–76) ATPR 15,901. A quarry agreed not to supply sand to other concrete manufacturers within a 30 mile radius without Pioneer's consent. This was held to be illegal because it prevented Pioneer's competitor from being supplied – transport costs limiting the geographic market.
[42] *Queensland Rugby Football League Inc* (1976–77) ATPR (Com.) 35–100 at p. 15,666.
[43] Heydon (looseleaf service, para 6.140).
[44] *Ibid*, para 6.160.
[45] (1974–75) ATPR 8,609.
[46] (1974–75) ATPR 8,650.
[47] United States courts generally make a detailed analysis of the market and the peculiar situation of requirements contracts etc – see *Tampa Electric Co. v. Nashville Coal Co.* 365 U.S. 320 (1961).

[48] (1974–75) ATPR 8,621.
[49] Prior to 1977 the Commission could grant a clearance which deemed a contract orunderstanding not to be in restraint of trade if the Commission believed the conduct did not have a significant effect on competition.
[50] (1975–1976) ATPR (Com) 16,701.
[51] (1975) 3 TPR 15 reprinted in Hurley (1991, p. 357).
[52] *Standard Stations* 337 US 293 (1949).
[53] (1979) ATPR 40–113.
[54] (1983) ATPR 40–376.
[55] *Nashua Australia Pty. Ltd.* (1974–1975) ATPR 8,720.
[56] *United States v. Jerrold Electronics Corp.* 187 F. Supp. 545 (1960).
[57] See *Fortner Enterprises, Inc. v United States Steel Corp.* 394 U.S. 495 (1969).
[58] Heydon, *supra* n. 43 at para 6.330.
[59] (1986) ATPR 40–751.
[60] (1978) ATPR 40–094.
[61] Hilmer (1993, p. 53).
[62] Trade Practices Commission (1993).
[63] Hilmer (1993, p. 79).

References

Blunt, R.G. (Chairman, The Trade Practices Consultative Committee), (1979) *Small Business and the Trade Practices Act.* Canberra, Australian Government Publishing Service.
Brunt, M. (1975) 'Economic Overview' in *Trade Practices Lectures*, Monash University.
Callaway, Francis H. (1980) 'Section 45 or 47?' *Australian Law Journal*, **54**, 200–205.
Corones, Stephen G. (1990) *Competition Law and Policy in Australia.* North Ryde, The Law Book Company Limited.
Griffiths, Alan (Chairman, House of Representatives Standing Committee on Legal and Constitutional Affairs) (1989) *Mergers, Takeovers and Monopolies: Profiting From Competition?* Canberra, Australian Government Publishing Service.
Hanks, Frances and Phillip L. Williams (1987) 'The Treatment of Vertical Restraints Under the Australian Trade Practices Act', *Australian Business Law Review*, **15**, 147–168.
Heydon, John D. (ed.) *Trade Practices Law.* Sydney, The Law Book Company Limited (looseleaf service).
Hilmer, Frederick G. (Chairman, The Independent Committee of Inquiry) (1993) *National Competition Policy.* Canberra, Australian Government Publishing Service.
Hurley, Anne (1987) 'The Castlemaine Tooheys Case and the Interpretation of Third-Line Forcing', *Australian Law Journal*, **61**, 415–420.
Hurley, Anne (1991) *Restrictive Trade Practices.* North Ryde, The Law Book Company Limited.
McEwin, R. Ian (1992) 'The Common Ground Between Section 46 and Section 47 (2) of the Trade Practices Act', *Australian Journal of Corporate Law*, **2**, 214–224.
McEwin, R. Ian (1994) 'Third-Line Forcing in Australia', *Australian Business Law Review* **22**, 114–137.
Mathewson, Frank, and Ralph Winter (1990) 'The Law and Economics of Vertical Restraints', in Frank Mathewson, Michael J. Trebilcock and Michael Walker (eds) *The Law and Economics of Competition Policy.* Vancouver, B.C., Fraser Institute.
Nieuwenhuysen, John P., and E.E. Oakley (1975) *Competition In Australian Bookselling.* Melbourne, Melbourne University Press.
Posner, Richard A. (1975) 'Antitrust Policy and the Supreme Court: An Analysis of the Restricted Distribution, Horizontal Merger and Potential Competition Decisions', *Columbia Law Review*, **75**, 282–327.
Swanson, T.B. (Chairman, Trade Practices Act Review Committee) (1976) *Report to the Minister of Business and Consumer Affairs.* Canberra, Australian Government Publishing Service.
Trade Practices Commission (1988) *Misuse of Market Power.* Submission to the Griffiths Committee of Inquiry into Mergers, Takeovers and Monopolies, Canberra.

Trade Practices Commission (1993) *Submission to the National Competition Policy Review*. Canberra.
United States Department of Justice (1985) *Vertical Restraints Guidelines*. Reprinted in (1985) 48 *Antitrust and Trade Regulation Report* (B.N.A) (Special Supplement).
Wang, Yuankuo. and Mark J. Davison, (1992) 'Resale Price Maintenance: Is the Per Se Prohibition Justified?', *Adelaide Law Review*, **14**, 35–101.

Review of Industrial Organization **9**: 649–670, 1994.

Threshold Tests for the Control of Mergers: The Australian Experience

BRIAN L. JOHNS
Trade Practices Commission, Belconnen, Australian Capital Territory, 2616, Australia

Abstract. Merger policy in Australia has been formulated for a small open economy. Tight merger control has been avoided in order not to impede rationalisation and improved international competitiveness. From 1977 to early 1993 a merger or acquisition was only prohibited if it would lead to a firm gaining a dominant position in a substantial market. As a result, few mergers were stopped and some which would probably have substantially lessened competition were allowed to proceed without detailed investigation. Since January 1993 a threshold test of substantial lessening of competition has applied – a reversion to the test included in the original 1974 Trade Practices Act. This is likely to mean that more proposed mergers will come under scrutiny and the trade-offs between efficiency gains and anti-competitive detriments will need to be evaluated in a greater number of individual cases. New draft merger guidelines released in November 1992 generally reflect contemporary thinking in industrial economics.

Key words: Mergers, dominance, authorization, guidelines, efficiency, concentration.

I. Introduction

The control of mergers and acquisitions was only introduced as an element of competition law in Australia twenty years ago, with the advent of the Trade Practices Act 1974. Since then, the merger provisions of the Act, in s. 50, have been substantially amended on four occasions, most recently in 1992. In addition, three separate public or parliamentary inquiries have devoted considerable time to an assessment of proposals for change in the section. There is little doubt that s. 50 qualifies as the most extensively debated section in Part IV of the Act. The extent and vigor of the debate reflects a number of factors.

First, the merger provisions deal with questions of market structure and not directly with anti-competitive conduct. All the other proscribed trade practices detailed in Part IV of the Act relate to observable market conduct. Second, in most proposed mergers there is a trade-off between the anticipated efficiency gains and the possible adverse effects on competition and the allocation of resources. This trade-off is difficult to evaluate, partly because the competition authority usually has less complete information than the proponents of a merger, and partly because a comparison has to be made between two future scenarios, one with the merger and one without. Third, under the Australian legislation, the balancing of the public benefits of a prospective merger (including the anticipated efficiency gains) against the likely anti-competitive effects is only made if the acquiring firm makes an application for authorization. Generally firms have been reluctant to apply for authorization, despite some urging to do so from the Trade Practices Commission (Australia's only antitrust enforcement authority). The reluctance arises from the delay occasioned by the authorization process and the public nature of the process. Publicity sometimes disadvantages the applicant against its competitors who may also be potential bidders for the target firm.

Fourth, the public attitude towards merger control depends a good deal on perceptions about the nature of the economy and its future direction. In Australia, with its small and now relatively open economy, government and business alike recognise the need for structural change, involving rationalisation and the construction of optimal size plants, in order to improve the international competitiveness of Australian industry. Tight control of horizontal mergers is seen by some as a potential obstacle to the achievement of these objectives and particularly to the realisation of economies of scale. Fifth, a related issue in the debate is the relatively high level of concentration in Australian markets – higher than in larger industrialised economies, including the United States, Japan and Germany but somewhat lower than in Canada.[1] One view is that such high concentration is an inevitable outcome when import competition forces domestic producers to utilise plants of minimum efficient scale (by world standards) in supplying a relatively small domestic market. But an earlier empirical study by Caves (1984) raised doubts as to whether the high concentration levels could be fully explained in this way. He found that average plant sizes in Australian manufacturing industries were typically well below minimum efficient scale in the corresponding United States industries.[2]

This paper reviews the twenty-year debate on merger policy and legislation in Australia. The major focus is on the appropriate threshold test to determine whether or not a merger should be prohibited. Should the test be that an acquisition if not authorised on public benefit grounds is illegal, if it would lead the acquiring firm to dominate the market in question or increase its existing degree of dominance in that market? This is the threshold test that applied between 1977 and January 1993. Alternatively, should a simpler but more stringent test apply, namely that an acquisition is prohibited if it is likely to result in a substantial lessening of competition (subject to possible authorization). This is the current test and the one that applied between 1974 and 1977. The choice between these two alternative tests cannot of course be made without considering the interpretation given to the merger provisions by the courts and the Trade Practices Commission (TPC) during the past 20 years. It is also necessary to consider the two merger guidelines issued by the TPC, in 1986 and, in draft form, in November 1992.

The paper is structured as follows. Part II provides a historical overview of merger policy and legislation in Australia from 1962 to the present, outlining the major amendments to s. 50 that have been made since the Trade Practices Act came into operation in 1974. Part III examines the dominance test in more detail, while Part IV briefly reports on three major court cases which considered mergers under the dominance test. The likely implications of the recent change to the substantial lessening of competition test are discussed in Part V. In Part VI the 1992 draft merger guidelines are examined from an economic perspective. Finally, Part VII provides some brief concluding comments.

II. Historical Overview

In 1962, the then Attorney-General, Sir Garfield Barwick put forward proposals for the control of anti-competitive mergers in Australia, designed to accompany other measures to combat restrictive trade practices. Barwick pointed out that, in the absence of any merger control, two firms could combine and engage in the very same restrictive practices that they were forbidden to do by collusive agreement. Nevertheless, these merger control proposals were never enacted and neither the Trade Practices Act 1965 nor its successor the Trade Practices Act 1971 contained any provisions to deal with mergers or acquisitions.[3]

In introducing the 1965 Bill, the then Attorney-General, Mr Billy Snedden said:

> "the problem of controlling mergers and takeovers is one of great complexity. Apart from devising a satisfactory criterion for deciding whether a merger or takeover should be permitted or prohibited, there is the real problem of the mechanism by which a system of control should be implemented."[4]

There the matter rested, until the Attorney-General in a new Labor Government, Senator Lionel Murphy, proposed much more radical trade practices legislation which culminated in the Trade Practices Act 1974. Section 50 of the Act, which was based on section 7 of the United States Clayton Act, prohibited any merger or acquisition likely to result in a substantial lessening of competition in a market for goods or services in Australia. The newly established TPC was empowered by the legislation to clear any merger or acquisition which it did not regard as significantly anti-competitive, and could grant an authorization to an anti-competitive merger on the grounds of substantial benefit to the public. Some 99 authorizations and clearances were granted in the first nine months (from 1 October 1974 to 30 June 1975) [5] of the Commission's operations.

Two interesting aspects of the authorization process under the new Act are worth mentioning. First, the TPC was required to grant an authorization if the proposed acquisition was by a foreign company which had received approval for the merger under the Companies (Foreign Takeovers) Act.[6] Second, the Attorney-General could issue a notice to the Commission on behalf of the Government indicating that special considerations existed and that in the interests of national economic policy a particular merger proposal should be authorised.[7] In the first nine months of the TPC's operation, notices were issued in respect of three merger proposals, although as the Commission remarked wryly in its first *Annual Report*:

> "The special considerations were not indicated, nor were the interests of national economic policy. In each case the Commission granted an authorization as it was required by the section to do."[8]

The Commission also suggested:

> ".... the power to direct the decisions of the Commission should be kept as a reserve power for use only in very exceptional circumstances .... The right of appeal from the Commission to the Trade Practices Tribunal in authorization matters should normally be sufficient check on the Commission."[9]

Over the course of the next three years both of these provisions requiring the Commission to grant authorizations were withdrawn from the legislation.

In the majority of cases the TPC had discretion whether or not to grant an authorization, provided that it was applied for. However, the conditions for granting authorization under the original 1974 Act were relatively difficult to meet. An authorization could only be obtained if the Commission was satisfied that the acquisition would result in a substantial public benefit *not otherwise available* (emphasis added) and that, in all the circumstances, the granting of the authorization was justified. As we shall see, this test was relaxed in the 1977 amendments when the words underlined were eliminated from the legislation.

In December 1975, less than 15 months after the Trade Practices Act came into operation, a Liberal/Country Party coalition was returned to government with an election undertaking to have a thorough review of the Act and its operation. The Trade Practices Review Committee (1976) was established to undertake the review and its report was published in August 1976. Business and other interested groups were invited to make submissions to the Federal Government commenting on the Committee's report. It became apparent that the merger control provisions of the Act were likely to be significantly relaxed and perhaps even repealed entirely. This was not solely the outcome of political considerations but was partly attributable to short-term economic factors. The Australian economy was in recession in 1977. The rate of unemployment was about 5.5 per cent – not high by today's standards, but much higher than the levels experienced in Australia during the previous forty years. Corporate profits as a percentage of GDP were at their lowest level for 20 years, while in the manufacturing sector employment had fallen by 7.5 per cent over the four years to 1977. Business leaders attributed much of the fall in manufacturing employment and some of the decline in the profit ratio to the 25 per cent across-the-board tariff cut which was instituted by the Whitlam Labor Government in 1973.[10] Facing much stronger import competition, they saw tight merger control as a threat to rationalisation and improved international competitiveness.

In the event, the amendments made to the Act in July 1977 did not include the repeal of the provisions prohibiting anti-competitive mergers, but the threshold test was made considerably weaker. Only mergers or acquisitions which would be likely to result in a corporation being able to dominate or control a *substantial* market for goods or services in Australia, a State or Territory, were proscribed. The right of a private person or corporation to seek an injunction to stop a proposed merger was withdrawn, leaving only the Attorney-General or the TPC with that power. Further, as noted earlier, the authorization of an anti-competitive merger was made somewhat easier by no longer requiring that the public benefits of the merger be benefits that would not otherwise be available. Finally, the clearance of proposed acquisitions was abolished. The Attorney-General told the House of Representatives that "the intended effect (of the amendments) was that the categories of mergers to be subject to the Act should be quite limited."[11] The rationale behind the changes was "to achieve economies of scale and to improve international competitiveness".[12]

The 1977–78 *Annual Report* of the TPC drew attention to the effects of these changes to the law. Merger activity increased and few companies applied for authorization "because they can now generally feel they are not at risk of breaching s. 50."[13] While the increase in the number of mergers could "have led in some cases to rationalisation of production or distribution by restructuring with better use of resources .... mergers can proceed ... whether or not they lessen competition, provided only they do not involve the acquisition or extension of control or dominance of substantial markets."[14]

The next milestone in Australian merger policy was not until 1986 when the Labor Government, now returned to power, put forward for discussion a Green Paper entitled *The Trade Practices Act – Proposals for Change*. Among the proposals was one that the threshold test for mergers should revert to that applying between 1974 and 1977, namely that a merger or acquisition likely to result in a substantial lessening of competition should be prohibited, unless authorised. The prohibition was only to apply where there was a lessening of competition in a substantial market for goods or services.

However, when amendments were made to the Trade Practices Act in 1986, only a minor change was made to s. 50. The reference to "control" of a market was deleted, leaving dominance or increased dominance of a market as the sole criteria for determining whether or not a proposed acquisition would breach the law. The deletion of any reference in the legislation to market "control" appears to have stemmed from the decision of Mr Justice Northrop in the *Ansett-Avis* merger case.[15] His Honor held that dominance meant something less than control, and hence the latter was redundant in the context of a merger investigation.

There followed, in quite rapid succession, reports from two Parliamentary Committees which had both been asked to examine the appropriateness of the dominance test for mergers. The House of Representatives Standing Committee on Legal and Constitutional Affairs (the Griffiths Committee) (1989) reported by a majority decision that it found insufficient evidence to justify a change in the existing dominance test. However, a minority report by two members of the Committee favoured a return to the substantial lessening of competition test, pointing out that "a corporation can be in a position to engage in anti-competitive conduct without dominating a market. The fundamental problem with the existing section 50 is that it fails to recognise this."[16]

The Government did not respond promptly to the Griffiths Committee's recommendations, and in the intervening period the Senate referred the matter of the

TABLE I. Recent merger activity in Australia. Proposed mergers considered by the TPC

	1992/93	1991/92	1990/91	1989/90
Total Mergers Considered	86	103	120	117
Authorization Sought	1	3	2	2
Court Action	3	0	1	3
Not proceeded with or amended following TPC concern	5	3	2	2

Source: Trade Practices Commission, *Annual Reports*.

appropriate test for mergers and acquisitions to its own Standing Committee on Legal and Constitutional Affairs (the Cooney Committee). The result was that the Government decided to await the report of the Senate Committee before taking a final position. Nevertheless there were straws in the wind. In August 1991 the Attorney-General indicated that the Government was not convinced of the need to revert to the substantial lessening of competition test. The Business Council of Australia also indicated its opposition to a change in the test. However, the TPC argued strongly before the Cooney Committee that the dominance test was inappropriate and inconsistent with the approach to other restrictive trade practices, which were generally illegal if they resulted in a substantial lessening of competition (and were not authorised).

The report of the Cooney Committee was eventually tabled in December 1991.[17] It recommended, by majority, an amendment to s. 50 to reintroduce the threshold test of "substantial lessening of competition in a substantial market." It also recommended the incorporation of certain merger guidelines in the Trade Practices Act itself (previously guidelines had been issued by the TPC but these were not included in the legislation), and proposed that there be compulsory pre-notification to the Commission of substantial mergers or acquisitions. Finally, it recommended strict time limits within which the TPC or the Trade Practices Tribunal should determine the outcome of applications for the authorization of mergers. In June 1992 the Government announced that it would accept these recommendations, and with one exception, the consequential amendments to the Act came into effect on 21 January 1993. The exception was the compulsory pre-notification of large mergers or acquisitions. It is intended that the detailed arrangements for this scheme will be worked out after comments are received on a planned exposure draft.

It is perhaps not surprising that a Labor Government should have been finally persuaded to change the threshold test for mergers back to the 1974 formulation of substantial lessening of competition. What is much more remarkable is that the decision to revert to the old, more stringent test was made in 1992, when Australia was in its most severe recession since the 1930s. The decision was taken against the advice of most business groups which had argued that the change in the threshold test would add to uncertainty and impede necessary rationalisation.

However, the 1992 amendments to the Act did include some concessions to business opinion. First, a new sub-section (s. 50(3)) listed nine factors that must be taken into account in determining whether an acquisition is likely to substantially lessen competition in a market. These factors will be discussed in detail in Part VI. A prime purpose in putting forward this list was to provide business with greater certainty about the principal factors that would be used to judge whether or not a proposed merger was in breach of the law. Second, the TPC was given only 30 days to determine an application for the authorization of a proposed merger or acquisition, although 45 days was allowed if the issues were complex.[18] The authorization was deemed to be granted if these tight deadlines were not met. This amendment was evidently meant to address business concerns that delays in the authorization process could damage the commercial interest of the acquiring firm to the point where the acquisition could become unattractive, even if the authorization were finally granted. Third, in considering an application for authorization of a merger, the TPC is now required to regard as a public benefit any significant increase in the real value of exports or in import replacement flowing from the merger and must take into account "all other relevant matters that relate to the international competitiveness of any Australian industry" (s. 90(9A)). This was designed to reassure business that international competitiveness would be given due weight in any comparison between the efficiency benefits of a merger and its adverse effects on competition. This amendment and that relating to the time limits for dealing with authorization applications can be expected to encourage more firms to consider applying for authorization for acquisitions which would substantially lessen competition in an Australian market.

What general conclusions can be drawn from this brief historical account of merger control legislation in Australia? First, although merger control has been a contentious issue, few proposed acquisitions have been stopped by the TPC or the courts. Table 1 shows that only a small number of firms have sought authorization in the last four years, and court action was taken against only 7 mergers. In the same period 12 additional proposed mergers were not proceeded with or were amended in the light of objections by the TPC. The main reason for the lack of activity has been the high threshold test of dominance (or increased dominance) which has applied for all but four years in the twenty year history of the legislation.

Second, the reluctance of governments to accept tighter merger control reflects the view that in a small open economy such control might endanger the achievement of economies of scale and improved international competitiveness. While many economists would question whether a substantial lessening of competition test for mergers would have that effect, the perception of the Australian business community has been different. Third, because of the limited number of authorization applications, there is not a great deal of case law on the public benefits of proposed mergers and how these are balanced against the anti-competitive detriments. Some of the information that is available, including a post-acquisition study of efficiency gains and effects on competition, is discussed later in this paper.

III. The Dominance Test

III.1 The Dominance Test in Operation

The Trade Practices Act did not define dominance in a market and the interpretation of the term was therefore left to the courts and the TPC. The Commission was usually the first port-of-call for companies contemplating a major acquisition, and its attitude was therefore important. To make a large acquisition without first consulting the Commission, or proceeding with one against its known opposition was to run the risk of an injunction, a fine of up to $250,000[19] and perhaps ultimately a Court order for divestiture of the company or the assets that had been acquired.

An indication of the way the TPC approached the question of dominance was provided by its merger guidelines published in 1986 (Trade Practices Commission (1986)). These guidelines stated that the Commission could be expected to inquire into all mergers or acquisitions which would result in the acquiring firm becoming the largest firm in the relevant market and having a post-acquisition market share of 45 per cent or more, or at least 15 percentage points more than its nearest competitor. In the case of a firm which was already dominant in a market, the Commission said it would usually investigate a proposed acquisition that would result in the dominant firm's market share increasing by 10 per cent or more. Mergers which involved lower post-acquisition market shares or smaller increases in market shares than those specified were likely to be safe from investigation.[20] It was clearly recognised by the TPC (and also by the courts) that an acquisition which resulted in the largest firm gaining a major share of the relevant market might not provide that firm with substantial market power. Other factors have to be considered, including the extent of actual or potential competition from imports, the height of barriers to entry, the existence of any countervailing power[21] and the presence of close substitutes. These factors were mentioned explicitly in the TPC's 1986 merger guidelines.

Generally, the position in Australia was that a firm could not be said to dominate a market, unless it could act independently in that market without the need to take much account of the competitive reactions of rivals, either actual or potential (including importers). As Mr Justice Beaumont said in the *Arnotts* case in 1990:

> "An enterprise will be in a position to dominate a market when there is a probability that the other enterprise or enterprises in the market will act in a way calculated not to affect adversely the dominant concern's short-term interests ... If the size or strength of a particular entity is such that, in practice, other entities are unable or unwilling to compete with it in a particular market that entity is dominant in that market".[22]

Given this interpretation of dominance it was inevitable that many acquisitions likely to substantially reduce competition would be allowed to proceed without intervention by the TPC. In addition some acquisitions went ahead despite the fact that, in the opinion of the Commission, they were likely to lead to market dominance or increased dominance. These fell into two distinct categories. In the first category was a small number of acquisitions authorised by the TPC itself after consideration of the claimed public benefits of the merger. In the second category were those cases where the Federal Court did not accept that there was a prima facie case that the merger would lead to dominance and accordingly did not grant the injunction sought by the Commission.[23]

In an unusual recent case, Mr Justice Spender found that a proposed acquisition by Davids Holdings of Queensland Independent Wholesalers (QIW)[24] would constitute a contravention of s. 50 (based on the dominance test), even though it had not been opposed by the TPC. The fundamental point at issue was the definition of the market. Davids maintained that the independent retailers in Queensland and northern New South Wales which bought supplies from the competing wholesalers Davids and QIW were in the same market as the big retail chains that conducted their own wholesaling operations. In other words, a small but significant price increase by the independent retailers (resulting from an increase in the price of their wholesale supplies) would mean a sizeable loss of customers to the retail chains. If this were true, the merged entity Davids/QIW would be restrained in its ability to raise wholesale prices after the merger and could not be said to dominate the market. The contrary view, accepted by Mr Justice Spender (and by the Full Federal Court on appeal[25]) was that the independent retailers and the retail chains were in different markets. They have different price zones and customers shop at the independent retailers for reasons of convenience and service, not price. The Court's acceptance that the relevant market was wholesale supplies to independent retailers alone meant that the proposed acquisition would lead to dominance, since Davids and QIW were effectively the only two wholesalers in this market. The chains were not willing to supply independent retailers and the likelihood of other entrants to the market was remote, partly because of economies of scale.

This case illustrates the general point that deciding whether there is likely to be a breach of s. 50 can sometimes depend on fine judgements about the appropriate definition of the market. Fewer cases are likely to require such fine judgement if there is a high threshold test for mergers, such as the dominance test, but this is only because fewer mergers come under scrutiny, not because it is easier to define the market in such cases.

There seems little doubt that under the dominance test, the TPC was unable to intervene in many acquisitions which were likely to substantially lessen competition in the relevant market. Some of the more important cases of this kind will now be discussed.

Early in 1991, the TPC decided not oppose the acquisition of McPhersons Ltd, a metal distribution business, by Tubemakers of Australia, the only vertically integrated metal pipe manufacturer and distributor in Australia.[26] Tubemakers had acquired a number of metal distributors over the previous ten years to the point where it held about 57 per cent of the distribution business, as well as a 60 per cent share of the market for the manufacture of steel pipe and tube.

The TPC recognised that further downstream acquisitions by Tubemakers might well damage the market position of Palmer Tube Mills, a major competitor of Tubemakers in the manufacture of steel pipe and tube. However, as Palmer's share of the manufacturing market would decline by only five per cent if the acquisition went ahead, the TPC considered that there would not be a breach of the dominance test in s. 50.

Three major horizontal takeovers that took place in the 1980s attracted considerable public attention at the time, because of their perceived adverse effects on competition. These were the merger of the retailers Coles and Myer to form the largest single retailing group in Australia; the takeover of East-West Airlines by Ansett, one of Australia's two major domestic airlines; and the acquisition by News Ltd. of The Herald & Weekly Times newspaper group in 1987. It is not possible to say definitively that the Coles-Myer merger would have breached the law if a substantial lessening of competition test had applied at the time. However it was apparent that the acquisition would significantly enhance Coles-Myer's market power, particularly in negotiating terms with suppliers. Nevertheless, it was not possible to conclude that the merged organisation would be able to act without taking account of the reaction of its competitors, partly because little evidence was forthcoming from competitors in the market place (who generally raised little objection to the merger at the time), and accordingly no case could be made out that the acquisition would result in market dominance.

The acquisition by Ansett of East-West Airlines involved potential market dominance in New South Wales and Western Australia, and a general reduction in competition on airline trunk routes in eastern Australia, the heaviest air traffic corridor in the country. The TPC sought to arrange voluntary divestiture of routes in both States to overcome dominance problems, but this was only partially successful. In Western Australia, it appeared that unless Ansett was allowed to continue its intra-state air services, passengers might have no such services available from an alternative carrier. The TPC therefore allowed Ansett to retain its dominant position in that State. The likely reduction in competition in the eastern trunk routes could not be overcome either by legal action or voluntary divestiture. Because Australian Airlines (the other major domestic trunk carrier) had a market share on most routes not far different from that of Ansett/East-West the latter group could not be said to dominate the markets concerned. Yet, one consequence of the merger was that the price competition that East-West had previously provided to the two major interstate airlines virtually disappeared.

The acquisition of The Herald & Weekly Times by News Ltd also involved dominance in some markets but not in others. As a result of the merger, News Ltd became the sole owner of daily metropolitan newspapers in Brisbane and Adelaide and divestiture of the afternoon newspapers in those cities to management buyout groups had therefore to be arranged. The substantial lessening of competition in other markets resulting from the withdrawal of The Herald & Weekly Times as an independent competitor could not be addressed as the law then stood.

III.2 Authorization Under the Dominance Test

The dominance test represented a market power standard[27] for judging a horizontal merger and a very high degree of post-acquisition market power was needed before there was a breach of the law. However, if the parties applied to the TPC for authorization of a prospective acquisition the likely efficiency gains and other public benefits of the merger could be taken into account as an offset to the costs imposed through the enhancement of market power. In this way a performance or efficiency standard could be said to override the market power standard in certain circumstances. The replacement of the substantial lessening of competition test by the dominance test in 1977 resulted in a considerable reduction in the number of acquisitions for which authorization was sought. Executives felt that the vast majority of mergers would no longer be at risk of breaching s. 50 of the Trade Practices Act and it was therefore unnecessary to seek authorization. Thus there are few cases indicating the nature of the public benefits taken into account by the TPC and how these benefits were weighed against the anti-competitive effects of the proposed acquisition.

One recent case is of particular interest because it raises the question of whether the required efficiency gains resulting from an acquisition should be sufficient to prevent any price increase to customers,[28] or whether an acquisition should be judged beneficial if the cost savings arising from the merger exceed the deadweight loss to customers (following Williamson (1968)). The case in question involved the 1991 takeover by ACI, Australia's largest glass manufacturer, of SCI's glass container division, which gave ACI a monopoly of glass container manufacturing in Australia. The acquisition was initially opposed by the TPC on the ground that it would lead to ACI being dominant in that market.

Subsequently, ACI applied for authorization[29] and the TPC accepted that there were likely to be some small efficiency gains, including a lower capital cost of constructing a new plant and reduced costs of retraining skilled workers. In addition, employment was likely to decline less than it would in the absence of the merger and the continuity of supply of glass containers to small customers would be improved. In the Commission's view, these anticipated public benefits by themselves did not outweigh the likely detriments to competition. However, it granted the authorization after certain undertakings were given by ACI. These required the merged entity to offer its customers contracts of several years duration. Most small customers were to be given the option of withdrawing from contracts without penalty, subject to 12 months' notice. The product prices ruling immediately prior to the acquisition were not to be varied, except in accordance with a variation in unit costs of production.[30] If productivity increases led to a reduction in unit costs this was to be reflected in a corresponding decrease in product prices. These undertakings effectively ensured that any efficiency gains arising from the merger were passed on to customers. However, a potential disadvantage of the arrangement was that it might have considerably reduced the incentive for the merged entity to improve its efficiency, encouraging it instead to enjoy a quiet (monopoly) life, largely insulated from import competition.

IV. Major Australian Merger Cases

Few merger cases involving an alleged breach of s. 50 of the Trade Practices Act have been fully argued in the Federal Court. However, these cases were hard fought and involved lengthy proceedings. The *Arnotts* biscuit (cookie) case,[31] for example, involved 110 days of court hearing between October 1988 and November 1990. In the *Australia Meat Holdings* case,[32] almost three years elapsed between the commencement of court proceedings by the Trade Practices Commission and the acceptance by the Federal Court that the assets acquired had been divested in an appropriate manner.

Apart from the time and cost involved in these cases, the Court's view of the admissibility of evidence given by expert economists has been a source of contention. In *Arnotts*, the judge of first instance and the Full Federal Court on appeal held that an economist witness could not properly offer an opinion on whether the acquisition would be likely to create or strengthen market dominance, based on his reading of all the evidence presented in the case. Both held it was the function of the Court, not the expert witness, to make such an assessment.[33] However, it would be admissible evidence if the economist had stated explicitly the assumptions that he was making (for example, regarding barriers to entry) and the implications that would follow if these assumptions were correct. There remains some concern that, unless there is a change in judicial opinion on this issue, expert economists will have a more restricted role in future merger cases.

The three principal merger cases described in this part all took place under the dominance test. The first related to the proposed acquisition in 1978 of the rental car company Avis by Ansett Transport Industries.[34] At the time, Ansett and Trans-Australia Airlines (TAA) were the only airlines providing interstate air services throughout Australia. It was estimated that Avis accounted for about 46 per cent of the national rental car market in Australia, with its closest rivals, Kay-Hertz and Budget each having about 16 per cent. There was broad agreement that the national car rental market could be distinguished from the local car rental market in which many small operators competed for local or regional business.

The strength of Avis in the national market derived partly from its exclusive authority to supply car rental services through counters at all Commonwealth airports in Australia following a successful tender for that right in 1969. Avis also enjoyed a monopoly of car rental advertising at airports. Despite this, the evidence suggested that other car rental operators did obtain airport business and the legality of this had never been challenged. The Minister of Transport had the power to disapprove of the car rental charges made by Avis at the airports, and it was said to be impractical for a different scale of rentals to be applied to non-airport business. Hence Avis was subject to potential price regulation across the whole range of its car rental business. The judge also took the view that entry into the national car rental market was relatively easy. For all these reasons he held that, prior to the proposed acquisition, Avis was not in a position to dominate the market.

More importantly, Justice Northrop concluded that Ansett would not obtain a position of dominance in the national car rental market if it acquired Avis. The critical factor in this decision was that the exclusive Avis concession at all Commonwealth airports was to expire at the end of June 1979 (twelve months after the Court's decision was handed down). The Minister of Transport had stated that from that date two or more rental car operators would be granted the right to provide services at the airports. Even if the merged entity were the successful tenderer for one of these concessions, it would be exposed to significant competition on and off airports. There was little doubt that Avis would suffer a significant decline in its market share whether the acquisition proceeded or not.

The second case related to the 1988 acquisition by Australia Meat Holdings (AMH) of two abattoirs in North Queensland operated by Thomas Borthwick, a company owned in the United Kingdom. The relevant product market was held to be the market for fat cattle (including feed-lot cattle). The geographic extent of that market was a key matter at issue in the case. Since data on cattle movements indicated that fat cattle were almost invariably sold to local abattoirs, the Court held that the relevant geographic market was the northern region of Queensland (excluding both the central and southern regions). In this region, AMH's abattoirs already accounted for about 58 per cent of the total capacity. If AMH acquired Borthwick's Bowen abattoir, this market share would increase to about 78 per cent.

The Court noted that Borthwick had been pursuing a relatively aggressive pricing policy and this had prevented AMH from exercising a dominant influence in the fat cattle market. The acquisition would eliminate this source of vigorous competition and would enable AMH to obtain a dominant position in the northern region, particularly as the remaining abattoir capacity in the region was largely in the hands of shareholders of AMH.

The third case involved the acquisition of Nabisco's biscuit operations in Australia by Arnotts, Australia's largest biscuit manufacturer. At the time of the proposed acquisition in 1988, Arnotts held about 62 per cent of the Australian biscuit market and Nabisco eight per cent. The only other major competitor was George Weston Foods with a market share of about 13 per cent. Mr. Justice Beaumont (and the Full Federal Court on appeal) found that Arnotts was already in a dominant position in the biscuit market prior to the acquisition. It had a large market share, was a price leader and enjoyed considerable brand loyalty. There also existed significant barriers to entry to the market, as well as barriers to expansion by small competitors, because of the scale and scope economies and brand loyalty enjoyed by Arnotts. The Court concluded that the acquisition would strengthen Arnotts' market dominance because, *inter alia*, it would enable it to eliminate its only competitor in the manufacture of dry and flavored snack crackers, which were fast-growing segments of the market.

V. The Substantial Lessening of Competition Test

In the hearings that took place before the Griffiths and Cooney Committees between 1988 and 1991, the likely consequences of changing from the dominance test to the substantial lessening of competition test were debated at considerable length. Those favoring the change maintained, as Sir Garfield Barwick had done about thirty years before, that it was not logical to prohibit two firms from entering into a restrictive agreement which substantially lessened competition in a market and yet condone a merger between the two which was likely to have the same effect. On this view, mergers and acquisitions which substantially lessened competition should be prohibited unless authorised, in the same way as most other restrictive practices and agreements covered by the Trade Practices Act. Although the 1992 amendments to s. 50 of the Act embodied this principle, there remains one significant difference between the treatment of mergers and that of restrictive agreements. Mergers and acquisitions are only prohibited if they substantially lessen competition in a *substantial* market in Australia, a State or Territory, while the prohibition of anti-competitive agreements, arrangements or understandings applies to conduct in any market in Australia.

In the Cooney Committee hearings, six main arguments were advanced for the retention of the dominance test. First, a reversion to the lower threshold of substantially lessening competition would make it more difficult for Australian enterprises to achieve scale economies and become internationally competitive. Second, the acquisition of an inefficient firm while it was still solvent was often less costly and less disruptive than waiting for that firm to wither and eventually fail. Third, a stricter merger test would impede the efficient working of the market for corporate control. Fourth, a change away from the dominance test would create uncertainty for some time about the interpretation of the amended s. 50, whereas the existing test and its application were well understood by business after many years' experience of its operation. Fifth, it was claimed that there was little or no evidence of any substantial adverse effects on competition resulting from the application of the dominance test. Finally, a lowering of the threshold test would mean an increase in the cost of administering the merger provisions of the Act, since more cases would require investigation by the TPC.

The first three of these arguments raise economic issues which warrant analysis. Empirical evidence does not support the view that firms in a small country must command a large share of the domestic market in order to achieve international competitiveness through economies of scale. The emphasis on economies of scale reflects a static view of the sources of competitive advantage. Dynamic factors such as product and process innovations, skill development and improvements in management practices are often more important. It is not clear that these dynamic sources of competitive advantage are strengthened by having few rivals in the domestic market. Indeed, the opposite is probably true, since it is competition which forces firms to upgrade their performance. In his book *The Competitive Advantage of Nations,* Porter (1990, p. 663) puts the point in the following way:

> "A strong antitrust policy, especially in the area of horizontal mergers, alliances, and collusive behavior, is essential to the rate of upgrading in an economy. Mergers, acquisitions, and alliances involving industry leaders should be disallowed. (Acquisitions of smaller domestic rivals by a firm in a related industry seeking to transfer skills are more potentially beneficial to competitive advantage and should be permissible.)"

Even in mature industries, where the rate of introduction of innovations is slow but economies of scale remain important, a merger between two leading Australian firms may not result in improved international competitiveness. One reason is that the combined output of the two Australian firms may still fall short of the output of firms of minimum efficient scale in a large exporting country. In that case, however, in the absence of a significant tariff barrier and high transport costs, the merged Australian entity is likely to encounter import competition in the domestic market.

If there is strong actual or potential import competition in the domestic market it is unlikely that the TPC would seek to challenge a merger, regardless of whether the threshold test was market dominance or a substantial lessening of competition. Business representatives who appeared before the Cooney Committee tended to overlook the significance of this point. They stressed the importance of improving international competitiveness as tariffs were progressively reduced in Australia. However, tariff cuts implied that imports would likely represent an effective constraint on the exercise of market power by large domestic firms in many Australian markets for internationally tradeable goods. In short, the lowering of tariff barriers significantly reduced the likelihood that mergers in the traded goods sector would breach the provisions of s. 50.

In any case, authorization is obtainable for a proposed acquisition in any sector of the economy, provided sufficient public benefits can be demonstrated by the parties concerned. Public benefits can include economies of scale, cost savings or efficiency gains arising from rationalisation, import substitution or improved export performance.[35] On balance, it seems unlikely that lowering the threshold test for mergers to substantial lessening of competition has made it more difficult for Australian firms to become internationally competitive.

Those opposed to a change from the dominance test implicitly assumed that *most* horizontal mergers which *substantially* lessened competition but did not create or strengthen dominance would bring substantial public benefits, outweighing the adverse effects on the allocation of resources. However if, contrary to this assumption, only some mergers would result in net benefits, the appropriate solution was to lower the threshold test and assess the net benefit of each anti-competitive acquisition individually, following an authorization application.

The Cooney Committee noted that empirical research on the effects of mergers in Australia was relatively sparse and concluded that the economic evidence generally was equivocal about the efficiencies generated by them. In its report it referred to case studies of mergers in three Australian industries conducted by the Bureau of Industry Economics (1990). The Bureau studied the outcome of mergers in the pastry products, roofing tiles and automotive batteries industries which had taken place between four and eight years earlier. Only one of these mergers had been authorised by the TPC. The others had been allowed to proceed on the basis that they were unlikely to lead to market dominance. The Bureau study found "that there was a substantial lag between the mergers and any apparent increases in productive efficiency and that other factors have had at least as great an impact on productive efficiency as the mergers."[36] These other factors included import competition and technological changes. In several of the acquisitions the costs of integrating two separate organisations and the time taken to put in place a new management structure had been significantly underestimated. The Bureau also found that there had usually been a lessening of competition in the relevant markets following the consummation of the mergers. However, competition had strengthened after an interval, due either to import competition or new entry. In general, concerns at the time of the merger about the probable adverse effects on competition were somewhat exaggerated.

The results of the Bureau's study suggest that mergers may be of secondary importance as determinants of competition and productive efficiency in the long run. However, in the short run a different story may apply. In the mergers studied, the efficiency gains began to emerge only two to three years after the consummation, but the adverse effects of enhanced market power were present much earlier. Discounting the costs and benefits to present day values would appear to suggest that few, if any of the mergers yielded positive net benefits.[37]

A further argument for retaining the dominance test for mergers was that any lowering of the threshold test would impede the efficient working of the market for corporate control.[38] There is no doubt that the threat of takeover acts as a spur to management efficiency in most public companies. Merger policy, by limiting the opportunity for acquisitions to be made because of competition considerations, tends to reduce the pressure on the managers of some companies to increase efficiency and maximise the value of their companies' shares. To avoid competition law having *any* impact on the market for corporate control, the merger provisions of the Trade Practices Act would have to be abandoned. Such a course does not appear to be justifiable. The overall benefits for the market for corporate control would be slight and the costs for the efficient administration of competition policy significant. For example, in the absence of merger control the competition authorities would have to rely mainly on s. 46 of the Act to prevent any misuse of market power by the merged entity. A breach of this section is difficult to prove because of the need to establish that the company concerned had the purpose of damaging competition. Moreover, the prohibition of mergers which might seriously endanger competition is clearly beneficial if it pre-empts later action by the merged entity to raise prices to a monopoly level, to collude tacitly with a small number of rivals, or to engage in anti-competitive conduct.

While the total repeal of the s. 50 merger provisions is not warranted, does the impact on the market for corporate control of lowering the merger threshold provide a case for not making this change? Probably not. The adoption of the substantial lessening of competition test would place only a small number of additional mergers at risk, although in a few isolated markets some firms may feel more secure from the risk of takeover by a large incumbent in that market. Further, it should be recognised that an acquiring firm could, in an authorization application, claim that there was public benefit in it gaining management control of the target company, because of the efficiency gain that could be realised. The TPC is concerned with the net public benefits of the proposed acquisition, not with protecting the interests of the target firm or its managers.

VI. The 1992 Draft Merger Guidelines

Following the lowering of the threshold test for mergers in the 1992 amendments to the Trade Practices Act, the Trade Practices Commission (1992) issued new draft merger guidelines in November of that year.[39] While the final version of these guidelines is unlikely to appear until late in 1994, the draft guidelines provide a good indication of how the Commission is currently approaching merger control issues under the amended legislation. It will be recalled that a new section (s. 50(3)) was included in the Act in the 1992 amendments, specifying a number of factors that must be taken into account in determining whether or not an acquisition would have the effect of substantially lessening competition. These statutory factors are incorporated in the TPC's draft guidelines. They include the actual or potential level of import competition; the height of barriers to entry; the level of concentration in the market; the degree of countervailing power; the availability of substitutes; the likelihood that the merger would result in the elimination from the market of a vigorous and effective competitor; and the nature and extent of vertical integration in the market. Two items in the list of statutory factors suggest that the approach will not be based solely on a traditional static structure-conduct-performance paradigm. First, account must be taken of "the dynamic characteristics of the market, including growth, innovation and product differentiation."[40] Second, the reference to the possible removal from the market of "a vigorous and effective competitor" suggests that attention will always be given to the qualitative aspects of competition pre-and post-merger and not simply to the anticipated change in market shares.

In the draft guidelines the TPC indicates that it will evaluate prospective mergers through a five stage process. The first stage involves defining the relevant market, taking into account its product, functional and geographic dimensions. Unless the market is a substantial one, the evaluation of the merger will not proceed further, since the Act does not prohibit mergers in markets which are not substantial. Market definition is seldom easy, although the concept that a market is an area of close competition or rivalry among firms seems simple enough. The Commission indicates that it will follow the North American antitrust approach and consider the appropriate market definition by assuming a small but significant non-transitory price increase by a hypothetical monopolist. If such a price increase would lead, in all probability, to consumers switching to alternative products or to suppliers significantly increasing the production of substitutes, these substitute products, on both the demand and supply side, should be considered as part of the same market as the product which has increased in price.

Once an acceptable market definition has been determined, the draft guidelines indicate that the next stage will be to examine market concentration as it is likely to be after the merger. This is intended as a screening device, so that many mergers which are unlikely to result in a substantial lessening of competition can be eliminated from further consideration. The TPC says it will give further consideration to a merger in which the merged firm will have a post-acquisition market share of 40 per cent or more. If concentration is very high (the four or five largest firms having a combined post-merger market share of 75 per cent or more), it is likely to investigate a merger which would result in the merged entity having a market share of 15 per cent or more. A comparison between these market share thresholds and those contained in the 1986 merger guidelines, when the dominance test applied, is instructive. The new thresholds are significantly lower, as might be expected, and it is likely that the TPC will need to consider many more mergers than previously, at least during the early stages of the evaluation process.

The third stage of the evaluation involves a consideration of import competition and the extent to which it may inhibit the exercise of market power by the merged enterprise. As pointed out by Hay and Walker (1993), however, the market share of imports will often be a poor indicator of their competitive impact. The volume of imports may reflect decisions by Australian manufacturers to locate part of their production offshore. In such cases the supply of imports may be inelastic with respect to higher prices on the domestic market. In addition, the historical share of imports in Australian markets may understate the importance of future import competition, in the face of Australia's progressive reductions in tariffs. Consideration also must be given to factors which may inhibit the growth of imports, including the additional cost of holding inventories of imported goods, consumer preferences for Australian-made goods, and government purchasing policies which may also favor domestic products. If, after consideration of these and other relevant factors it is apparent that actual or potential import competition will prevent the merged enterprise from exploiting its market power, the investigation will not proceed further.

However, if strong import competition is unlikely to emerge, the next step would be to evaluate barriers to entry into the market. The TPC identifies as possible barriers, regulatory restrictions, economies of scale, brand loyalty, better access for the incumbent to essential facilities, and pecuniary cost advantages favoring the incumbent. The importance of sunk costs in determining whether or not the market is contestable is also recognised. The critical test is whether the acquiring firm is able to demonstrate that, if it should use its market power to raise prices after the merger, entry would be likely to take place within two years "on a sufficient scale and sufficiently attractive to consumers"[41] to prevent that conduct persisting. The onus is placed on the parties to the merger to demonstrate that such entry is likely. If they cannot do so, the evaluation would proceed to the final stage to see whether there are any other factors which might suggest that the proposed merger would not substantially lessen competition.

Perhaps the most important of these other factors is countervailing power. Buyers in a market may be able to exercise effective countervailing power against suppliers if they are few in number, can shift to alternative products at little cost, or would be unable to pass on the higher cost of the intermediate products to the markets that they supply. For example, a merger involving leading manufacturers of glass bottles may lack the market power to raise the price of beer bottles because the major brewers could within a relatively short period switch to metal cans as an alternative to bottles. If a countervailing power or some other valid defense cannot be established at this stage of the evaluation, the TPC is likely to find that the proposed merger would substantially lessen competition.

This still leaves open the possibility that the merger may be allowed through the authorization process. The new draft guidelines do not attempt to spell out in detail the various public benefits that could be taken into account in considering an authorization application. However there is some emphasis on improved international competitiveness, innovation and the introduction of new technology, the onus being on the proponents of the merger to establish that there is a direct causal link between the proposed acquisition and the attainment of these (and any other) public benefits.

VII. Concluding Comments

Merger policies have to be shaped to suit the particular circumstances of an economy. In Australia, a relatively light-handed approach to merger control has been in operation for 20 years, designed to take account of the small size of the economy and its exposure to international trade. The lowering of the threshold test for mergers in 1992 can be seen as a tightening of merger control, although in effect it re-established a threshold that was incorporated in the original 1974 Trade Practices Act. A major aim of the 1992 change is to prevent undue increases in market power in the markets for non-tradeable goods and services. To the extent that it is successful in that regard, some of the benefits should take the form of lower input prices for Australian firms exposed to international competition.

The intensive debate about merger policy in Australia over the past four years has centered on the appropriate threshold test. However, this is only the starting point in the evaluation of a merger. The threshold test is concerned solely with the increase in market power that is likely to result from an acquisition and whether this will amount (under the 1992 test) to a substantial lessening of competition. If the answer is in the affirmative, it does not directly follow that the proposed acquisition should be stopped. The likely efficiency gains and other public benefits of the acquisition should be assessed, although this can only be done under Australian competition law if the parties concerned apply for authorization of the merger. With the 1992 threshold test in place it can be expected that more companies will apply for authorization, enabling the trade-off between efficiency gains and the costs of greater market power to be made more explicit. The public nature of the authorization process is helpful to transparency, but sometimes disadvantages the acquiring firm. The streamlining of authorization procedures following the 1992 amendments to the Trade Practices Act should alleviate that problem to some degree.

Notes

[1] See Bureau of Industry Economies (1990) pp. 34–36.
[2] However, since the Caves study related to a period preceding the recent program of substantial scheduled tariff reductions in Australia, it is quite possible that the results would be different if the study were replicated using current data.
[3] The 1971 Act replaced the 1965 Act because of the High Court of Australia's decision in the *Concrete Pipes Case* ((1971) 124 C.L.R. 129) that the earlier Act as drafted was unconstitutional.
[4] Hansard, 19 May 1965, quoted by Nieuwenhuysen and Norman (1976) at p. 51.
[5] See Trade Practices Commission (1975) at p. 27.
[6] See section 90(11) of the original 1974 Trade Practices Act.
[7] See section 90(9) of the original 1974 Trade Practices Act.
[8] *Supra* n. 5, at p. 28.
[9] *Ibid*, at p. 10. The Trade Practices Tribunal is a quasi-judicial body whose function is to review the authorization decisions made by the TPC.
[10] However economists were more sceptical of the view that the 25 per cent tariff cut was responsible for major employment losses in manufacturing. See Gregory and Pincus (1982).
[11] Hansard, House of Representatives, 3 May 1977, at p. 1478.
[12] *Loc. cit.*
[13] Trade Practices Commission (1978), at p. 44.
[14] *Ibid*, at p. 4.
[15] *Trade Practices Commission v. Ansett Transport Industries (Operations) Pty. Ltd. & Ors. (1978)* ATPR 40–071, at p. 17, 717.
[16] House of Representatives Standing Committee on Legal and Constitutional Affairs (1989), at para 5.4.22.
[17] Senate Standing Committee on Legal and Constitutional Affairs (1991).
[18] See s. 90(11) of the amended Trade Practices Act.
[19] The maximum fine for a corporation was raised to $10 million in late 1992.
[20] Acquisitions which are expected to create or strengthen a position of market dominance are prohibited in other countries, including Germany and the European Community (see Hawk (1990)). It is noteworthy, however, that in these countries an investigation into possible market dominance could be instituted when the acquiring firm would have a much smaller post-acquisition market share than the one indicated in the 1986 TPC guidelines.
[21] The countervailing power in the market might be from buyers able to restrain the exercise of market power of a few sellers or from sellers constraining the actions of one or a few buyers in the market.
[22] *Trade Practices Commission v. Arnotts Limited & Ors.* (1990) ATPR 41–062, at p. 51,821.
[23] See, for example, *Cope Allman (Australia) Pty. Ltd. & Ors. v. Trade Practices Commission & Ors.* (1983) ATPR 40–347 and *Trade Practices Commission v. Bowral Brickworks Pty. Ltd. & Ors.* (1984) ATPR 40–480.

[24] *QIW Retailers Ltd v. Davids Holdings Pty. Ltd. & Ors.; Attorney-General of the Commonwealth v. Davids Holdings Pty Limited & Anor* (1993) ATPR 41–226.
[25] *Davids Holdings Pty. Ltd. & Ors. v. Attorney General of the Commonwealth and QIW Retailers Pty. Ltd.*, unreported decision of the Full Federal Court of Australia, 22 April 1994.
[26] For further details see Trade Practices Commission (1991), at p. 11.
[27] Comanor and White (1992) draw the distinction between a market power standard and an efficiency standard for judging whether a proposed merger would breach antitrust laws.
[28] A price increase to consumers may be avoided by regulation. If price regulation does not occur, the efficiency gains of the merger would have to be of such magnitude that the profit maximising price of the merged entity was at or below the pre-merger price (see Crampton (1993)).
[29] Details of the application and the Trade Practices Commission determination are to be found in Trade Practices Commission (1991a).
[30] As there is likely to be a greater number of applications following the re-introduction of the substantial lessening of competition test, the implications of a requirement that product prices be not raised after the merger will need to be carefully analysed in the future.
[31] The first instance judgment is referred to at *supra* n. 22. The Full Court decision on appeal may be found at *Arnotts Limited & Ors. v. Trade Practices Commission* (1990) ATPR 41–061.
[32] The first instance decision is *Trade Practices Commission v. Australia Meat Holdings Pty. Ltd. & Ors.* (1988) ATPR 40–876 and continued in *Trade Practices Commission v. Australia Meat Holdings Pty. Ltd. & Ors. (No.2)* (1988) ATPR 40–893, while the Full Court judgment on appeal is *Australia Meat Holdings Pty. Limited v. Trade Practices Commission* (1989) ATPR 40–932.
[33] These decisions are also considered by Brunt and French in their papers in this issue.
[34] *Supra* n. 15.
[35] As noted earlier, the 1992 amendments to the Trade Practices Act made it mandatory to consider an increase in the real value of exports or import replacement as public benefits when considering an application for authorization.
[36] Bureau of Industry Economics (1990), at pp. 105–6.
[37] Crampton (1993) also points out the need to discount to present values the costs and benefits of a merger.
[38] Sheard (1992) criticises merger policy because of its impact on the market for corporate control.
[39] For a more detailed discussion of the 1992 draft merger guidelines see Hay and Walker (1993).
[40] This is one of the factors listed in s. 50(3) of the Act.
[41] Trade Practices Commission (1992), at para 4.59.

References

Bureau of Industry Economics (1990) *Mergers and Acquisitions*, Research Report 36. Canberra: Australian Government Publishing Service.

Caves, Richard E. (1984) 'Scale, Openness and Productivity in Manufacturing Industries' in Richard E. Caves and Lawrence B. Krause, eds, *The Australian Economy: A View from the North*. Sydney: George Allen & Unwin.

Crampton, Paul S. (1993) 'The Efficiency Exception for Mergers: An Assessment of Early Signals from the Competition Tribunal', *Canadian Business Law Journal*, **21**, 371–394.

Comanor, William S., and Lawrence J. White (1992) 'Market Power or Efficiency: A Review of Antitrust Standards', *Review of Industrial Organisation*, **7**, 105–116.

Gregory, R.J., and J.J. Pincus (1982) 'Industry Assistance', in Webb, L.R., and R.H. Allan, eds, *Industrial Economics. Australian Studies*, Sydney: George Allen & Unwin.

Hawk, Barry E. (1990) 'The EEC Merger Regulation: The First Step Towards One Stop Merger Control', *Antitrust Law Journal*, **59**, 195–235.

Hay, George, and Jill Walker (1993) 'Merger Policy and the TPC's Draft Merger Guidelines', *Competition and Consumer Law Journal*, **1**, 33–48.

House of Representatives Standing Committee on Legal and Constitutional Affairs (the Griffiths Committee) (1989) *Mergers, Takeovers and Monopolies; Profiting from Competition*. Canberra: Australian Government Publishing Service.

Nieuwenhuysen, J.P. and N.R. Norman (1976) *Australian Competition and Prices Policy*. London: Croom Helm Ltd.

Porter, M.E. (1990) *The Competitive Advantage of Nations*. New York: The Free Press.

Senate Standing Committee on Legal and Constitutional Affairs (the Cooney Committee) (1991) *Mergers, Monopolies and Acquisitions: Adequacy of Existing Legislative Controls*. Canberra: Australian Government Publishing Service.

Sheard, Paul (1992) 'Competition Policy and Microeconomic Reform in Australia', in Peter Forsyth, ed, *Microeconomic Reform in Australia*. St. Leonards, NSW: Allen & Unwin.

Trade Practices Commission (1975) *First Annual Report Year Ended 30 June 1975*. Canberra: Australian Government Publishing Service.

Trade Practices Commission (1978) *Fourth Annual Report Year Ended 30 June 1978*. Canberra: Australian Government Publishing Service.

Trade Practices Commission (1986) *Guidelines for the Merger Provisions of the Trade Practices Act 1974*. Canberra: Trade Practices Commission.

Trade Practices Commission (1991) *Annual Report 1990–91*. Canberra: Australian Government Publishing Service.

Trade Practices Commission (1991a) *Determination on Application for Authorisation by ACI Operations Pty Ltd in relation to proposed acquisition of Glass Containers Pty Ltd and SCI Operations Pty Ltd* (Application No. A40058). Canberra: Trade Practices Commission.

Trade Practices Commission (1992) *Merger Guidelines – Draft for Comment*. Canberra: Trade Practices Commission.

Trade Practices Commission (1992a) *Annual Report 1991–92*. Canberra: Australian Government Publishing Service.

Trade Practices Commission (1993) *Annual Report 1992–93*. Canberra: Australian Government Publishing Service.

Trade Practices Review Committee (the Swanson Committee) (1976) *Report to Minister of Business and Consumer Affairs*. Canberra: Australian Government Publishing Service.

Williamson, O.E. (1968) 'Economies as an Antitrust Defense: The Welfare Tradeoffs', *American Economic Review*, **58**, 18–36.

Review of Industrial Organization **9:** 671–694, 1994.

The Role of Antitrust in a Small Open Economy: The Commerce Act in New Zealand

ALAN E. BOLLARD[1]
At time of writing: Director New Zealand Institute of Economic Research, 8 Halswell Street, Wellington, New Zealand; Now: Chairman, New Zealand Commerce Commission, P.O. Box 2351, Wellington, New Zealand

Abstract. This paper reviews the New Zealand antitrust regime represented by the Commerce Act 1986. The context is a rapidly liberalising, small open economy with light-handed regulation. New Zealand antitrust draws on recent US microeconomics for its underlying economic principles, but more on the Australian Trade Practices Act for its legal framework. The influences of these and other countries on the operation of New Zealand antitrust are traced through precedent and an analysis of major cases. Increasingly interpretations have differed from those in Australia, with more weight being put on the promotion of efficiency and less on traditional competition objectives.

Key words: Commerce Act, New Zealand antitrust

I. Introduction

I.1. The New Zealand Economy

New Zealand is a group of large islands but with a population of only 3.35 million. It is a major primary producer of temperate agricultural products; until the post-war period most of this was sold on the British market. It had one of the highest standards of living in the world, which in turn funded a generous system of universal social security, state provision of education and health, and a wide range of government involvement in utilities, financial and other services. UK entry to the European Community in 1973 and increasing difficulty with market access restrictions and large terms of trade shocks have led to a relative fall in New Zealand's standard of living since then. Hit by the 1970s oil price shocks, the New Zealand Government initiated a major state-funded investment program in energy and related industries, known as the "Think Big" program.

This was a time of large fiscal deficits, high public debt, high inflation, high tax rates and strategic currency devaluations in an unsuccessful attempt to improve trading competitiveness. The traded sector continued to be insulated from these world price movements through import protection (a widespread system of quotas and high tariffs on most goods that could be manufactured domestically), tight controls on entry and operating conditions, and widespread price control. Special protection was in place for industries considered strategically important (including steel production and car assembly). The farm sector was assisted through a price support scheme for livestock, concessional financing, and compulsory marketing boards.

In the 1970s and early 1980s New Zealand productivity rates were poor compared to OECD averages, and growth rates were significantly below trading partner averages. In 1950 New Zealand's GDP per capita was 26 per cent above the OECD average. Forty years later it had dropped to 27 per cent below average. As the economic reality of this situation emerged, there was widespread acceptance of the need for major change. Following the election of a Labour Government in 1984, New Zealand commenced a program of rapid and widespread economic liberalisation. A comprehensive set of policy reforms were put in place quickly, the constraint being how fast they could be enacted into new law.[2]

I.1.1. *Factor market deregulation*

Reforming factor markets was an important early focus: finance, transport and energy were regarded as three strategically important sectors. In a series of measures the Government removed most market entry restrictions, price controls, regulated monopolies and operating restrictions in these areas. Traditionally restricted sectors such as banking, aviation, and electricity generation have now been effectively deregulated. In 1991 the Employment Contracts Act was enacted, to deregulate employer/employee bargaining arrangements.

I.1.2. *Industry deregulation*

In the agricultural sector, price support and concessionary financing was ended. The prevailing general wage and price freeze was terminated, price controls were ended, quantity licensing requirements were terminated and state regulated monopoly rights in electricity, telecommunications, postal services and other sectors were removed. Most utilities now face no industry-specific regulation. Some aspects of securities, company and intellectual property legislation regulation have also been reformed.

I.1.3. *International trade reform*

New Zealand's manufacturing sector traditionally sheltered behind a high protective wall of tariffs, import licenses, capital controls and fixed exchange rates. By 1987 import licensing had been phased out and the tariff structure has now been rationalised and reduced to OECD averages. Almost all regulation on the movement of international capital has been removed, and investment in New Zealand in portfolio or equity form is virtually free of restriction. In 1985 the New Zealand dollar was freely floated on foreign exchange markets without direct control.

I.1.4. *Government sector reform*

The New Zealand Government has long been a key provider of services in a wide range of sectors. During the reform period almost all its trading activities were set up in corporate form with boards of directors on an arms length basis from the shareholder. Since 1987 two thirds of these assets have been privatised, with the payments devoted principally to reducing public debt. More recently local authority trading enterprises and government health enterprises have been put on a similar path with corporatisation and the tendering out of services. In addition, there has been substantial monetary and fiscal reform. However, traditional macroeconomic objectives of stabilisation and equality did not figure prominently in all of this restructuring. Policymakers saw the new system delivering improvements in efficiency, and they saw these as being driven by increased competitive pressures arising from internal markets and from international competitive pressures. The 1986 Commerce Act was intended to play the central role in delivering these competitive rewards.

I.2. Antitrust's Role in Reform

The modern New Zealand antitrust regime was conceived out of a period of radical change in which the corporate sector of the country emerged from a protected and regulated environment, into one that recognised the predominant role of world prices. Antitrust policy was seen as one of the key mechanisms to implement and regulate this change. The antitrust regime in New Zealand is unusual in that it was designed to provide key new regulatory support for a relatively deregulated economic system. The timing was such that it could incorporate recent economic thinking and practical experience from other countries' legal experiences.

This paper focuses on New Zealand deregulation, the role that antitrust plays in regulating a small, open economy, and New Zealand antitrust's derivative links from Australian antitrust and from American microeconomic theories. It was the Australian Trade Practices Act 1974 that New Zealand's antitrust reform leant upon most heavily. The New Zealand Commerce Act 1986 was designed at a time when the Australian legislation had been in operation for a decade, and it provided the most appropriate model from which to draw. Common political experiences and social ties between the countries, and growing business integration (especially following the 1983 Closer Economic Relationship Agreement) helped reinforce this common perception.[3] In addition, as the closest country to New Zealand, Australian firms are seen as the major source of international competitive constraints on domestic operations. But there are also important differences in New Zealand antitrust policy that result from the extra decade of legal and economic experience, from differences in the two countries' economies, and from differences in the underlying views about the appropriate role of antitrust in the economy.

II. The Theory of Antitrust in a Small Open Economy

A small closed economy is *ceteris paribus* likely to display a number of characteristics that have implications for competition. These include a smaller number of domestic operators, a higher level of concentration, and an increased incidence of natural monopoly.[4] The principles of competition policy in a small country can change radically when such an economy is opened up. There are several mechanisms through which this might work.

Liberalisation of import protection makes it relatively cheaper to source inputs and final goods from foreign suppliers. This offers a new degree of competitive restraint in domestic markets, helping to alleviate the monopsonist problem in factor markets and the monopolist problem in consumer markets, restraining local producers from pricing above the import parity price. In practice, however, the degree of substitutability between imports and local production will never be perfect, as transport costs offer some natural protection and buyers may put a premium on local supply for stock-holding, special design, or nationalist reasons.

Removal of capital controls makes it easier for foreigners to become domestic producers by investing in their own plant, or to become domestic suppliers by investing in warehouses and sales/distribution outlets. This increases local competition directly. In contrast, if foreign capital takes over existing capacity, there will be a more neutral effect on competition, although it is possible that a foreign investor in a non-tradeable sector might be in a stronger position than a local producer and could try to monopolise the sector.

Liberalisation of exports would likely have less direct competitive effect, although if the product involved is consumed domestically and if there are economies of scale, then exporting could lead to reductions in the unit costs of production. Whether these are passed on to domestic markets, to foreigners, or retained by the company depends, among other things, on the extent of domestic competition. If the liberalisation involves the removal of export incentives, as in the New Zealand case, then the opposite effect could occur.

Removal of exchange rate regulation could also be relevant. A systematically overvalued exchange rate means that imports are relatively cheap in the domestic market, and hence that they exert more competitive pressure on local producers. An undervalued exchange rate has the opposite effect. The converse impact on exports probably has less impact on competition. The issue, however, becomes more complex when the importer has to consider the possibility of future exchange rate moves. A freely floating but highly volatile exchange rate could dissuade importers from competing with local firms more than a regulated undervalued exchange rate would.

The view of imports as a constraint on market power in a small country is now an accepted one. Pickford (1991) reviews the arguments in the case of New Zealand. He notes the arguments about the constraining power of imports in a large country is based on the assumption that for such countries the foreign (excess) supply curve is upward sloping – foreign firms can divert supplies to the US when US domestic prices rise. However in a small country like New Zealand, the foreign supply response is likely to be perfectly elastic, as domestic importers can make their relatively small purchases without influencing the price on world markets. The economic analysis of import competition changes as a consequence, focussing attention on the degree to which import barriers raise horizontal foreign supply curves, and how domestic firms might incorporate that barrier into their pricing behavior.

While admitting that import competition might assist antitrust policy, Pickford argues that an import constraint policy suffers from several potential disadvantages. For example, international trade patterns are less stable than domestic trade patterns and may not be relied on for a consistent competitive effect; second, a domestic monopolist might use a range of strategic behavior designed to keep out imports; third, import competition does not provide a uniform restraint on domestic firms, as this depends rather on the individual impact of trade barriers, exchange rates and competitiveness; and finally, established local firms may be able to nullify the competitive impact of actual entry.

In their determinations the New Zealand antitrust authorities have generally included potential import competition as a determinant of dominance, but their precise stance has varied from case to case.[5] Pickford comments on the *ad hoc* matter of import barrier measurement; the fact that most goods and services are not tradeable and therefore are not directly susceptible to import competition, and that domestic supply is often preferred anyhow because of non-price costs or disadvantages associated with imports; and also the fluctuating nature of the barrier caused by movements in floating exchange rates. He concludes that the correct focus should be on the degree to which import barriers allow the limit pricing firm to exercise market power as measured by profit.

New Zealand is an economy that has moved from being relatively closed to relatively open within the last decade. Exports and imports now each represent about 30% of GDP, and this proportion is expected to rise further. New Zealand firms are largely price takers in world markets. There are major international capital flows and these are largely unregulated. However with nominal tariffs at about 10 per cent of output and high transport costs, there is still some degree of protection for domestic manufacturers. The effective competitive limit for manufacturers is the import parity price, often the cost of landed imports from Australia. The removal of monopoly rights from most operations in New Zealand, together with the removal of barriers on foreign direct investment on most forms of inward and outward capital flows, means that a similar international competitive constraint also applies to many non-traded sectors.[6,7] Thus foreign investors have set up operations (e.g. in domestic aviation and telephone communications) in competition with established operators. In practice, given the widespread factor market deregulation, the traded/non-traded sector distinction in New Zealand has become less clear-cut, with competitive pressures flowing indirectly into most sectors of the economy.[8]

III. The Theoretical Underpinnings of New Zealand Liberalisation

The New Zealand program of economic liberalisation can be thought of as unusually comprehensive and consistent policy reforms. This is a result of its having been for the most part based on a consistent theoretical framework. In this section we outline the boundaries of that framework.[9]

New Zealand business structures presented particular regulatory problems because the country has a low population and a high degree of market concentration with national monopoly present in a number of sectors. Traditionally this has been reflected in views about the anticompetitive effects of dominant firms, a distrust of market allocation mechanisms, little confidence in domestic industries' abilities to survive under competition, and a belief in the destructive effects of competition. A number of industries, particularly state-owned utilities, have operated with monopoly rights. There has been a history of concern about firms "profiteering" and contributing to inflation, and direct price control was seen as the appropriate way to protect against this. This traditionally meant a preference for stable (and non-dynamic) market systems, and thus for a century New Zealand policymakers took the view that the State had a major role to play in funding, owning, providing and regulating the provision of products and services.

The economic reforms commencing in 1984 took a markedly different view. This was partly for the practical reason that the New Zealand economy had become demonstrably more sophisticated, mature, and globally-integrated. The reforms relied heavily on a number of schools of new microeconomic thinking that had arisen in the U.S., which are summarised in Table 1. These theories broadly supported policies that aimed at decreasing the economic role of the state, namely corporatisation, privatisation and deregulation. In particular, the development of transactions cost and contestability theories was seized on by policymakers as providing attractive new ground on which to build regulatory policy. Such theories lessen regulatory attention on the numbers of competitors and concentration levels and refocus it on barriers to entry, and threats of entry both by domestic operations and via imports.

Because of the timing of the Baumol, Panzar and Willig (1982) book and the accompanying economic debate on contestability theory, the new New Zealand antitrust legislation that was occupying policymakers' minds from 1984 to 1986 was the first that was in a position to incorporate the principles of the (as yet largely untested) theory. Contestability theory appeared particularly attractive to

Table I. Changes in theoretical base of government policies in New Zealand.

Policy:	Pre-1984	Post-1984
Public Funding	Market failure theory	Public choice and property rights theories
Public Ownership	Equity and nationalism arguments	Principal-agent theory
Provision of Services	Distrust of private sector motives and ability	Public sector crowd-out thinking
Regulation	Direct price and operational controls	Contestability & transactions cost theories Light-handed regulation

New Zealand policymakers, because it seemed to offer them a way through their on-going problems of small numbers of local competitors, and pointed to the importance of removing import protection to allow foreigners to act as potential entrants and hence to help regulate local producers.

The New Zealand approach may be criticised as confusing the technical and popular usages of the term "contestability". Policymakers made wide use of the term in areas as widespread as trade policy and labor market deregulation, and in situations where the tightly defined preconditions of perfect contestability clearly did not hold. In particular many potential foreign competitors were unable to operate as hit-and-run entrants, and sunk costs abounded in most markets. Nevertheless, the attractiveness of contestability theory for the New Zealand economy was that it appeared to offer a light-handed regulatory option for the many markets in which there were but a few established players. Contestability theory was also used as an *ex post* justification for the removal of some regulatory controls during the 1980s, and particularly for the reduction in import protection.

In interpreting the Commerce Act, the Commerce Commission has been prepared at least partly to embrace a contestability framework.[10] Writing in 1985, the then Chairman of the Commission said:

> "Contestability theory has the important practical consequence that, in the absence of independent sellers in the market [i.e. monopoly], there need be no concern if there is reasonably costless entry and exit for potential competitors."[11]

In practice, the Commission and the Courts have only rarely mentioned contestability, but rather have focussed on the importance of barriers to entry. This approach has partly been derived from influential Australian cases, especially *QCMA*,[12] although some Commerce Commission decisions have been placed more explicitly within a (loose) contestability framework.[13] This framework has also been used by counsel in pleading cases before judicial authorities. However, as shown by Bollard (1987) there are considerable difficulties in proving the existence of a sufficient degree of consistency with the assumptions to be sure this theory's outcomes hold true in any particular case.

Many competitively sensitive industries are dominated by sunk costs, and Baumol (1986) argues that sunk cost economics is the valid domain of transactions cost theory. This theory offered policymakers some confidence that efficient allocation decisions might still be made in such circumstances through market-based or internal governance decisions. This approach also held sway in New Zealand business law design. Oliver Williamson's theories of markets and hierarchies, and his framework of unilateral, bilateral and trilateral governance provided the foundations for the New Zealand Treasury's proposals for securities and takeovers law reform. The Coasian view that firms act to minimise their transactions costs through various forms of internal/external reorganisation also underlies the Commerce Act's tolerance of a wide range of intra-firm and market trade practices.[14]

Why was New Zealand antitrust policy so sympathetic to the new U.S. microeconomic theories, in contrast to Australia? By the early 1980s, the New Zealand economy was highly interventionist, badly underperforming, and more in need of structural reform than its neighbor. The thinner political system meant that such reform was easier to carry out, and the timing of the new theoretical developments made them attractive to incorporate. When it came, the whole program of economic liberalisation went far further than it had in Australia.[15]

IV. The Design of the New Zealand Commerce Act

Since 1908 New Zealand trade practices law had been based principally on U.K. legislation. This relationship was particularly clear in the Restrictive Trade Practices Act 1956, which used the formal and pragmatic approach of listing types of practices which could be investigated. The Australian Trade Practices Act 1974 marked a movement away from this U.K. case-by-case style, towards a more U.S. style of antitrust code. At the time, however, New Zealand retained the British approach when it enacted the Commerce Act 1975. A decade later, this legislation was felt to be inadequate for the needs of a deregulating economy.

The Commerce Act 1986 was designed as a key piece of New Zealand legislation. It was to represent the new rules of the game for an open competitive economy, and it was seen as having a central role to play in New Zealand's economic liberalisation process. The Act was to guide the behavior of firms that had been recently exposed by the removal of import protection, price control and other regulation, and were being propelled towards efficient operation, or else to exit. The Act was passed into law with the objective "to promote competition in markets within New Zealand", and is designed to prevent the establishment or operation of business arrangements reducing competition; to prevent firms from using market power for anticompetitive purposes; and to provide for the regulation of mergers and takeovers to prevent any undesired acquisition of market power.

The Act has two substantive parts: Part II governs trade practices and Part III regulates mergers and takeovers. Part IV allows for price controls (and is currently unused). The rest of the Act is largely administrative. Its main features are summarized in Table 2. The essence of Part III of the Act (in its 1986 form) was that companies seeking to merge or acquire assets were subject to an asset threshold test, above which they must notify the Commerce Commission of their intentions and proceed through a two stage test to gain clearance or authorisation. This test first involved assessing whether the merger would lead to the acquiring or strengthening of a dominant position in a market, and if so, then whether it would likely result in a benefit to the public which would outweigh any detriment resulting from that increased dominance. In Part II, the Act prohibits arrangements between competitors that substantially lessen competition in a market (section 27), arrangements between competitors that reduce the competitiveness of a rival (section 29), arrangements that lead to prices being fixed amongst competitors (section 30), and a company dominant in a market using its position to prevent competition (section 36).

The Commerce Commission was established as a combined regulatory and judicial authority to administer the Act (and also the Fair Trading Act which governs consumer rights). There are no comparable industry-specific statutory regulatory authorities, so the Commerce Commission has generalised sectoral powers, including coverage of all utilities. Decisions may be appealed to the High Court and then to the Court of Appeal. Commerce Act proceedings that are initiated in the High Court can be appealed ultimately to the Privy Council in London.[16] Private rights of action are available for most contraventions. The Commission is an independent statutory authority, but the Government can direct it to "have regard to" the latter's economic policies.

The Act was controversial when initially introduced.[17] For that reason the Minister of Trade and Industry undertook to review it after two years of operation. This review was undertaken in 1988–89.[18] As a result, a 1990 Amendment was passed, making a number of changes. In order to clarify the intentions of the legislation, the Commission was now required to include in its assessment of public benefits, any efficiencies resulting from the conduct under examination. The Amendment also extended the application of the Act to any firms resident in Australia, to the extent that their actions would affect markets in New Zealand, and hence the amended Act established the concept of a trans-Tasman market for competition purposes. Resale price maintenance became authorisable on application to the Commission, and other restrictive trade practices could also be authorised, provided they were new practices and were not being used for anticompetitive purposes.

Table II. Summary of major changes to NZ antitrust legislation.

	1986 Commerce Act	1990 Amendment	1993 Review [1]
Merger notification	Mandatory prenotification	Voluntary prenotification. Clearance and authorisation options	Fast track and slow track applicati procedures
Merger authorisation	Market dominance and public benefit tests	Bare transfer of dominance excluded	–
Public benefit test	Public benefit not defined	To have regard to resulting efficiencies	Defined as 'benefit NZ'. No account to be taken of who benefi consumers or producers.
Market dominance	Illegal to restrict entry, prevent or eliminate competition	Dominance test extended to Australasia	–
Trans-Tasman issues	No focus	Extension to certain anti-competitive trans-Tasman behavior. Anti-dumping regime superseded by antitrust	No further harmonisation
Price-fixing	Per se illegal	–	Presumed to lessen competition unless otherwise establishe
Resale price maintenance	RPM prohibited	RPM authorisable	–
Other trade practices	Arrangements lessening competition prohibited	–	–
Labour market	Applies if anti-competitive effect in product markets (unless relates to pay/work practices).	–	–

[1] For details see Ministry of Commerce (1992).

A further review of the Act was carried out in 1993, focussing on a number of issues, including whether special conditions should be applied to markets for primary produce, whether the Act should apply more broadly to labor practices, and other trans-Tasman harmonisation subjects.[19] In particular, attention was paid to the nature of the economic cost-benefit analysis and the scope of the public benefit test to be applied. It was decided by the Government that the Act will be amended in a number of ways, and its views have been announced.

Following experience in a number of merger cases, it was argued that the Commerce Commission should not operate, even indirectly, as an instrument of social policy, and that it should therefore be distributionally neutral in its rulings, in the sense that benefits/detriments to customers should not be weighted any differently from benefits/detriments to shareholders or any other domestic parties. The Government has provisionally agreed to this approach, and to clarify this procedure it has said it will change the wording of the Act from "public benefit" to "benefit to New Zealand". This is a more radical move, with the implication being that a merger might be judged very harmful to consumers yet still be approved because of its benefits to shareholders. In addition, the Government has indicated that it wishes to see more economic quantification being undertaken for the purpose of assessment of the net benefit. This debate was partly influenced by practices under the Canadian Competition Act. Currently, levels of quantification in New Zealand are relatively unsophisticated compared with North American practice; econometrics is used only rarely in the courtroom. Finally, the Government has also provisionally accepted further implicit liberalisation in the treatment of price fixing, that most restricted of all trade practices; price fixing will no longer be *per se* illegal, but would be presumed to lessen competition unless otherwise established.

V. Australian and Other Influences

V.1. Legislation and Policy Influences

The Commerce Act 1986 looked to the new U.S. microeconomics for its underlying economic principles. But for its legal framework it relied heavily on the Australian Trade Practices Act 1974. The attraction of the Australian Act was obvious: it was felt the Australian approach was broad enough to incorporate New Zealand requirements for light regulation in a liberalised economy. Australia used a similar judicial and economic regime within the Westminster tradition, which New Zealand could draw on for institutional design and legal precedence. In 1983 New Zealand signed ANZCERTA, a free trade arrangement with Australia which allows unimpeded trade in all merchandise goods between the countries and has been extended to cover some services (ANZCERTA was one of the role models used by NAFTA). This Agreement was both a reflection of and a contributor to the growing economic integration of New Zealand with Australia, especially in manufacturing, and it marked a convergence in the two countries' corporate structures and raised issues of business law harmonisation.

The Commerce Act is structured in a broadly similar way to the Australian legislation, except that the consumer protection clauses constitute a separate piece of legislation, known as the Fair Trading Act. The Australian section 45 on contracts, arrangements or understandings restricting dealings or affecting competition broadly covers the same ground as sections 27, 29 and 30 of the New Zealand Act. Section 46 of the Trade Practices Act on the misuse of market power is generally parallelled by section 36 of the Commerce Act, to the extent that similar wording is used. However, the New Zealand legislation departs from the Australian model in two significant ways. First, the Commerce Act does not specifically single out particular trade practices for attention. For example, exclusive dealing and price discrimination are not mentioned specifically, and there is no prohibition of secondary boycotts. Second, the concept of misuse of a dominant position is ultimately derived from Article 86 of the Treaty of Rome 1957 (EEC). The definition and treatment of the exploitation of a dominant position therefore rests on some earlier key European Court cases such as *Re Continental Can* (1972), *Hoffman La Roche v ECC* (1979) and *United Brands* (1978).

The institutional arrangements to administer the Acts are similar in the two countries. In New Zealand the Commerce Commission performs similar roles to the Australian Trade Practices Commission in policing and authorising trade practices. Appeals against decisions of the Commerce Commission are considered by the High Court of New Zealand with the assistance of lay members.[20] This follows the composition of the Australian Trade Practices Tribunal, which comprises a Federal Court judge and lay assessors, and whose methodological approaches and arguments have been instrumental in influencing Federal Court judges to incorporate economic and business principles into their judgments.

As the Closer Economic Relationship between the two countries has developed, business integration has put pressure on policymakers to bring the two regimes further into line. In addition, authorities realised that in the absence of restrictions on direct foreign investment, Australasian companies were becoming increasingly mobile between the two countries and were ready to exploit differences in the two regimes. Parry (1989) and others have argued the case for closer harmonisation between the two trade practices regimes and in particular the need to replace anti-dumping trade provisions with appropriate trade practices legislation; for recognition of the trans-Tasman dimension to the market; and for explicit recognition of trans-Tasman issues in the public benefit test.[21] Thus, in 1988 a Memo of Understanding was signed between Australia and New Zealand on the harmonisation of business laws, aimed at identifying where differences might restrict trade. The two countries undertook to consult one another on changes to their regimes. The 1988 ANZCERTA Review agreed that from 1990 the countries would no longer take anti-dumping action against goods arising in the other territory, and that any such concerns would be dealt with by

Table III. Use of legal precedent in NZ Commerce Act cases cited by country of jurisdiction.

	Commerce Act Guidebooks [1]	Commerce Commission Decisions [2]	High Court Decisions [3]
New Zealand	43%	77% [4]	47%
Australia	40%	18%	22%
US	7%	3%	17%
UK	8%	2%	13%
EC	1%	–	1%
Other	1%	–	–

This table is based on an analysis of the citations of legal precedents that have been used in Commerce Act judicial decisions and in advisory handbooks. These citations are classified by the country of relevant judicial authority, according to the frequency with which they arise.
[1]Derived from 485 citations in Van Roy (1992) and 333 citations in Hill & Jones (1986). Note that the first reference also includes cases relating to the Fair Trading Act.
[2]Derived from 106 Commerce Commission decisions from 1986 to 1993, citing 231 cases.
[3]Derived from 23 major High Court cases involving the Commerce Act between 1986 and 1992.
[4]Note that most of these relate to former Commission decisions.

the two countries' competition laws. In addition, the New Zealand Commerce Commission and the Australian Trade Practices Commission have since agreed to undertake preliminary investigations on behalf of one another into anticompetitive conduct.

While initially there was some convergence of the Commerce Act towards the Australian legislation, more recently there has been a divergence in approach. The Australian direction has been to tighten up its prohibitions on anticompetitive conduct, while New Zealand is moving to a more liberal regime. Currently there is some concern in New Zealand regarding the Australian Government's move from a dominance standard for mergers to a substantial lessening of competition standard (which generally implies a lower threshold).[22]

V.2. Influences from Legal Precedent

New Zealand relied heavily on U.K. precedent for its interpretation of its earlier antitrust legislation. However, in interpreting the Commerce Act, recourse has been made principally to New Zealand and Australian legal precedent, although increasingly to the U.S. Table 3 presents an approximate assessment of the various jurisdictional influences by quantifying the use of legal precedent used under the Commerce Act, interpreted from three sources: guidebooks to the Act written by lawyers, Commerce Commission decisions, and High Court cases.

The guidebooks compiled largely before the 1986 Act was in force predicted major recourse to Australian cases for guidance as to likely interpretation. The Commerce Commission has been more strongly anchored in New Zealand precedent, most of it being its own. There was some recourse to U.K. law in the earlier days, with the Commission frequently quoting from U.K. and earlier New Zealand decisions made under abuse control law. In contrast the High Court of New Zealand was quick to recognise that the Commerce Act was, like the Australian Trade Practices Act, a prohibition law based on the Sherman Act, and it was more likely to look abroad for appropriate legal precedent. It has observed:

> ". . . there is a wealth of Australian precedent on which New Zealand Courts have drawn and should continue to draw. The close relationship between the New Zealand Act and the Australian Trade Practices Act 1974, the goal of harmonisation of commercial statutes and an increasingly shared interpretation of commercial law in both common law and statutory areas, makes reliance on Australian precedent almost inevitable . . . Despite the common ancestry which both the New Zealand and Australian statutes derive from United States anti-trust statutes, caution has to be exhibited before adopting uncritically developments in law and economics from that country. Not only are there different statutory regimes, but there are vast differences in the markets."[23]

Table 4 lists the six major High Court cases heard under the Commerce Act so far, and notes the antitrust precedents that the judgments cite and appear to have drawn on. While a body of New Zealand precedent is now building up, these seminal cases have drawn heavily on some key Australian judgments. In particular *QCMA* and *Queensland Wire* have guided market definition, the role of competition, the definition of market power, and the interpretation of anticompetitive purpose and effect.[24] Paterson (1992) and Brunt (1990) discuss this further, and point to some different interpretations of similar concepts in market definition and market power thresholds in the two countries. Hay (1990, p. 20) explains the different market power thresholds as stemming from the smaller size of the New Zealand economy requiring larger market share to achieve minimum efficient scale:

> ". . . if "dominance" under the New Zealand statute is intended to signify a different (and presumably higher) threshold than that used in Australia, it seems to me that what ought to be meant is that a firm which has the minimum degree of market power to satisfy the New Zealand threshold will be able to charge higher prices than a firm which has the minimum degree of market power to satisfy the Australian threshold."

Analysis of these key cases shows the emergence of an overriding focus of concern in New Zealand with the role of dominant firms, especially where the question is about access to the facilities that they control.[25] All the High Court cases cited in Table 4 involve allegations of dominance, in fields as diverse as ports, apple marketing, major domestic household appliance manufacturing, and telecommunications. As noted above, judgments in these cases have relied heavily on Australian precedent for rulings on market definition, competition, and public benefit. When assessing the issue of market dominance, European Community and increasingly, Australian, precedents are being cited. Most of the New Zealand cases have also involved pricing or access problems with bottleneck facilities. Here the legal recourse has been more to U.S. precedent, but judges have warned against over-reliance on an American approach and have declined to accept more formal U.S. procedures such as the essential facilities doctrine.

The only High Court trade practices case of any major importance in the sense of extending and applying economic thinking, involved an appeal against a majority Commerce Commission judgment against the validity of an exclusive dealing arrangement for domestic appliances like refrigerators and washing machines (the *Fisher & Paykel* case). Here the Court admitted to difficulties in finding useful overseas or New Zealand precedent, and referred to several older U.S. and Australian cases, but warned that it felt these paid insufficient attention to the role of efficiencies in vertical arrangements and that there may be need for further interpretation.

VI. The Major High Court Cases

The six major cases identified in Table 4 are described briefly in this section.

VI.1. *Auckland Regional Authority v Mutual Rental Cars Ltd and Others*

The ARA sought a declaratory judgment as to whether its contracts with two car rental companies which excluded other operators from car rental booths at Auckland airport were in breach of sections 27, 29, and/or 36. The Court found that the appropriate market was for rental car services at Auckland airport, that the contracts had the purpose of substantially lessening competition in that market, and that despite the motive of maximising rent, the ARA had used its dominant position to exclude other rental car competitors.

VI.2. *Applefields Ltd v New Zealand Apple and Pear Board*

The NZAPB is a marketing board with statutory powers. It used these to apply a levy on new growers and established growers increasing their production. This levy constituted about 8 per cent of typical development costs. The High Court held that it represented a barrier to entry that had the effect of substantially lessening competition in a market. The Board appealed the decision to the Court of Appeal, which confirmed the judgment of lessening of competition, but concluded that the Board's actions were exempt under section 43 of the Commerce Act (which exempts any Act specifically authorised by another statute). Applefields then appealed to the Privy Council, which ruled that the Board did not have specific authorisation to impose this levy.

Table IV. Citation of Precedent in Six Major New Zealand High Court Cases.

	Objective of Commerce Act	Market Definition	Competition	Anticompetitive Purpose/Effect
1. ARA/Mutual Rental (1987)		Edmond Foods QCMA* Tooth & Co* Outboard Marine* Dandy Power*		
2. Applefields/APMB (1989, 91)		Tru Tone		ARA/Budget QCMA* Tooth & Co* Queensland Wire*
3. Union Shipping/Port Nelson (1990)	Tru Tone	Tru Tone	ARA/Budget QCMA* Tooth & Co* Queensland Wire*	ARA/Budget Tru Tone Magic Millions Outboard Marine* Queensland Wire*
4. Fisher & Paykel (1990)	Tru Tone		Watties/Taylor Freezer	Outboard Marine* Tillmans* Dandy Power*
5. Telecom/Commerce Commision (1990)		ARA/Budget Tru Tone QCMA* Queensland Wire* Tooth & Co*		
6. Clear/Telecom (1992)				Electricorp/Geotherm Tru Tone Port Nelson

The cases listed are those that have been cited as being influential in the judgments. The cases are New Zealand ones, exce where marked:

* Australia

+ United States

\# European Community

Australian lay members were present in the High Court for cases 3–6.

Market Dominance	Bottleneck Facilities	Public Benefit	Vertical Restraints/ Trade Practices
Continental Can#	Australian Bankcard* Terminal Railroad of St Louis+ Hecht/Pro Football+		
ARA/Budget Queensland Wire* Hecht/Pro Football+ MCI Communications+ Grinnell Corp+	ARA/Budget Queensland Wire*		
QCMA* Queensland Wire*			GTE Sylvania+ Roland Machinery+ Ford Motor Co* John Lysaght* Outboard Marine*
Magnum Corp Welgas NZ Coop Dairy QMCA* Queensland Wire* Arnotts* United Brands# Hoffman La Roche#		QCMA* John Dee Ltd* Rural Traders Coop (WA)*	
Port Nelson Magic Million Queensland Wire*	Olympia Equipment+		

Cases:

1. *Auckland Regional Authority v Mutual Rental Cars & Others*, (1988) 2 NZBLC 103,041; [1987] 2 NZLR 647.
2. *Applefields & Others v NZ Apple & Pear Marketing Board & Other*, (1989) 2 NZBLC 103,564 (HC).
3. *Union Shipping NZ Ltd & Other v Port Nelson Ltd.* (1990) 3 NZBLC 101,618.
4. *Fisher & Paykel Ltd v Commerce Commission* (1990) 3 NZBLC 101,655.
5. *Telecom Corporation of NZ Ltd v Commerce Commission and Others*, Wellington, AP279/90, 1990.
6. *Clear Communications Ltd v Telecom Corporation of NZ Ltd and Others*, Wellington, (1992) 5 TCLR, 166.

VI.3. *Union Shipping NZ Ltd v Port Nelson Ltd*

Port Nelson is a duly corporatised Crown-owned company which owns the wharves, land, buildings and equipment at Nelson. On corporatisation it imposed a newly amalgamated wharfage charge on customers. In addition, it insisted that stevedores (with whom it was looking to compete) sign a contract tying them to use the full port facilities exclusively. It then introduced a wharf user levy which double-counted some of these costs for stevedores who used their own staff and equipment. The High Court ruled that Port Nelson constituted a natural monopoly and was dominant in all relevant wharf activity markets. Port Nelson's demands for use of its own plant or for payment in lieu were judged to represent misuse of its position, being aimed at elimination of other plant in contravention of section 36. The Court recommended the Port recalculate the basis for its charges.

VI.4. *Fisher & Paykel Ltd v Commerce Commission*

Fisher & Paykel is the major New Zealand producer of whiteware (refrigerators, washing machines and similar domestic appliances), and used an exclusive dealing clause in its agreement with retailers, forbidding them from stocking competing brands. Simpson, an Australian whiteware producer, applied for a declaration that this clause substantially lessened competition in the market. The Commerce Commission (by a split decision) had refused an application for the authorisation of this practice. The High Court supported Fisher & Paykel's counter claim and appeal against the Commission decision. It judged that the clause did not necessarily represent a barrier to entry, and that Fisher and Paykel was significantly constrained by competition from other firms, despite its very high market share. The Court also commented that private benefits in the form of cost savings achieved through greater efficiency had an element of public benefit, even though not shown to have been directly passed on to consumers.

VI.5. *Telecom NZ Ltd v Commerce Commission*

The Commerce Commission declined to authorise Telecom NZ Ltd to acquire the AMPS-A frequency band to extend its operation of cellular mobile telephones. The Commission ruled that this would result in Telecom strengthening its dominant position in the market. Telecom (principally owned by Bell Atlantic and Ameritech) was one of two companies (the other being Bell South) to own management rights to cellular frequencies. The High Court broadly supported the decision of the Commission. However in 1992 the Court of Appeal allowed Telecom's appeal against the previous decisions. A majority of judges concluded that acquiring the AMPS-A band would strengthen Telecom's dominance in the mobile telephone market, but went on to decide that the public benefits outweighed the detriments.

VI.6. *Clear Communications Ltd v Telecom NZ Ltd*

In 1990 Clear Communications, a joint venture company, entered the New Zealand telecommunications industry as a significant competitor to Telecom (which had previously been the state-owned monopolist operator). Clear used Telecom's local network and there was considerable dispute over the terms of access. In 1991 Clear alleged that Telecom had breached (among other things) section 36 of the Commerce Act, by charging too much for interconnection, and by requiring an access code. The High Court ruled that Telecom was dominant in the market and that it used this position for an anticompetitive purpose, though without loss to Clear. The Court particularly noted the 'Baumol-Willig pricing framework' as a basis to pricing for access to the network.[26]

VII. The Impact of Deregulation and the Antitrust Regime in New Zealand

The program of economic liberalisation has had a major impact on the structure and behavior of firms in New Zealand. From the viewpoint of the typical firm, pressures to adjust may be thought of as arising from two sources: directly from specific industry deregulation, and indirectly from other changes resulting from macroeconomic policies and exogenous events. Deregulatory pressures on firms to adjust in New Zealand have derived from the removal of entry restrictions in a range of industries (statutory monopoly rights, quality licensing, etc); from the removal of barriers to direct foreign investment (opening up the prospects for foreign-owned domestic competition); from removing barriers to imports (opening up the prospects for foreign-originated competing products); from the removal of operating restrictions (including price controls and internal sub-market operating restrictions); and from the deregulation of factor markets (including finance, labor, energy and transport). These pressures have particularly affected New Zealand industry structures, changing the type of industry participants, leading to increased entry and later to increased exit, new classes of owners, new types of operation, and changing levels of concentration. Simultaneously, New Zealand firms have also been under pressure from other sources: from changing world prices, and from a sharply rising real exchange rate between 1985 and 1988. Initially the traded sector was the focus of these pressures, but by 1987 the non-traded sector was starting to feel these competitive pressures indirectly. As a result the New Zealand economy went into sharp and prolonged recession, with no per capita GDP growth between 1986 and 1991, and an increase in unemployment from 4 per cent to 12 per cent.

As these pressures started to impinge upon performance, New Zealand firms took a range of reactive measures, initially developing new products, cutting unprofitable operations and making new investments. Gradually more fundamental attempts were made to cut costs, with subsequent layoffs and corporate restructuring. By 1991 one third of the manufacturing sector had gone out of

Table V. Numbers of Commerce Commission applications.

	1986/87	1987/88	1988/89	1989/90	1990/91	1991/92
(i) Mergers & Acquisitions						
Applications Registered	311	525	624	400	159	53
Clearances/Authorisations	258	488	537	384	171	48
Applications Declined	–	8	2	–	3	6
(ii) Restrictive Trade Practices						
Applications Registered	27	4	2	1	1	–
Authorisations	–	1	2	1	–	–
Applications Declined	–	1	–	2	1	–

Period 1986/87 covers only 11 months.
Numbers cited do not balance due to withdrawals and transfers of applications, rulings of no jurisdiction, and applications remaining on hand.
The change to a voluntary notification system in 1990/91 makes comparison of the numbers somewhat arbitrary.
Authorisations for restrictive trade practices include letters of comfort.

business.[27] Since 1991 there has been a growth in business confidence and a significant upturn in firm profits, with improvements to competitiveness and productivity.

How effectively was the Commerce Act able to regulate these major firm adjustments? As pressures came to restructure there was a very large number of mergers and acquisitions of companies or assets, as well as some hive offs and closures. Feil (1990) records a large increase in listed company mergers in New Zealand in the mid 1980s as a result of restructuring, peaking in 1988 and then reducing. Table 5 shows the number of applications for mergers and acquisitions from 1986/87 to 1991/92. In the early years these numbers are inflated by the strong growth in the deregulated financial sector, and by the large amount of restructuring under way. In later years more defensive mergers have taken place for rationalisation reasons. As can be seen, almost all merger applications were granted, with less than one per cent of applications being declined. In almost all cases this was due to concerns about the likely strengthening of dominance by an existing large firm. Most of these refusals were in the forestry, gas and telecommunications sectors. A few applications sought rationalisation arrangements through which industry capacity could be reduced, occasionally relying on a failing company defense. The Commerce Commission usually regarded such applications with more suspicion, fearing either that the company was not really failing, or that helping it to merge would not assist the competitive process.

In overall terms, the merger and acquisition regime of the Commerce Act should be described as one that has been highly enabling for restructuring. This has attracted some criticism. Greer (1988, p. 57) has argued that the New Zealand standard for determining dominance is far too permissive and that it should move towards an Australian standard. He says:

> "It would not be inaccurate to summarise New Zealand merger policy by saying that virtually all mergers are approved, except those that leave a monopoly protected by high barriers to entry (and even then the monopoly creating merger may be approved if the Commission believes the claim to public benefits will outweigh the detriments. . .)"

The issue of whether the corporate sector has become more concentrated as a result of a permissive merger regime is inevitably complicated, especially given the degree of turbulence in ownership during the period. Hamilton (1991) found evidence of increasing concentration within some sectors of New Zealand manufacturing between 1984 and 1989, as measured by Herfindahl indices (but not adjusted for imports and exports). On the other hand, when Harper (1992) adjusted concentration measures for international trade, he found that between 1987 and 1990 most sectors had actually become less concentrated. With its small economy, New Zealand industry has always been relatively concentrated. On balance there is no strong evidence that it has become more concentrated as a result of the Commerce Act.

The restrictive trade practices legislation has affected the economy in a somewhat different way to the merger/takeover regime. New Zealand industry traditionally had been characterised by a wide collection of explicit and implicit trade arrangements amongst groups of firms. For example, a 1986 survey of retailers and wholesalers found that three quarters of them indulged in some form of vertical trade agreements (Ayto and Bollard, 1986). Some of these practices (e.g. resale price maintenance) became specifically illegal under the 1986 Act, but the vast majority fell into a category which were not specifically prohibited and would therefore have to be judged on their specific anticompetitive effects. With restructuring, many firms sought to review their inter- and intra-firm arrangements. Generally this was done without application to or influence from the Commerce Commission, which was focussing at that stage on mergers and acquisitions and Fair Trading Act contraventions. The first significant restrictive trade practices application was on the question of exclusive dealing arrangements in 1989–90.[28] Since 1986, 35 applications have been made, resulting in only 4 authorisations and 4 refusals, as shown in Table 5.

The restrictive trade practices regime of the Commerce Act was originally drafted in a relatively permissive way, and it was eased further in the 1990 and 1993 reviews. It is generally agreed that, like section III on mergers and acquisitions, section II of the Commerce Act has not obstructed corporate growth and rationalisation. However, there has not yet been sufficient experience of trade practices cases to draw overall conclusions as to the efficacy of this part of the Act.

VIII. Conclusions

The Commerce Act 1986, which applies to all commercial sectors, is liberal in its design and has been implemented in a very light-handed way, allowing major restructuring to proceed with relatively little constraint. The Act was designed on an Australian framework, but driven by efficiency-focussed U.S. microeconomic theories. Increasingly it is being interpreted differently from Australian antitrust legislation. In contrast to Australia and the U.S., mergers with very high resulting market shares (even 100 per cent) have been allowed to proceed, in recognition of New Zealand's need for economies of scale. Restrictive trade practices have been more loosely defined. Public benefit has been interpreted widely to include benefits to the company.

The Commerce Act represents legislation that is in the spirit of the New Zealand economic liberalisation experience. Although its stated objective is to promote competition, and much of its wording is similar to the Australian Trade Practices Act, it was actually designed with more weight on the promotion of efficiency. This is how the judiciary has interpreted it, sometimes at the cost of more traditional competition objectives, and in contrast to some Australian judgments. It is still too early to draw overall conclusions about the Act's net effects on economic welfare.

1. Notes

[1] I acknowledge the assistance of G. Connors, J. Feil, D. Round, G. Sellens and M. Malan. The views expressed are those of the author, and not the institutions with which he is associated.

[2] The accepted economic arguments on sequencing were not given much consideration in the New Zealand case (see Bollard (1992)). Officials felt the Commerce Act 1986 was so important in driving reform that it had to be accorded an early spot on the legislative agenda.

[3] The Closer Economic Relationship Agreement between Australia and New Zealand, first signed in 1983 and since extended, allows for free trade in all manufactured goods and most services between the two countries.

[4] The principles of merger policy in a small economy and the implications of liberalisation are usefully surveyed by Khemani (1991).

[5] The direct relationship between trade policies and the effectiveness of competition laws is discussed by Farmer (1987). He notes that the role of imported goods in a local market is expressly recognised by both the Australian Trade Practices Act and the New Zealand Commerce Act (sections 4 (1) and 3 (3) respectively).

[6] The only remaining non-agricultural regulated monopoly of commercial importance in New Zealand is the letterpost market, but deregulated courier/post/parcel competitors are well established throughout this market.

[7] Permission is still formally required (and usually granted) for foreign investment in broadcasting, rural land, and commercial fishing.

[8] A significant proportion of New Zealand's exports remain regulated through statutory producer marketing boards. These mainly affect sectors where New Zealand has a major international comparative advantage, and the local price is often well below the traded world price (and sometimes far below the intervention price in markets like the EC). In these cases the threat of imports is not an effective domestic competitive constraint. In cases where the domestic competitive price has crept up above the import parity price, foreign suppliers have been reluctant to enter the market because of the ability of New Zealand agricultural producers to drive them out by limit pricing.

[9] For a more detailed discussion see Bollard (1992).

[10] The Commerce Commission is the major antitrust regulatory authority in New Zealand, and is described in the next section.
[11] Quoted by Greer (1988, p. 57). Greer comments: "This has, in effect, become the policy of the Commerce Commission."
[12] *Re Queensland Co-operative Milling Association Ltd., Defiance Holdings Ltd. (Proposed Mergers with Barnes Milling Ltd.)* (1976) ATPR 40–012.
[13] These decisions have covered industries such as food products, trucking and packaging.
[14] In contrast to Australia, the Act makes no preemptive judgment about the *per se* undesirability of conduct such as price discrimination and third line forcing. The only exceptions are price fixing (illegal though likely to be treated differently in 1994) and resale price maintenance (illegal until the 1990 Amendment, now authorisable).
[15] For more details on the political economy of the reform process see Bollard (1993).
[16] One such Commerce Act case was *Applefields Ltd and Others v The New Zealand Apple & Pear Marketing Board and Others* (1989) 2 NZBLC 103, 564 (HC).
[17] The history of New Zealand competition law is outlined in Donaldson (1991).
[18] See Department of Trade and Industry (1988) and Ministry of Commerce (1989).
[19] In the end any such extension to the Act was rejected for both practical and legal reasons. However, the Act has always applied where labor market practices have an anticompetitive effect on product markets "unless the practices primarily relate to remuneration and work practices used". See Ministry of Commerce (1992).
[20] To date, two of the most influential lay members have been Australians.
[21] Dellow and Feil (1991) note that the competition laws of the two countries had effectively already been harmonised to a significant extent, although the process of moving together has been a one-way process, with New Zealand following Australian practices and experience. They argue that in the future Australia could look more to New Zealand's experience in dealing with particular areas such as network monopolies and other essential facilities, as these problems are particularly acute and have received considerable attention in New Zealand.
[22] The Australian Trade Practices Commission has since said that these changes could lead to a different treatment of the same trans-Tasman merger by the two countries' competition authorities, and this could cause practical problems (Rotherham, 1992). See also Gascoigne and Limbury (1991).
[23] *Fisher & Paykel Limited v Commerce Commission* 1990 NZAR 241 at 271.
[24] *Supra* n. 11, and *Queensland Wire Industries Pty. Ltd. v The Broken Hill Proprietary Company Limited & Anor* (1989) ATPR 40–925.
[25] The Commerce Commission and the Courts are now increasingly focussing their attention on the problem of utility regulation. The *Clear Communications* (telecommunications) case has gone to the Court of Appeal. Ultimately at issue is whether non-specific light-handed utility regulation is possible in New Zealand, in contrast to the utility-specific regulatory bodies used in Australia.
[26] The case has been appealed, and judgment is awaited at the time of writing.
[27] This adjustment is summarised in Harper and Malcolm (1991).
[28] *Fisher & Paykel Ltd; Re* (1989) 2 NZBLC (Com) 104, 377, and *Fisher & Paykel Ltd v Commerce Commission* (1990) 3 NZBLC 101, 655.

References

Ayto, J. and, A. Bollard (1987) *New Zealand Distributive Trades: Pricing, Regulation and Structural Change*, Research Paper 37. Wellington: NZ Institute of Economic Research.

Baumol, W.J. (1986) 'Williamson's "The Economic Institutions of Capitalism"', *Rand Journal of Economics*, **17**, 279–286.

Baumol, W.J., J.C. Panzar, and R.D. Willig (1982) *Contestable Markets and the Theory of Industry Structure*. New York: Harcourt Brace Jovanovich, Inc.

Bollard, A. (1987) *Contestability Theory and its Relationship to Competition in Law and Policy*, Working Paper 87/4. Wellington: NZ Institute of Economic Research.

Bollard, A. (1992) *New Zealand: Economic Reforms 1984–1991*, Country Studies Series No 10. San Francisco: International Centre for Economic Growth.

Bollard, A. (1993) 'The Political Economy of Liberalisation in New Zealand', in J. Williamson, ed, *The Political Economy of Policy Reform.* Washington: Institute for International Economics.
Brunt, M. (1990) '"Market Definition" Issues in Australian and New Zealand Trade Practices Litigation', *Australian Business Law Review*, **18**, 86–128.
Dellow, T., and J. Feil (1991) 'Competition Law and Trans Tasman Trade', chapter 3 in R.J. Ahdar, ed, *Competition Law and Policy in New Zealand.* Sydney: The Law Book Company Limited, 24–43.
Department of Trade and Industry (1988) *Review of the Commerce Act 1986: A Discussion Paper.* Wellington.
Donaldson, H.M. (1991) 'The Development of New Zealand Competition Law', chapter 2 in R.J. Ahdar, ed, *Competition Law and Policy in New Zealand.* Sydney: The Law Book Company Limited, 11–23.
Farmer, J. (1987) 'Resolving Trans Tasman Competition Issues', *Trade Practices Workshop.* Auckland: New Zealand Centre for Commercial Law and Applied Legal Research.
Feil, J. (1990) *The Incidence and Motivations of Mergers in New Zealand*, Research Monograph 55. Wellington: NZ Institute of Economic Research.
Gascoigne, D.R., and A.L. Limbury (1991) 'Trans Tasman Mergers', *Workshop of the Competition Law & Policy Institute of New Zealand.* Wellington.
Greer, D. (1988) 'Contestability in Competition Policy: Replacement, Supplement, or Impediment?', chapter 2 in A. Bollard, ed, *The Influence of American Economics on New Zealand Thinking and Policy*, Research Monograph 42, 39–68. Wellington: NZ Institute of Economic Research.
Hamilton, R.T. (1991) 'Diversification and Concentration in New Zealand Industry', *New Zealand Economic Papers*, **25**(2), 151–170.
Harper, D. (1992) *Industrial Concentration in New Zealand 1987–90*, Occasional Paper No. 6. Wellington: NZ Commerce Commission.
Harper, D., and G. Malcolm (1991) *Surviving the Change: How Firms Adjusted to the New Environment*, Research Monograph 56. Wellington: NZ Institute of Economic Research.
Hay, G.A. (1991) 'Market Power Thresholds Under the New Zealand and Australian Statutes', *Workshop of the Competition Law and Policy Institute of New Zealand.* Wellington.
Hill, B., and M. Jones (1986) *Competitive Trading in New Zealand: The Commerce Act 1986.* Wellington: Butterworths.
Khemani, R. (1991) 'Merger Policy in Small vs Large Economies', chapter 9 in R. Khemani and W. Stanbury, eds, *Canadian Competition Law and Policy at the Centenary*, 205–223. The Institute for Research on Public Policy.
Ministry of Commerce (1989) *Review of the Commerce Act 1986: Reports and Decisions.* Wellington.
Ministry of Commerce and others (1992) *Review of the Commerce Act 1986.* Wellington: The Officials Group.
Parry, T.G. (1989) 'CER and Competition Policy: The Need for Harmonisation?' in M. James, ed, *Regulating for Competition? Trade Practices Policy in a Changing Economy*, 141–150. Sydney: Centre for Independent Studies.
Paterson, R.H. (1992) 'Market Power Thresholds Under the Commerce Act and the Trade Practices Act', *Workshop of the Competition Law and Policy Institute of New Zealand.* Wellington.
Pickford, M. (1991) 'Imports as a Constraint on Market Power in a Small Country', *Workshop of the Competition Law and Policy Institute of New Zealand.* Wellington.
Rotherham, F. 'Competition Law Tests Trans Tasman Harmony', *National Business Review*, 24 July 1992.
Van Roy, Y. (1991) *Guidebook to New Zealand Competition Laws.* Auckland: Commerce Clearing House.

Studies in Industrial Organization

1. H.W. de Jong (ed.): *The Structure of European Industry.* 1981
   2nd Revised edition, 1988: see below under Volume 8
2. M. Fennema: *International Networks of Banks and Industry* (1970–1976). 1982
   ISBN 90-247-2620-4
3. P. Bianchi: *Public and Private Control in Mass Product Industry.* The Cement Industry Cases. 1982 ISBN 90-247-2603-4
4. W. Kingston: *The Political Economy of Innovation.* (1984) 1989 2nd printing
   ISBN 90-247-2621-2
5. J. Pelkmans: *Market Integration in the European Community.* 1984
   ISBN Hb: 90-247-2978-5; Pb: 90-247-2988-2
6. H.W. de Jong and W.G. Shepherd (eds.): *Mainstreams in Industrial Organization.* 1986
   Book I: *Theory and International Aspects.* ISBN 90-247-3461-4
   Book II: *Policies: Antitrust, Deregulation and Industrial.* ISBN 90-247-3462-2
   Set ISBN Book I + II: 90-247-3363-4
7. S. Faltas: *Arms Markets and Armament Policy.* The Changing Structure of Naval Industries in Western Europe. 1986 ISBN 90-247-3406-1
8. H.W. de Jong (ed.): *The Structure of European Industry.* 2nd revised ed. (of Volume 1). 1988 Third Revised Edition, 1993: See below under Volume 18
9. I.L.O. Schmidt and J.B. Rittaler: *A Critical Evaluation of the Chicago School of Antitrust Analysis.* 1989 ISBN 90-247-3792-3
10. B. Carlsson (ed.): *Industrial Dynamics.* Technological, Organizational, and Structural Changes in Industries and Firms. 1989 ISBN 0-7923-9044-X
11. Z.J. Acs and D.B. Audretsch (eds.): *The Economics of Small Firms.* A European Challenge. 1990 ISBN 0-7923-0484-5
12. W. Kingston: *Innovation, Creativity and Law.* 1990 ISBN 0-7923-0348-2
13. B. Dankbaar, J. Groenewegen and H. Schenk (eds.): *Perspectives in Industrial Organization.* 1990 ISBN 0-7923-0814-X
14. P. de Wolf (ed.): *Competition in Europe.* Essays in Honour of Henk W. de Jong. 1991 ISBN 0-7923-1050-0
15. C. van der Linde: *Dynamic International Oil Markets.* Oil Market Developments and Structure (1860–1990). 1991 ISBN 0-7923-1478-6
16. D.B. Audretsch and J.J. Siegfried (eds.): *Empirical Studies in Industrial Organization.* Essays in Honor of Leonard W. Weiss. 1992 ISBN 0-7923-1806-4
17. R.J. Gilbert (ed.): *The Environment of Oil.* 1992 ISBN 0-7923-9287-6
18. H.W. de Jong (ed.): *The Structure of European Industry.* Third Revised Edition. 1993 ISBN Hb: 0-7923-2160-X; Pb: 0-7923-2253-3
19. D.K. Round (ed.): *The Australian Trade Practices Act 1974.* Proscriptions and Prescriptions for a More Competitive Economy. 1994 ISBN 0-7923-3228-8

Kluwer Academic Publishers – Dordrecht / Boston / London

SPRINGER NATURE

GPSR Compliance

The European Union's (EU) General Product Safety Regulation (GPSR) is a set of rules that requires consumer products to be safe and our obligations to ensure this.

If you have any concerns about our products, you can contact us on ProductSafety@springernature.com

In case Publisher is established outside the EU, the EU authorized representative is:

Springer Nature Customer Service Center GmbH
Europaplatz 3
69115 Heidelberg, Germany

FSC
www.fsc.org
MIX
Papier | Fördert
gute Waldnutzung
FSC® C083411

Kolibri 360 GmbH
Ferdinand-Jühlke-Straße 7
99095 Erfurt, Deutschland
produktsicherheit@kolibri360.de